D1626965

CALIFORNIA COMEBACK

ALSO BY NARDA ZACCHINO

*Boots on the Ground by Dusk: My Tribute
to Pat Tillman* (with Mary Tillman)

AS EDITOR

The Los Angeles Lakers: 50 Amazing Years in the City of Angels
(with the *Los Angeles Times* sports staff)

*Journey to the Ring: Behind the Scenes with
the 2010 NBA Champion Lakers* (by Phil Jackson)

Four Seasons of Yosemite: A Photographer's Journey

The Washington Post Cookbook: Readers' Favorite Recipes

CALIFORNIA COMEBACK

The Genius of Jerry Brown

NARDA ZACCHINO

with Christopher Scheer

Heyday, Berkeley, California

Copyright © 2016 by Narda Zacchino
Reprinted by arrangement with Thomas Dunne Books, an imprint of St. Martin's Press
First Heyday paperback edition, 2018

All rights reserved. No portion of this work may be reproduced or transmitted in any form
or by any means, electronic or mechanical, including photocopying and recording, or by
any information storage or retrieval system, without permission in writing from Heyday.

The Library of Congress has cataloged the hardcover edition as follows:

Names: Zacchino, Narda, author.
Title: California comeback : how a "failed state" became a model for the
    nation / Narda Zacchino.
Description: New York : Thomas Dunne Books, 2016.
Identifiers: LCCN 2016002477 | ISBN 978-0-312-64935-7 (hardback) |
    ISBN 978-1-250-10089-4 (e-book)
Subjects: LCSH: California—Politics and government—1951– | Political
    planning—California. | BISAC: HISTORY / United States / State &
    Local / West (AK, CA, CO, HI, ID, MT, NV, UT, WY). | POLITICAL
    SCIENCE / Public Policy / Economic Policy. | POLITICAL
    SCIENCE / Public Affairs & Administration.
Classification: LCC F866.2 .Z33 2016 | DDC 979.4/053—dc23
LC record available at http://lccn.loc.gov/2016002477

Paperback ISBN: 978-1-59714-450-6

Cover photo by Russell Yip, *San Francisco Chronicle*, Polaris
Cover design by Ashley Ingram

Orders, inquiries, and correspondence should be addressed to:

Heyday
P.O. Box 9145, Berkeley, CA 94709
(510) 549-3564, Fax (510) 549-1889
www.heydaybooks.com

Printed by in East Peoria, IL, by Versa Press, Inc.

10 9 8 7 6 5 4 3 2 1

For my husband, Robert Scheer,
who is never boring,
and for my family—Peter, Josh, Isa,
Tamayo, Christopher, and Ben—who inspire me

CONTENTS

PREFACE

The genius of Jerry Brown is that he has fundamentally reinvented both himself and California, arguably the most significant state in the country. Through two separate four-year terms as governor, he has established a bold model for progressive governance that is an inspiration for a nation mired in despair and frustration.

It has been a remarkable journey for a nation-state that was exposed early on to the reactionary nostrums of cultural xenophobia and nativism. But Californians have come to soundly reject at the polls these politics of meanness, defying the national swing to the right because divisive politics ultimately failed in a state that has historically thrived through growth and inclusion.

It has also been quite a journey for Jerry Brown. During his first two terms as governor of California from 1975 to 1983, Brown developed a reputation that was as much about style as substance. He was young and inexperienced in governance and could be downright quirky. "Governor Moonbeam," a moniker he still disdains, attached to his image like icky glue. Today—seasoned by years of ruminating on mistakes and unfinished business; helming the large city of Oakland as mayor; and serving as attorney general, the state's top law enforcer—he is the respected leader of the most influential and important state in the country and one that is admired throughout the world.

With a $2.6 trillion GDP, California is the largest economy on the planet behind number five United Kingdom and ahead of France. California climbed up from number ten just five years ago after Brown pulled the state back from the financial abyss with a 2012 voter-approved tax increase on the wealthy, saving California from bankruptcy and a dire future.

Brown has earned status on the world stage as a master player in combatting climate change, from which California has suffered tremendously due to punishing droughts, fires, and floods, with more predicted. This international role became more important when President Donald Trump withdrew from the Paris Climate Accords, foolishly leaving the United States as the only country in the world to not be part of the pact.

By November 2017, seeing his final term in office approaching the 2018 finish line, Brown donned his track shoes and began his sprint around the world to deliver the message that no president of the United States has the power to demolish sound environmental policy devised to combat human-caused global warming. He traveled to the Vatican and a United Nations conference in Bonn for major addresses on climate change action. In Bonn he accepted for the State of California a climate action award for outstanding policy. He also delivered opening remarks at a climate conference in Brussels organized by the European Union, and in Oslo he met with Norway's prime minister and convened a meeting of the world's leading scientists on climate change.

Acting more like the head of a nation than the governor of a state, Brown held a meeting in June 2017 with China's President Xi Jinping, reported in the *Los Angeles Times* under the headline, "China is now looking to California—not Trump—to help lead the fight against climate change." This was followed by a visit to the Eastern Economic Forum meeting in Vladivostok, Russia, where he spoke about the same topic to international government and business leaders.

In the United States, Brown is an effective counterweight to the dismantler-in-chief in the White House and the conservative Republican majority in

Congress, whose strong desire is to undo much of what makes California the success it is. Under the leadership of Brown and the state's Democratic legislature and attorney general, California stands in strong opposition to Trumpism and its attacks not just on climate change action but on Muslim immigrants; the rights of gay, lesbian, and transgender people; gun control; taxes; healthcare; and walling off the Mexican border.

The state continues to chart its own course, in some cases flaunting its independence by filing lawsuits against the administration for its policies that run counter to values supported by most Californians. The same day Trump established a new federal policy to allow employers to deny health insurance coverage for birth control, Attorney General Xavier Becerra filed a lawsuit alleging the president's action was unconstitutional for violating anti-discrimination laws. Another suit was filed to stop Trump from building a wall at the Mexican border, and others challenged the Muslim travel ban, the plan to end the Deferred Action for Childhood Arrivals (DACA) program, changes to healthcare, and Trump's action to roll back greenhouse gas and vehicle mileage standards.

Brown and the legislature earmarked $30 million in legal services and financial aid to undocumented students when Trump made his decision to cancel the DACA program. In October 2017, in the face of attacks by Trump and U.S. Attorney General Jeff Sessions, Brown signed into law a measure declaring California a sanctuary state, limiting what state law enforcement agencies can do to cooperate with the feds on deportation efforts. State officials had already told federal immigration officials to stay out of state buildings and courtrooms, where they seemed to be trolling for undocumented immigrants who might have been in court as witnesses, family members, or defendants.

Immigration bashing is a loser in a state where agriculture and other segments of the economy are dependent on immigrants, and where intermarriage of Latinos and Anglos brings happiness one day and fear the next, as Anglos worry about their new family members being deported.

While Trump and his education secretary Betsy DeVos favor school vouchers and charter schools, the right to a good public education is cherished by Californians, who voted themselves the 2012 tax increase when the main recipients were the state's public schools. In October 2017, Brown signed a bill making the first year of community college tuition-free.

When transgender people serving in the U.S. military became the president's target, California became the first state in the nation to enable people who do not classify themselves male or female to mark their driver's licenses and change their birth certificates to "nonbinary," to be designated by an "X" or "NB."

The 2016 election demonstrated that people were yearning for change. Bernie Sanders represented a progressive populist response to what is not working, and Trump also expertly tapped into the pain of people, though he offered a reactionary, scapegoating view that is all too familiar now. The Democratic party establishment represented by Hillary Clinton failed to acknowledge the popular discontent in the nation, and it cost the election. The state's party registration figures are an indication of the voting public's mood, with 44.8 percent Democrats, 25.9 percent Republicans, and 24.5 percent "no preferred party," or independent, up from 20.9 percent in 2013. The headline is that independents stand just 1.4 percent away from making the Republican party the third party of choice in California.

Brown has been able to fulfill his agenda by appealing to the better nature of Californians, drawing on the legacy of traditional progressive politics of his father, Governor Pat Brown (from 1959 to 1967), and his own earlier terms in the governor's office. While much of the nation turned to the right in November 2016, California rejected that path, having long ago ended its flirtation with a sometimes mean-spirited conservatism for the simple reason that it did not work, examples being the anti-immigrant and anti-minority propositions in the 1990s, the energy deregulation crisis in 2000–2001, and tough-on-crime measures that in recent years were moderated by voters. All of these are dealt with in this book.

None of this is to suggest that California is free of issues that leave many of its residents feeling pain. While it is true that Brown governs the richest state in the union, it is also the poorest, with too many in the middle class for whom housing, healthcare, a college education for their children, and social mobility are increasingly unaffordable. California has the highest poverty rate in the nation at 20 percent, factoring in cost-of-living expenses, with another 20 percent "near poverty" according to the Public Policy Institute of California.

A contributing factor is increasing homelessness and unaffordable housing. In 2017, for example, while 425 people were living in tents in a since-demolished encampment in an old riverbed near the Anaheim Angels ballpark, the wait for affordable housing in Anaheim was about ten years. Los Angeles, with a shortage of half a million affordable housing units, counts about fifty thousand homeless people living in tents and cardboard shelters or on the pavement. In San Francisco the median price of a home was $1,380,000, while a house with less than two thousand square feet in the Silicon Valley city of Sunnyvale sold for $2.47 million, $782,000 over its listing price. The state's overall median home price in August 2017 was $565,000, more than double the national average, and one-third of Californians say they spend most of their income on housing. This is not sustainable.

After months of sometimes tense negotiations with Democratic legislators, Brown signed into law fifteen housing bills to encourage development of more affordable housing and shelters for the homeless by cutting red tape, easing zoning laws, putting a $4 billon housing bond measure on the ballot, and other means to generate new housing for all Californians.

There are other serious issues. The state abides a justice system that unfairly puts too many black, brown, and poor white people in prison (some of them innocent) and a crowded prison system that provides little to no rehabilitative effort to prevent recidivism. Brown's support of fracking leaves those who support his other environmental efforts scratching their heads and exercising their vocal chords in loud protest that mars his public appearances. In November 2017, Brown took on public employee labor unions in an attempt to fix a looming pension deficit in the billions by arguing that such pensions could be lowered for current as well as future public employees. With his term ending and no political race in his future, Brown can fight such battles that are unpopular with large numbers of steadfast Democratic voters.

The overall positive message of this book is that the country's most vibrant and important state has firmly established itself as a model for the nation—certainly not for the white separatist crowd that adulates Trump, but for the general populace. Instead of tiptoeing around the issues of immigration, climate change, deregulation, and human rights, the state is now deep blue precisely because it has offered an uncompromising alternative that embraces immigration as an asset, establishes climate change action as a bedrock policy, pays more to strengthen public education, and protects the rights of all people. This book is an examination of the struggle between the regressive vision of Trump and the progressive vision of Jerry Brown, and how these battles were fought and won in California and exist to be emulated elsewhere.

The California Dream

Living in California is like living in a bowl of
granola; what ain't fruits or nuts, is flakes.

—GALLAGHER, COMEDIAN

This popular late '70s East Coast rip on a state already then famous for trendsetting, cultural liberation, and technological innovation was notable for its ubiquity, so common that young children shared it without understanding who, exactly, it mocked: radicals and rebels, new agers and hippies, gay men and women. One of those made fun of was Governor Jerry Brown, whose unconventional and often quirky methods of governance and personal lifestyle landed him in the "flake" category of Gallagher's commentary.

But today, that dismissive stereotype, still repeated from time to time, is absurdly out of place. The second coming of Jerry Brown, prophet of revitalized notions of liberalism, progressive governance, and sound fiscal policy, has guided California's ascendance from the economic mire of the recession and near "failed state" status a mere six years ago to prominence, rising again as the most important state in the nation and seventh largest economy in the world.

California has become the economic, social, and political model of the twenty-first century, which stands in contrast to the alternative examples of Texas, Kansas, Florida, and others hobbled by right-wing ideology. In just one area, Brown's actions, with the support of a Democratic legislative majority and the people of his state, has cemented California's place in the universe of nations as a leader in the move to combat climate change, while conservative governors and Republican candidates for president deny the problem exists or that there is any human harm that can be reversed. (Florida's Rick Scott banned state employees from using the words "climate change" or "global warming" in reports and documents.[1])

Now in his fourth term heading the state, seasoned in the art of governing, Brown has contributed significantly to making California great again, to borrow from the Trumpian slogan. He has done this by balancing the budget (not always as his fellow Democrats would like), and funding a multibillion-dollar rainy-day fund, pushed by Republicans, while crafting social and government policy that is more sensitive and forward thinking than back in the 1970s, when he ran the state according to his self-described "era of limits."

Even back then, the "nuts and flakes" slam was way off base. And while the jibe was light, the mocking hinted at a larger American defensiveness, an attempt to write off the previous decade's dramatic social and political upheavals as nothing more than a goof. Because if California wasn't the site of all the nation's conflicts over civil rights, the war in Vietnam, and the attempt to depants "the Man" and his "system," it certainly had seemed to be the symbolic locus of changes many "mainstream" Americans were bemoaning as the root of a host of social ills. Meaner quips, in fact, often centered on the notion that if an earthquake pushed the state off the continental shelf into the Pacific, it would be no great loss.

From the rise of a bold Chicano culture in Los Angeles to the decadence and "obscenity" of an increasingly artistic and unchained Hollywood, from the myriad communes and cults dotting the forests and coastal towns along Highway 1 to columnist Herb Caen's radical "Berserkeley" and Oakland, home of the Black Panthers, Hells Angels, and even the renegade Raiders, California seemed to have exploded with color, strife, and new ideas, some silly, some scary, some brilliant.

Nor was it all "airy-fairy" stuff, another popular dismissal of the Left Coast from Manhattan's towers: The home-garage invention of the personal computer and the inventive commodification of the Internet created overnight fortunes even Wall Street had to respect—at least, that is, until the dot-com collapse that began in 1999 drew national mockery for the hubris and chutzpah of twentysomethings blowing billions on concept companies built around nothing more than a URL. And, perhaps a bit jealous of all the attention San Francisco's overheated housing market had attracted pre-mortgage meltdown, the East Coast media was quick to celebrate presidential candidate Rick Perry's mocking of California's foreclosure crisis after the recession.

Of course, as early as the gold rush, the East Coast establishment had chuckled at those crazy left coasters, perhaps smugly glad to have emptied their cities of so many dreamers, hustlers, and con artists making the migration westward. Yet the powerful draw of California, the final frontier of continental manifest destiny, ultimately prevented it from being perceived as a backwater for outcasts in the way, say, that the British saw their old penal colony Australia.

Instead, California became the seductress of the Wild West, bedazzling her suitors with shiny gold trinkets and promises to make them rich. They came in hordes and most stayed, if only to bask in her beauty. She was starkly different from what they'd left back home, warm and welcoming, her spirit conveying a sense of adventure and abandon. Over time, she would become the envy of the entire country, while those behind were left pouting, like jilted lovers.

Occasionally, she stumbled, yet she has always recovered her balance and run ahead, racing to embrace the future. Today, several years removed from a devastating recession that deeply challenged her confidence, California is surging once more—economically, politically, and culturally—as its quirky, "ruthlessly practical" leader, Governor Jerry Brown, aggressively pushes forward a new, trimmer, yet still essentially compassionate and optimistic version of the California dream.[2]

As historian H. W. Brands described the birth of the California dream after the staged "discovery" of gold near Sacramento: "The old American dream . . . was the dream of the Puritans . . . of men and women content to accumulate their modest fortunes a little at a time, year by year by year. The new dream was the dream of instant wealth, won in a twinkling by audacity and good luck. [This] golden dream . . . became a prominent part of the American psyche only after [gold was found at] Sutter's Mill."[3]

The dream proved remarkably enduring, even as reports began drifting back about the hell that was a miner's life and the bawdy lawlessness of the nation's new Paris-style theme park of debauchery, San Francisco, where venereal disease and earthquakes were equally terrifying facts of life. New Yorkers, Bostonians, Philadelphians, and the rest assumed that California would never be more than a distant novelty; the real power would always reside with the bankers on Wall Street, the industrialists in Chicago, the politicians in D.C. Let those westerners send us some fine, rowdy tall tales to read by the fire in our brownstone—tales of cowboys and sailors, miners and naturalists—and then let us get back to work.

But by 1963, California had knocked off prideful New York as the most populous state in the nation[4]—and it seemed to have become the most interesting one, too. That many of the nation's young people had been streaming west for more than a century left the nation's elite a bit queasy, especially since by then the region had several bona fide industries of towering global importance: aerospace, technology, and entertainment. So it is perhaps not surprising, then and now, that when bad times befall California, pundits, historians, and leaders of other states often appear unseemly in their haste to pronounce the California dream on life support, if not already dead.

"The California Dream is a love affair with an idea, a marriage to a myth,"[5] wrote historian Claudia Jurmain, explaining the rank disappointment of the farmers who fled the 1930s Dust Bowl for the sustained poverty they found in California—the same scenario that subsequent destitute immigrants from China, Mexico, Guatemala, Vietnam, Cambodia, and other parts of the developing world would find upon arrival.

"California is a tragic country—like Palestine, like every Promised Land," wrote Christopher Isherwood. "Its short history is a fever-chart of migrations—the land rush, the gold rush, the oil rush, the movie rush, the Okie fruit-picking rush, the wartime rush to the aircraft factories—followed, in each instance, by counter-migrations of the disappointed and unsuccessful, moving sorrowfully homeward."[6]

It's true that the dream, regardless of how it was marketed or perceived, could never be a promise, but many found that the strip of desert, mountain, plain, and coast spanning one thousand by four hundred miles offered greater opportunities than the rigidly stratified and frequently war-torn societies they had fled. With each receding echo of the post–World War II population and economic booms, the dream is renewed, reinvigorated. The place is just so fertile, spawning cultural trends and whole industries as easily as it produces grapes, or olives, or avocados, and this tends to alleviate the often harsh realities that threaten to tarnish the veneer of the Golden State: racial tension, exploitation of immigrants, massive and, since the 1970s, increasing economic inequality.

In fact, by the eve of the Great Recession of 2008, California had navigated a thirty-year period of increased political polarization, exacerbated by a steady stream of reactionary citizen-initiated ballot measures—targeting immigrants, people of color, and gays and lesbians—to become dominated once again by the centrist Democratic Party; the state also was a key bulwark for the historic election of Barack Obama. Host to the dominant corporate engines powering the again-booming and synergistic technology and entertainment industries and the "cool factor" they accrued, the state was in the midst of another astonishing housing boom, financed by easy credit and equity loans based on seemingly ever-rising property values.

Sure, no matter how high the share prices of Google or Apple climbed, the state was still struggling to fulfill its promise to those not able to afford a $95,000 Tesla Model S. And the once shiny educational and infrastructure systems were widely perceived as still in decline thirty years after a national "taxpayers' revolt" was kicked off with the shocking passage of Proposition 13. But, hey, the laser, iPhone, blue jeans, and the summer blockbuster were invented here; there was even a macho, charming, cigar-chomping actor in the governor's mansion. And the weather was still nice.

Then the roof caved in. *The Guardian*'s Paul Harris summarized the crushing Great Recession well, noting that the Golden State, for all its glitter and gloss, its image of success and boundless opportunity, by 2009 was in a state of collapse: "From its politics to its economy to its environment and way of life, California is like a patient on life support."

The financial meltdown had walloped the state. The government, collapsing under a crippling deficit, began issuing IOUs to pay its bills and made huge cuts in education and healthcare funding. Large numbers of state workers lost their jobs and others were forced to take unpaid "furlough" days and lengthier unpaid leaves. Local governments suffered a similar fate. The unemployment rate of 12 percent was the highest since 1939, further contributing to the deficit through loss of tax revenue. The mortgage meltdown wiped out the wealth of a large swath of the middle class and cost tens of thousands of families their homes, lost to foreclosure. It did not end there.

"Its political system is locked in paralysis and the two-term rule of former movie star Arnold Schwarzenegger is seen as a disaster," Harris noted. "The crisis is so deep that Professor Kevin Starr, who has written an acclaimed history of the state, recently declared: 'California is on the verge of becoming the first failed state in America.'"[7]

Et tu, Professor Starr? The fact that as revered a scholar as Starr, California's historian emeritus and perhaps the state's biggest fan, would deploy such an epithet showed the depths to which the mighty had quickly fallen after Wall Street inflated and then burst the biggest bubble in decades.

Even Mitt Romney, running another failed presidential campaign, took a crack at the state where he had one of his many luxury homes—even though he wasn't facing any California politicians in the race. "At some point America is going to become like Greece or like Spain or Italy, or like California," he smirked, listing political states where capitalism had recently run aground in dramatic fashion.[8]

Economists at California Lutheran University were even harsher in their judgment. "California is fast becoming a post-industrial hell," wrote Bill Watkins, director of the Center for Economic Research and Forecasting, for "almost everyone except the gentry class, their best servants, and the public sector."[9] He defended his hyperbole: The state's unemployment rate at 12 percent was higher than the national average, and the poverty rate adjusted for the high cost of living more than twice that. Two of the country's ten poorest large cities were here, Fresno and San Bernardino, with the latter second only to bankrupt and burning Detroit. Beneath the glitz and techie gleam, there were enormous reservoirs of pain.

Even access to the state's free natural beauty was being curtailed; in 2011, state officials announced that by July 1, 2012, seventy parks across California would be closed completely to save a measly $22 million.[10]

By that point, three years after the mortgage crisis began, disastrously declining tax revenues had begun savaging the state's budget, like a rabbit slowly being digested by a snake. Both the elementary and higher education systems were absorbing historic decreases in funding—$7 billion, or 13.8 percent, statewide for K–12—with school and district administrators being asked each year to trim absurd amounts of fat off budgets that already had long been on a diet.

In Oakland, for example, the high-poverty district of nearly forty thousand students saw its budget shrink from $615 million in 2008 to $445 million just four years later; schools were shuttered, staff and teachers laid off, a new contract was unilaterally imposed on teachers who had not had a raise in a decade, and nearly the entire adult education program was dismantled overnight. At the city's biggest public high school, Skyline, where most students are from low-income families, the school shed its librarian, all its counselors, and most of its untenured teachers. This was not uncommon in schools throughout the state.

Governor Arnold Schwarzenegger, brought to power in 2003 with much populist fanfare after the successful recall campaign against his predecessor, centrist Democrat Gray Davis, had himself been humbled in 2005 by the total rejection of a slew of ambitious Republican reform initiatives he brought to the electorate through a special election. Chastened, especially by his failure to weaken the power of public unions, he retreated into moderation, and by 2010 his second term was ending on a down note, with his leaving behind a high budget deficit, a debt that grew from $34 billion to $91 billion during his tenure, and embarrassingly low approval ratings.

"Do you ever feel like you're watching the end of the California dream?" a reporter asked him at a press conference concerning a state budget featuring billions in cuts. "I think the California dream is as strong as ever,"[11] he replied with a straight face.

What Schwarzenegger presided over was a seismic political shift based on long-developing demographic changes that had shrunk the power of conservative and elderly whites alongside a shocking series of excesses spawned by a lack of controls on the free market: the inflation and crash of the tech bubble that began the new millennium, the humiliation of California and Governor Gray Davis by rapacious Wild West energy companies in the deregulation crisis of 2001–03, and now the foreclosure crisis, high unemployment, and economic recession that was leaving millions of Californians in pain and hardship.

Homeowners were losing their claim on middle-class security, bedrock liberal programs such as public education were under threat in a way not seen since the Depression, and a popular movement called Occupy Wall Street had spread across the country in 2011 as if cultivated in a petri dish overnight, planting the issue of economic inequality front and center in the national conversation. After months of protests, the impromptu urban encampments dispersed, shattered by police violence, liberal versus radical splits—and the intervention of Mother Nature throwing rain and snow into the mix—but not before Occupiers had raised the national consciousness.

For decades, California had been drifting stutteringly rightward, from the rise of Reagan through the tax revolt that made the state highly dependent on a narrow slice of wealthy taxpayers and the value of their stock options, to the bipartisan immigrant bashing of Proposition 187, which sought to turn every nurse and elementary school teacher into a border cop, and which would have disastrous ramifications for the Republican Party. Now, at last, the state's pendulum seemed to be moving back toward center.

Certainly, Schwarzenegger's successor, with impeccable timing honed by decades in the electoral trenches, was tacking hard that way. After decades of fighting back toward mainstream acceptance from the fringes to which his career had been banished, an iconic and once forgotten California leader arrived back on center stage well prepped for a leading role.

Lampooned by the media in his first youthful governorship in the 1970s as a proverbial California flake, or some sort of weird if engaging eccentric, political scion Edmund "Jerry" Brown Jr. actually had always been more of a zig-zagging pragmatist and clever political animal than the quasi-hippie space cadet East Coasters liked to imagine. In 2010, facing former eBay CEO Meg Whitman, a living embodiment of the smug corporate and financial world that had so recently humbled the great state and created misery for millions, the veteran pol crushed the dilettante on his home turf with the wind at his back.

Now, with the state at a historic crossroads after the shattering recession, the unlikely triumphant return of the still enigmatic Brown, presenting himself as a nonideological problem solver, posed as many questions as answers. There were many sacred cows on the chopping block—not just programs, but even the state's values and core beliefs about itself—and Brown was now the butcher, wielding enormous power with a Democratic supermajority in the state legislature in 2012 (for the first time since 1883) and line-item veto power. What would he do? To which of the myriad furious voices assaulting Sacramento would he listen?

The stakes were sky high. Brown and his thirty-eight million constituents were facing major decisions about the future, and, as so often for the nation's bellwether, the repercussions would be global in impact. California in the 1990s and into the early 2000s had cut taxes[12] even as it built an enormous prison gulag and kept giving select groups of public workers fat pensions and steady raises; something had to give.

As long as the state was riding the tech and housing booms, windfall capital gains taxes on the stock sales of a tiny number of the megawealthy cashing in on IPOs had kept the budgets in the black, but those days were over. Between 2007 and 2009, the percentage of the general fund covered by capital gains revenue fell from 12 percent to just 3—the main reason, according to Standard & Poor's, being that the state's credit rating had fallen to an embarrassing A-.

The upshot was that Californians had to decide whether to raise taxes or cut spending, or create a new ratio of both. With the abrupt rise of the Tea Party movement—a Koch Brothers–funded renewal of the traditional populist small-government mind-set always endemic in the West and South—many portrayed the economic crisis as an opportunity to dramatically shrink the ambitions of liberal governance: Slash the bureaucracy, ax environmental protections, limit or halt social services, cut taxes on the rich.

The deregulation and tax cuts of the Reagan revolution, they insisted, had not caused the economic problems; in fact, they argued, they had not gone far enough. This conveniently ignored the disastrous effects of repealing the Glass-Steagall Act, engineered by Bill Clinton and company, and of further deregulating the banking and financial industry in ways friendly to Wall Street lobbyists, through the Financial Services Modernization Act.

These proponents of a return to frontier-style limited government had a new favorite model, and it happened to be California's bitter longtime western rival in economics, political leadership, and even sports: Texas. The Lone Star State, led through the financial meltdown by the increasingly hard-line governor Rick Perry, had weathered the recession better than most of the country through a quirk of history: Populist anger against a prestatehood foreclosure crisis in the 1830s led to the state's imposing long ago some of the most stringent bank regulations, particularly about so-called predatory lending, and so Texas suffered fewer foreclosures on overleveraged homeowners. Only Alaska had fewer foreclosures than Texas in the mortgage meltdown.

Despite these protective—and, in this case, effective—regulations, which Tea Partiers might mock as products of a "nanny state," modern Texas is generally marked by an unabashed probusiness, low-tax, minimal-services approach to governance. "Building a business is tough," Perry drawled in radio commercials aired in California, "but I hear building a business in California is next to impossible." With the state working its way out of recession purgatory and Texas less damaged, Perry and a national chorus of Republicans began to frame the California-Texas rivalry as something akin to a referendum on the future of the American experiment.

After serving as a model for the country in the 1960s and 1970s, "California, like so many other states facing budget shortfalls, is a victim of decades of reckless spending and unsustainable budgets," wrote former Speaker of the House Newt Gingrich in 2009 in the *Financial Times* under the headline "Texas Leads as California Dreams On." Instead of admitting that banking regulation had been key to saving the Texas economy, the Georgia Republican credited that state's success in part to the fact that the legislature only meets every other year for 140 days and "Texas lawmakers have also made it clear that they like jobs enough to like people who create jobs. There is no state income or capital gains tax, and state enterprise funds and creative governments have fostered dramatic economic growth."[13]

In his book *The Texas Model: Prosperity in the Lone Star State and Lessons for America*, former California Republican state assemblyman Chuck DeVore was even more clear in casting the two states as "two opposing versions of the American Dream, one based on liberty, the other, government," and claiming that Americans were voting with their feet by "moving to Texas while Californians have been fleeing as fast as they can sell their home and pack." A spate of other books and magazine articles piled on to the meme: *Texas Got It Right* and *Big, Hot, Cheap, and Right: What America Can Learn from the Strange Genius of Texas*; as well as a *Time* magazine cover story headlined "Why Texas Is Our Future."

It was simple, the now ubiquitous argument went: Shrink your government, pass a balanced budget, keep taxes low—at least for the wealthy—and get out of the way. Never mind that Texas had the lowest percentage of high school graduates, the highest percentage of adults lacking health insurance, and the most hazardous waste and carbon dioxide emissions in the nation.[14] By 2009, California had run aground on the shoals of history, critics were bellowing—the once-enviable state was drowning in deficit, and the sooner Sacramento started emulating Austin, the better. Conventional wisdom that year held that Texas was now a "miracle," while California was a "failed state." It was obvious which one should be the model for the future.

Or was it?

By 2012, a mere three years later, the situation hardly looked so clear-cut. California's economy was again booming,[15] unemployment was falling,[16] and the state had voted for the Brown-crafted Proposition 30, which raised both sales and income taxes for several years in order to fend off, at the eleventh hour, the harshest probable budget cuts.

Meanwhile, the "Texas Miracle" that Governor Perry had been driving was being questioned by those willing to look under the hood. In a lengthy examination of the underlying economics of the Texas job-creation boom, *Washington Monthly* senior editor Phillip Longman argued that many of the bolder claims made by Texas booster in chief Perry "crumble under inspection."[17] Specifically, he showed convincingly that the reasons the Lone Star State had been able to add jobs—and pretty good ones, too—at a higher rate than the rest of the country was primarily because of a huge oil and gas boom supported by new drilling technologies and strong global prices. The state's oil production increased 126 percent between 2010 and 2013, carrying the rest of the state's economy with it.

Longman also established, using hard numbers, that any sort of Cal-to-Texas stampede was strictly a myth promulgated by agenda-driven politicians. In 2012, for example, the net migration for the two states was a negligible 19,697 toward the East—or .00051 percent of Californians.

"Far from proving the merits of the so-called Texas model, it shows just how few Californians have seen fit to set out for the Lone Star State, despite California's high cost of housing and other very real problems," he wrote.[18]

"The real Texas miracle is that its current leaders get away with bragging about it," Longman concluded.[19]

The reality, of course, is that California is a complex and massive state, and attempts to simplify it as "failed" are not much more accurate than calling it "golden." It is, after all, the state that almost simultaneously spawned the conservative Reagan revolution, the radical Black Panther Party, and the world's biggest annual celebration of being lesbian, gay, bisexual, and transgender: San Francisco's Pride weekend. Its diversity is not just racial, ethnic, or linguistic, but cultural and political, too.

In fact, there are two competing narratives of California's greatness that have alternately contended as explanations for the state's success. Both have had a legitimate claim to dominance. One, which came to be so ably marketed by Ronald Reagan himself, emphasizes the creative power of the free market and, in particular, individual entrepreneurs, using their ingenuity to make

God's gift of California ever more bountiful; it stresses the market-driven aspect of wealth creation and denies that the state requires strong government intervention as a key to its development.

Fitting neatly into this vision are celebrated examples of ambitious individuals and corporations, starting with the original hardscrabble forty-niners and the founders of banks like Wells Fargo and Bank of America that cashed their gold and continuing through the early-twentieth-century rise of the great Hollywood studios; the great "garage" success stories, from Disneyland and Mattel to Apple and Hewlett-Packard; the birth of Google; and real estate giants like billionaire Eli Broad, whose KB Homes spun an endless procession of suburbs out into the deserts and valleys of the state.

The other story, less heroically portrayed because it relies on unglamorous bureaucracies and unpopular taxation, is one of government intervention—at both the federal and state levels—which set the stage for economic growth. While everybody agrees California is beautiful, the reality is that much of it is rugged, vast, and inhospitable to many types of human activities. Until the advent of massive public works projects—aqueducts, bridges, freeways, port dredging, electrification, schools, universities, and even the Defense Department's subsidized aerospace industry and its role in creating the Internet—civilization in the state primarily had been dominated in its early days by the "Barbary Coast" image of San Francisco, farming in the valleys, and the forlorn desert backwater of Los Angeles.

In this version of the story, regulation and "good government" progressivism would ensure the state developed a reputation as much less corrupt than the rest of the country. Environmental protections started early here, with the banning of hydraulic mining in 1884 because it was polluting the farmers' precious water. The reality was that capitalism has always benefited from an honest broker, balanced laws, and public infrastructure created for the commons.

Spurred by the Depression and subsequent New Deal repudiation of pure laissez-faire capitalism, this latter vision—public, liberal, optimistic—had gained ascendancy in California, and its greatest policy successes, under a series of moderate Republican and Democratic governors, were conveniently supported by a post–World War II boom that made it easy to pay for it all.

California became famous for its state-of-the-art highway and water infrastructure and, especially, for its world-famous University of California and state college systems, with their impressive array of massive campuses in every corner of the state. In China, villagers who knew nothing else about California wanted their children to one day attend "Harvard or Berkeley," to be taught by what seemed an ever-refreshing army of Nobel Laureates.

Less than one hundred years after achieving statehood, California had become the national model, an enthusiastic ally in President Lyndon Johnson's ambitious if underfunded Great Society program. However, just as the disastrous war against Vietnam was bringing Johnson to his knees and setting the stage for a Republican to capture the White House, the pendulum in California was swinging to the right.

Running in 1966 on a twin platform of small government—sending "the welfare bums back to work" was his pungent analysis—and a crackdown on student protesters to "clean up the mess at Berkeley," former actor and General Electric spokesmodel Ronald Reagan upset the incumbent, the liberal's liberal, Edmund G. "Pat" Brown Sr.,[20] and was reelected four years later.

Reagan's developing vision, which came to be called the Reagan revolution after he went on to two terms as president, was oddly, if not always obviously, embraced by his successor, Pat's son, Jerry. Leading opposing parties, the two nevertheless shared a common view that government, in California at least, had become too big, too bureaucratic, too unwieldy. Both men were also uncanny in their ability to work the media and political symbols.

Ironically, considering their divergent historical reputations, Jerry Brown was even more successful in his first term at trimming Sacramento's sails than his Republican predecessor had been. Not so subtly rebuking his father's policies, which he perceived as no longer politically tenable, he called in his second State of the State speech for belt-tightening. The Organization of Oil Producing Countries' (OPEC) oil shocks of the early 1970s and a period of stagflation were sobering, and Brown, personally frugal with both money and sentiment, would remain in character.

He spoke of the nation's "sluggish economic growth, increasing social instability, widespread unemployment and unprecedented environmental challenges" and announced "Something has to give. . . . The choice to do one thing may preclude another. In short, we are entering an era of limits. . . . We face a sober reassessment of new economic realities; and we all have to get used to it."[21]

The rise of these political curmudgeons, including President Nixon, another California pol, was abetted by and fed upon a rising individualism, or selfishness, as times got tougher, and anger at allegedly being forced to solve "other people's problems," whether through taxation, school busing, mental asylums, or public transportation improvements. While some racial and ethnic minorities embraced this mood, it was particularly popular with suburban and rural whites, still the majority in the state but able to see a time not far off where they would no longer be so.

When a housing boom in the 1970s abruptly sent property taxes tied to home values soaring year over year, this retrenchment from the compassionate optimism of earlier decades found its full flowering expression with the historic "tax revolt" in the form of Proposition 13, led by proto–Tea Party leader and angry white male Howard Jarvis and his sidekick, Paul Gann. For the state's liberals and progressives decades later, this initiative would eventually become the sort of original sin blamed for California's alleged decline as a global model, even as conservatives focused on the state's still massive bureaucracy and powerful public unions.

These competing ideological tendrils, both singly and in combination, have spawned their share of positive and negative consequences—many of them unintended. Public works underpinning private industry led to polluted cities, suburban sprawl, labor exploitation, and illegal immigration while simultaneously providing good jobs, technological innovation, and much of the arsenal that defeated Nazi Germany and imperial Japan. When the state's facilities for the mentally ill were largely decommissioned by Reagan in the early 1970s, supporters of the move, including the American Civil Liberties Union, pointed to the end of inmate abuses, while critics would link the move to a historic and persistent rise in urban homelessness.

But complexity and subtlety are not in fashion in our "What have you tweeted lately?" era. California, dominated politically by middle-class Democrats, is nevertheless still home to millions of conservative evangelical Christians;

naturalized, legal, and undocumented immigrants; and unevenly educated children in inequitable schools. Toss in a few Google buses' worth of multimillionaires and billionaires who like to throw their considerable weight around and an amorphous but real Left Coast sensibility that questions received wisdom, and it becomes clear that any expectation of ideological consistency in such a diverse place is woefully misplaced.

Despite its size and lack of homogeneity, or perhaps because of it, this book argues that today California represents a model for the nation, having boldly rejected the idea that government, operated for the good of both the majority and minority, is a dirty word. From raising taxes on those with annual incomes over $250,000 to shifting money toward schools in low-income communities, from seeking environmental alliances with other countries to limit global warming to the rejection of military solutions to illegal immigration, there are clear, if not always consistent, indications that Californians are not content to pursue the "race to the bottom" neoliberal model that has catapulted conservative politics in recent years.

This latter vision is exemplified by conservative Republicans such as Perry, Sam Brownback of Kansas, and Rick Scott of Florida and rejected by the pragmatic liberal Brown. It is a blueprint for government that endorses privatization, deregulation, reductions in government spending, minimal government "interference" in business, and a tax system that disproportionately favors the wealthy.

To develop this hypothesis, this book seeks to move away from generalities and examine in depth some of the state's most important conflicts, leaders, issues, and watershed moments of the past half century that have influenced the state's evolution from a red state to solid blue. Subsequent chapters will examine two very different landmark taxation measures, Propositions 13 and 30, bracketing the political transformation; the state of public education; the long, quirky, and calculated political career of Jerry Brown, whose leadership has been key to the state's rebound; and the crucial state battleground issues of immigration, education, energy, the environment, and, of course, taxes.

2

The Pendulum Swings Right

t was 1978, and my mother was about to lose her Southern California home. Twenty-five years after she and my father, both of them World War II Marine Corps veterans, realized the American dream of buying their own home in a suburb of San Diego for the barely affordable price of $13,500, she was going to be forced to sell it. Living on a fixed income from Social Security and veteran's benefits, she could no longer pay the skyrocketing property-tax bill she received from the San Diego County tax assessor. The imminent possibility of forcing her to sell her home to avoid foreclosure created in her an overwhelming fear, wiping out the years of security and stability she and my father had enjoyed as first-time homeowners.

My parents were transplants from the East Coast, part of the large postwar westward migration of former veterans who either stayed in the state or returned after having been stationed at one of its many military bases during the war years. Leaving the freezing winters and hot, muggy summers of Providence, Rhode Island, for the temperate clime of Southern California was irresistible. The Golden State was paradise.

My father preceded my mother, brother, and me, coming to find a job before sending for us. He found one almost immediately, in the burgeoning aerospace industry, and we soon followed him. We took a train west in 1951, crossing the continent when I was four and my brother was five. My father told me we were moving to a place where it never rained; when it did, I cried.

World War II, and the Cold War that followed, spurred massive federal spending in California in the state's defense-related industries. Building ships and planes and bombs was big business, and jobs were plentiful. Workers flooded the state, and California's population boomed. Between 1940 and 1965, when I graduated from high school, the state's population grew from 6.95 million to 18.5 million residents. As the population grew, so did housing construction. Seemingly overnight, acres of land were cleared and tract homes sprouted near two-lane roads that eventually would expand into superhighways. I witnessed this phenomenon firsthand as my parents, who had rented for two years, bought their 1,280-square-foot, four-bedroom tract house while it was still being built, allowing my mother to choose countertops and colors to personalize our home.

We moved in as construction crews worked feverishly all around us to finish the houses our future neighbors would occupy. Unpaved dirt roads kicked up dust all day, as heavy tractors leveled plots and dump trucks hauled away dirt, to the utter fascination of my brother and me. The smell of fresh-cut lumber lingered in the air, as did the excitement of each family who moved into its new home. Tiny tree and plant sprouts dotted the parkways and front and back yards, leaving entirely to one's imagination the thick foliage that would one day produce the color and life that would break up the monotony of these tract houses. It seemed that schools could not be built fast enough, so going to class in temporary buildings and then being moved to partially constructed schools was not uncommon for us new young suburbanites.

Three years after we moved into our home, there were so many children in the neighborhood that a new elementary school had to be built. It was just a few blocks from our house, and we started our classes there in portable prefab buildings while the main school buildings were being completed. This was happening all over California, its infrastructure expanding to keep pace with its growing population. Taxes were raised to support building multilane freeways, bridges, and water systems to meet the people's needs.

Lifelong Roosevelt Democrats, my parents had never been opposed to paying taxes. My mother knew the levies she and my father paid contributed to the fine public schools my brother and I attended, to the local library where we had borrowed wonderful books, to the municipal pool we visited almost daily in the hot summer months, not to mention the public services we all took, and still do take, for granted: the water and sewer systems, parks, buses, well-paved roads, and more.

She knew those very community benefits had resulted in her home's value increasing to a worth she could not have imagined when she and my father purchased it, tens of thousands of dollars more. It seemed unfair that she now was faced with selling her home because on her fixed income she could no longer pay the escalating taxes needed to maintain that comfortable middle-class lifestyle her taxes had helped create.

Her dilemma in 1978 was similarly faced by hundreds of thousands of other homeowners in California, many of whom had seen their property taxes double and then double again in just a few years. In the four years between 1968 and 1972, property tax revenue for local governments grew an average of 11.5 percent, accompanied by the boom in home prices; the median price of a home in the state doubled from $31,460 in 1973 to $62,290 in four years.[1] In 1978, the average home value in California was $85,000.[2]

Conversations in coffeehouses, PTA meetings, posh private clubs, and backyard barbecues inevitably turned to real estate—what a friend or co-worker paid for a house, how much the neighbors got for theirs, where or how one could get a really good deal. Homeowners who wanted to sell their houses enjoyed large profits.

But for others, such as those on a fixed income who wanted to stay in their homes and leave something of value to their children, the soaring property values invited higher and higher taxes. Ultimately, for many who had neither the desire nor the finances to move, or the income to pay a higher mortgage payment if they took out an equity loan to pay the taxes, the only options were foreclosure or sale of their treasured home.

There had been several attempts by California legislators and citizens using the ballot initiative process to pass tax-reduction measures. Some modest efforts were successful, but voters rejected the most radical of the tax-cutting measures. It was clear to them that in order to pay for the services they had been enjoying, a "robbing Peter to pay Paul" scenario would force increases in income, sales, and other taxes to offset a decrease in property taxes.

Howard Jarvis, the man who would ultimately gain national fame as California's tax cutter in chief, failed to qualify a property tax decrease initiative for the 1972 ballot, when two hundred thousand signatures were disqualified because they could not be validated due, as Jarvis put it, to "boobs who were hired off the street . . . who didn't know what they were doing."[3] Many considered the man's frank style attractive.

Jarvis, who today is lionized by his followers as a hero of the antitax movement, back then was a political wannabe who had sought public office several times, unsuccessfully. He first opposed the popular moderate Republican senator Thomas Kuchel, a ten-year incumbent, in the 1962 Republican primary; he considered Kuchel too liberal. He lowered his sights in 1970 for a seat on the State Board of Equalization and again was rejected by voters. A final attempt for elective office came in 1977, when he unsuccessfully tried to unseat the popular two-term Los Angeles mayor, Tom Bradley, the city's first African American mayor.

Exposing an inflated view of himself in his 1979 memoir, *I'm Mad as Hell*, Jarvis said of that race: "I made a pretty damn good showing."[4] In fact, he got only 10 percent of the vote. After his 1972 tax-cutting initiative failed to qualify, he supported the alternative initiative proposed by the Los Angeles County assessor, Philip Watson, to cap property taxes at 1.75 percent but raise sales, corporate income, and the so-called "sin" taxes on liquor and cigarettes. It also would have capped local per-pupil expenditures. The official ballot document included the mandatory "Financial impact: A net ascertainable decrease in revenues to state and local government of $1,233,000,000 per year."[5] Voters rejected it 66 percent to 34 percent.

That year the California legislature gave property-tax payers a small break in the process of changing the way schools were funded in the state. Senate Bill (SB) 90, the so-called Tax Relief Act of 1972, was a highly contentious measure passed by the legislature and signed into law by Reagan. This measure provided some property-tax relief by increasing the homeowner's exemption to $7,000, but it also took care of a major problem facing the state: complying with the landmark 1971 California Supreme Court decision *Serrano v. Priest,* which found that relying on local property taxes to fund schools resulted in rampant inequality among schoolchildren.

To comply with the *Serrano* decision, the state needed a new mechanism to take funding of schools away from local governments. That was accomplished with SB 90, which limited a school district's authority to raise local property taxes to meet its local budgetary demands and established state support for schools for the first time. As a consequence of SB 90, the state handed school districts more than $1 billion in aid and tax relief to help schools transition from local property-tax revenue to a state-funded system.

Getting SB 90 enacted into law involved a major compromise between Reagan and the Democratic assembly speaker, Bob Moretti, the state's second most powerful figure. To comply with *Serrano,* there had to be a tax shift; the Democrats, who controlled both legislative houses, preferred a switch to a progressive income tax, while the Republicans and the governor preferred to rely on the more regressive sales taxes. Both sides finally struck a compromise: a modest sales tax increase and higher bank and corporation taxes.

Although SB 90 was signed by Reagan on December 1, 1972, it left him brooding. Reagan, who had presided over a deficit-induced large tax increase shortly after he took office in 1967, had spent years trying to rein in government spending, pushing against the legislative tide, and he put the full weight of his office and all of his political capital behind a constitutional amendment the following year to do just that.

Proposition 1, the Revenue Control and Tax Reduction Initiative, appeared on the ballot in a special election on November 6, 1973. The measure, written in part by Nobel Prize–winning laissez-faire economist Milton Friedman, who taped television commercials for the campaign, would have tied annual growth in state expenditures to the increase in state revenues. It would have capped the amount of income tax that could be collected from Californians and would have required a two-thirds vote of the legislature to pass any tax measure.

The campaign received national media coverage. All eyes were on Reagan, as pundits suggested that the measure's success would be the former actor's springboard to a presidential bid in 1976. The governor tried mightily to sell Proposition 1 to Californians, personally engaging in a $1 million campaign in which he talked up the "taxpayers' revolt" in a flurry of speeches around the state.[6] In those speeches and in taped telephone messages to Republican households throughout California, he enticed voters to approve this "once in a lifetime" chance to trim taxes.[7]

Moretti also traveled the state, but his message was a dire warning of the consequences—the "walls [will] come crashing down"—if the measure passed.[8] Voters by a 54-46 percent margin decided to keep the walls up, spurning the popular governor. However, the closeness of this vote compared with previous tax-cutting measures, two of which lost by more than two-to-one margins, was a sign of growing voter discontent. State lawmakers, who had grown accustomed to voters rejecting big tax cuts out of fear of the repercussions, failed to recognize this. But the message was not lost on one persistent man who had been waiting offstage.

The indefatigable Jarvis, director of a Los Angeles association of apartment-house owners, who remained on his eternal quest to cut taxes, reentered the electoral picture three years after the special election, once again with a statewide initiative for the 1976 ballot. He had managed to obtain 489,000 signatures on petitions for another tax-limitation constitutional amendment but fell short by about 10,000 (the required number based on a percentage of the gubernatorial vote in the previous election). Philip Watson also tried again and also failed to get his measure qualified. Jarvis was undeterred. Like the child's Bobo doll that's knocked down only to immediately bounce back up, Jarvis popped back into the electoral process and launched another effort aimed for the June 1978 ballot.

This time, Jarvis, who was also head of the Los Angeles–based United Organization of Taxpayers, teamed up with Paul Gann, a former Sacramento Realtor and head of his own antitax group. Together, the two men had several years of experience in the initiative business and a valuable resource: lists of hundreds of thousands of antitax supporters from Northern and Southern

California. They could cover the entire state, with Jarvis focusing on Southern California and Gann spearheading efforts in the North. Their formula worked. They obtained 1.2 million signatures, nearly three times what was needed, to qualify Proposition 13 for the 1978 June ballot.

Patience and persistence finally paid off for the tax-cutting pair, but they were significantly aided by a growing panic among homeowners afraid of losing their homes, as well as a brewing general discontent with politicians who didn't seem to care about them.

A conservative backlash had been developing in the state since the early 1960s in reaction to emboldened protest movements and legal gains made by minorities. A bill banning discrimination in housing passed the legislature in 1963. It was later repealed by voters, but the courts nullified that action by declaring the repeal unconstitutional. This, coupled with increasingly aggressive actions of campus protesters at the esteemed—and taxpayer-supported—University of California campuses, most notably Berkeley, infuriated older suburban moderates in both parties. In Reagan's campaign for governor in 1966, the so-called Great Communicator convinced voters that Pat Brown was coddling the protesters. Once elected, he duly cracked down on them, on occasion turning Berkeley into a war zone patrolled by the National Guard.

Voters were also riled by another popular measure that was overturned by the courts, this time when Reagan supported and signed a 1970 law banning the busing of schoolchildren without parental consent. After the courts threw it out, voters passed an antibusing statewide initiative in November 1972, with a margin of two million votes. That, too, was nullified as unconstitutional by the Supreme Court of California in 1975.

In addition, while a series of moderate Democratic and Republican governors up through Pat Brown had fostered an era of development and growth—building freeways and bridges and college campuses—Californians now increasingly wanted development to slow down or stop and thus blocked the construction of low-to-moderate-income housing, as well as expensive development along the California coastline. Californians took control of that issue by voting to preserve open space and public access to the state's beaches in the California Coastal Act of 1972. The landmark constitutional amendment re-created the California Coastal Commission and six regional commissions to oversee regulation of development along the state's 840-mile coastline. This slow-growth movement contributed in part to driving up the prices of existing housing, resulting in higher assessments and property taxes. This was the lay of the land in 1978, when Howard Jarvis was blasting his antitax messages. To have achieved the American dream of homeownership only to face the nightmare of losing it was a specter that resonated with property owners.

Jarvis was a skilled orator of the common-man variety, appealing to discontented voters with made-for-TV rhetoric the media could not resist. His bombast reminds one of today's Donald Trump. Jarvis campaigned on the airwaves, in newspaper interviews, and through public appearances, using his booming voice to rail about laggards living on welfare, forced school busing, a lax criminal justice system, lazy bureaucrats, and waste in government. He pushed every hot button there was, acting as the 1970s version of today's Tea Party zealot or right-wing personality prattling on about bloated government. In fact, one of his followers was way ahead of her time. As he wrote in 1979, "Some of the people who wanted to reduce taxes had turned to gimmicks, without my approval. A gal out in the [San Fernando] Valley came up with the idea of using a tea bag as a symbol, to remind everyone of the Boston Tea Party."[9]

To many, the seventy-four-year-old Jarvis was a folk hero. He made *Time*'s cover. He fired up voters. In his book he noted that going door-to-door with petitions, as he'd done in previous campaigns, took too much time. "It was much more efficient to have our people at shopping centers and office buildings," he said. "We learned the best approach to use on someone when you want to get their signatures on a petition [is to tell them]: 'Sign this—it will help lower your taxes.' That usually worked."[10]

And it did work, even if it wasn't true for everyone, since renters did not have property tax to lower, though they did have higher rents to pay if landlords asked for more in rent to cover escalating tax bills.

A bumbling but quite energetic grandfather type, Jarvis was a colorful personality who attracted attention as he traversed the state. "On a typical day during the campaign," he wrote, "I would do a couple of interviews with the press, give a speech at lunch, cut a radio or TV spot, have dinner with the local tax leaders in whatever area I was in, and appear at an evening rally . . . in two or three or four different cities and towns around the state."[11]

He claimed to have hit "a responsive chord" in two coastal communities in particular. One was Los Angeles's southern neighbor, Orange County, arguably the most Republican bastion in the state, where home values and property taxes, particularly along the Pacific Ocean, had skyrocketed. The other was in Santa Cruz, "where they had about 1,800 surfers from all over the country, aged sixteen to thirty-four. They didn't do anything but surf and draw welfare and food stamps. The guy who owned a home got hit with a huge tax increase in order to support these surfers . . . I told them after [Proposition] 13 passed, the sun was going to come up the next day and all the surfers were going to evaporate. Proposition 13 went over real well in those places."[12]

Jarvis made a masterful decision when he decided to hook up the Prop 13 campaign with two men who would become famous—infamous, more accurately—for their work in direct marketing. Bill Butcher and Arnold Forde, doing business as Butcher-Forde Consulting in solid-red-Republican Newport Beach, Orange County's upscale coastal city, ran an unrivaled political campaign fund-raising apparatus that targeted sympathetic groups of voters to raise enormous amounts of money in small denominations. They were skilled in crafting mailings that instilled fear in taxpayers, particularly the elderly, as a tool to raise money. Butcher and Forde called themselves the "Darth Vaders of direct mail,"[13] and they and Howard Jarvis established a lucrative years-long relationship: Jarvis made them extremely wealthy; they, in turn, delivered a heap of money to the Proposition 13 campaign. As *Sacramento Bee* columnist and author Peter Schrag described the pair's common practice on behalf of Proposition 13:

> One of Butcher-Forde's favorite devices, which would be further honed and refined in the 1980s, was to mail their pitches in official-looking envelopes

that mimicked the mailings of their archenemy, the tax collector, advising the recipient that there was "IMPORTANT TAX INFORMATION INSIDE" that should be opened immediately. Often that important information included the amount of the recipient's current property tax, a warning that it might soon double, and an appeal to send money at once to stop it.[14]

Send money they did, in whatever amounts they could afford. Many were elderly and retired, a fixed-income group most vulnerable to losing their homes to escalating property taxes through foreclosure or forced sale. Other major contributors were apartment owners, homeowners' associations, and antitax organizations led by Gann's People's Advocate and Jarvis's United Organization of Taxpayers. The "Yes" campaign raised more than $2.25 million and spent that amount on television, radio, and direct-mail advertising.

One of the biggest obstacles for Proposition 13 opponents was that at this time, in 1977–78, when homeowners were desperately in need of tax relief, the state was holding a surplus that was about $4 billion, the equivalent of more than $14.6 billion in 2015 dollars. The surplus would give Brown fiscal-responsibility bragging rights in his 1980 run for the presidency, but he later directed $2.2 billion to schools and $1.85 billion to cities and counties to offset revenue losses due to Prop 13.[15]

The Democrats were the majority in both the state assembly and senate, but they did not have a supermajority to pass a tax reform measure, which required a two-thirds vote, a condition that would create gridlock well through the next three decades. Nor were they of one mind on what kind of tax relief to hand out, with ideas ranging from closing corporate loopholes, giving money directly to homeowners, and providing some of the surplus to renters.

In 1977, while Jarvis and Gann were signing up tens of thousands of voters flush with tax revolt fever to qualify Proposition 13 for the June ballot, Governor Brown and legislators stalled in coming up with an alternative tax relief measure, failing even to agree on a seemingly fair and innovative measure that would tie a person's property tax to his or her income (that proposal fell just two votes shy of the necessary two-thirds majority). The lawmakers went home after the session ended and heard about their do-nothingness from their constituents, who were growing angrier than ever, their fury fueled by fear of ever-growing tax bills. Perhaps because voters had rejected three previous tax-cutting efforts—two of them by two-to-one margins—the legislature and governor were neither on top of the crisis facing them nor adequately comprehending the voters' growing antitax sentiment.

Gray Davis, Jerry Brown's chief of staff, who would later become lieutenant governor and then governor, recalled this period vividly in an interview in his Century City law office:[16]

> Jerry had asked me to run his reelection campaign, so around late April, early May [1978] I came down to L.A. Prop 13 is on the ballot the first week in June. And so every night on [television]—it seems like it was every night; it was probably two or three times a week—Howard Jarvis is debating some . . . what he would call, "pointy-headed bureaucrat." And just through his histrionics and theatrics, he would kind of win the debate, in part because the other person was trying to answer the question and be logical, and he was just playing to people's emotions and understandable anger over rising property taxes.
>
> Plus, he came back every day, and the other person didn't. . . . So I remember telling him, "Jerry," I said, "I don't think you guys get it. This is going to be big. This is not just going to pass, this is going to be big." And no one would believe me, because they weren't seeing what I was seeing . . . you have all these people saying "look, this failed four times before . . ." Unless you're getting a property tax bill that's going up 300 percent, you don't get it.[17]

In February 1978, just four months before the election, legislators returned to the state capital and crafted another compromise measure based on the split-roll concept. With the exact number of votes needed, they passed a measure that would allow local governments to tax owner-occupied residences at a lower rate than commercial and other properties. It would cut taxes for homeowners by about 20 percent, compared with Jarvis-Gann's 57 percent.

A companion bill provided renters with small benefits and levels of exemptions for senior citizens. It was sensible, but it was doomed.

Governor Brown signed the bill and enactment mechanism, which would become Proposition 8 on the June ballot. Had Brown and the legislature taken action before they left Sacramento for their break, they and the powerful forces that opposed Prop 13 would have had more time to convince voters to choose Proposition 8 over the more draconian measure; they were left with just over a dozen weeks. It was nigh impossible to stop the momentum of the Prop 13 train speeding down the track.

Opponents of 13 were an influential group of people representing organizations that were rarely on the same side of issues: chambers of commerce, statewide industries, banks, the state's most powerful newspapers, the California Taxpayers Association, utilities, labor unions, key moderate Democratic and Republican political figures, and such civic-minded groups as the League of Women Voters and Common Cause, as well as two prominent Republicans who would each later serve as the state's governor: George Deukmejian and Pete Wilson.

It is true that big business stood to gain millions of dollars in tax relief under Proposition 13, more than it would get with Prop 8. But there was apprehension that if Proposition 13 passed, the Democratic-controlled legislature would seek to recover lost revenue, either through heavier levies on corporations or a split-roll system that would increase property taxes on businesses to an even greater extent than under Proposition 8.

The battle was fought on the airwaves. In one corner it was Butcher-Forde, and in the other, Winner/Wagner, a Democratic consultant firm run by Ethan Wagner and Chuck Winner. Each side spent more than $2 million in advertising, an enormous amount of money for that time.

Scare tactics were pervasive in advertisements and attention-grabbing media events. The strategy of Winner/Wagner was to frighten voters so thoroughly with dire statistics that they would be afraid to vote for Proposition 13, as had been the case with previous tax-cutting measures. They cited documents prepared by the graduate school of management at UCLA stating that a victory for Proposition 13 would result in a loss of 451,300 jobs, that unemployment in the state would rise from 6 percent to more than 10 percent, and that the total income in the state would drop by $4.8 billion. Winner/ Wagner painted a much rosier picture of life under Proposition 8: a job gain of 48,000 jobs; unemployment dropping four-tenths of a point, to 5.6 percent; and a $2 million increase in income for Californians.

There was no sound reason to disbelieve the dire warnings about what would happen to schools, libraries, cultural institutions, and public services if voters enacted Prop 13. Massive layoffs of thousands of public sector workers were anticipated. Cities and counties throughout the state were furiously re-drafting already approved budgets and preparing for life under a new tax code, and their new spending plans deleting services people had taken for granted got much media attention.

A month before the election, Los Angeles city government departments released proposed cutbacks that would have to be instituted under Proposition 13. Mayor Tom Bradley announced that 13,500 employees would have to be fired for the city to withstand the expected $237.6 million in lost property tax revenues. The city's Board of Library Commissioners let the public know that the library system would have to close sixteen branch libraries, lay off eight hundred of the system's two thousand employees, and drastically curtail benefits such as bookmobiles and service to incapacitated individuals.

At the Los Angeles County Museum of Art, which was jammed with visitors to the popular King Tut exhibit a week before the election, nearly one hundred arts supporters and employees held a lunchtime protest, chanting, "Don't close our museum!"[18] Museum officials talked about a range of cuts, including layoffs of 178 employees and possible closure of the museum. Similar protests were held at other cultural institutions in the state.

The city of San Diego's contingency budget called for slashing nearly $88 million from the county's original $462 million budget. There would be severe cuts in health programs, law enforcement, and library services, includ-ing a 50 percent cut in staffing; administration services projected the firing of 1,500 workers.

The anti-13 forces emphasized the damage that would be done to schools and education. California's state superintendent of public instruction, Wilson

Riles, the first African American elected to statewide office, warned that passage of Prop 13 would destroy education in California, forcing districts to cut their budgets by almost 40 percent and increase class size to as many as sixty students. State law mandates that teachers be warned by March 15 every year if their job is in jeopardy, so thousands of letters—21,000 in Los Angeles city's school district alone—warned teachers they might be laid off in June.

Education and environmental issues in California are hot buttons for voters. Cutting educational opportunities and standards, increasing class size, and cutting the school day or year to save money concerned parents seeking a quality education for their children, as well as big corporate interests that relied on an educated workforce for even the most menial jobs.

Many were swayed by Riles's argument. But not Howard Jarvis. In typical form, he railed to a *Sacramento Bee* reporter that Riles was "of low IQ and doesn't understand the amendment. Education has already been destroyed in California by Riles and the school system that doesn't teach kids anything . . . the initiative is to cut property taxes in California and to save a couple of million people from losing their homes. They are a lot more important than twenty thousand schoolteachers."[19]

The print and broadcast media onslaught resulted in an election that was too close to call in the closing weeks, according to polls. The education argument, and a recitation of all the services that would have to be eliminated, took a toll on Prop 13's popularity. The less severe Proposition 8 seemed a reasonable alternative to many voters, since not all voters were property owners, but all state residents stood to lose services if Proposition 13 was approved. Prop 8's proponents were winning the rhetorical arguments in April. That month, according to the Field Research Corporation's California Poll, Proposition 8 was leading slightly, but by May, according to a Field poll released just days before the election, Proposition 13 was slightly ahead, 42-39, with 19 percent undecided.

Then the bomb dropped. On May 16, 1978, just three weeks before the election, a quorum of three Los Angeles County supervisors, armed with the knowledge that the new reassessments would be the highest in a decade, exercised their power to unleash that information to the public, an action that was certain to guarantee the course of the election. With two fellow supervisors absent, they voted 3-0 to direct Los Angeles County's assessor, Alexander Pope, to accelerate the mailing of upcoming assessments to more than seven hundred thousand property owners by June 1, ensuring that they would be in hand before the June 6 election. Normally, the assessor's office would have started mailing out the notices on July 1, almost a month after the election.

The Board of Supervisors chairman, Pete Schabarum, a staunch conservative and, like another member of the board, James Hayes, a supporter of Proposition 13, knew that compelling the assessor to release the new assessments would likely affect the election's outcome when he said, "Maybe an immediate awareness of record percentage increases will be best for all concerned. Some will say it may impact on the decision come June 6, but isn't that what the political system is all about?"[20]

Pope had only been in office ten weeks when he received the supervisors' order. Before that, he had offered to make one's information available to any homeowner who came into the assessor's offices throughout the county. There was a lot of curiosity about the reassessments, and among many who had been able to take advantage of that offer, there was shock and dismay.

At that time, under previous state law, the county would assess one-third of the properties each year, then those properties would not be reassessed again for three more years. In 1978, many of those properties reassessed were on the tony west side of Los Angeles, which includes the beach cities of Santa Monica and Malibu, as well as Beverly Hills and Bel Air, known nationally for their glitz and celebrities, and real estate prices were shooting upward fast here. The assessor also followed the practice of calculating new assessed values by using recent sales of properties in the area, which in many cases resulted in homeowners' receiving a tax bill double their previous one.

In some neighborhoods, there were increases of 50 to 100 percent and higher. Supervisor Hayes's coastline district was hit hard because the housing values had escalated so dramatically. A constituent in the posh community of

Palos Verdes lamented that her new tax bill was going to be $6,000, a 110 percent increase over the previous assessment and up from $600 just ten years earlier. "She says it is now a question if she and her husband can pay the tax bill," he said, echoing what thousands of other county residents were wondering.[21]

In an article Pope wrote the following year for the *University of Southern California Law Review*, he noted that "the impact of the three-year [assessment] cycle, which went into effect in early 1978, would have been to impose an *average 120 percent increase in assessed value* on the one-third of the residences reappraised by the department for the 1978–79 tax roll."[22]

He noted that his own home in 1974 was valued at $34,900, with taxes of $1,224. Just four years later, the assessed value on his home had jumped to $90,800, and, had Prop 13 failed, his property taxes would have increased to $3,130.[23] He wrote that more than one-third of all the assessed value in the state of California was in Los Angeles County, which helps explain why, once the assessments were made known to homeowners, the election was in the bag for the Jarvis-Gann forces.

The release of the Los Angeles County assessments, which made headlines statewide, created a surge of support for Proposition 13. The respected California Poll reported that among voters surveyed in late May, just days before the election, 57 percent said they would vote for the measure, and 34 were against it. The 42-39 percent lead for Prop 13 announced earlier in the month became history, with the 19 percent of undecided voters accounting for most of the vote shift. As Schrag described it:

At that point it was all over: Jarvis, ever the master of blather and hyperbole, had been making what appeared to be wild predictions that taxes here or there would double. Now, night after night, the evening news on Los Angeles television stations, with their three million viewers, was filled with pictures of tearful old ladies whose assessments had in fact more than doubled and who told interviewers they saw no alternative but to sell their homes, young mothers declaring that they would have to go back to work to pay the tax- man, and public officials scurrying to come up with yet one more fix.[24]

The final tally for Proposition 13 was made by the largest turnout of voters for a primary election in state history, and the result was a 65 percent to 35 percent victory for Jarvis and company.

But consider the numbers: While this revolutionary new law would impact every man, woman, and child in California, only three in ten California adults voted for Proposition 13—the other 70 percent of adults were not registered to vote, did not go to the polls, or voted against it. Nonetheless, among those who did vote, the victory was overwhelming—only two of California's fifty-eight counties had more nay votes for Prop 13 than yeas. On a personal note, I was among the nays and my mother with the yeas, voting to save her home; it remained in our family for another thirty-five years.

The 1978 taxpayer revolution fundamentally changed the course of California history, both fiscally and politically, and fractured the security of education and public services. Damage was delayed for a short while, with the aforementioned handover of nearly $4 billion from the existing budget surplus to schools and local governments, but this merely lent a false credibility to the contention of the pro-13 forces that the anti-13ers were exaggerating. They weren't.

The bailout was scathingly criticized years later as "Stupid!" by John Burton, state Democratic Party chairman, and arguably the most astute Democrat strategist in the state. He represented his district in San Francisco in both houses of the state legislature and in Congress, where he was serving when Proposition 13 passed. The dean of liberals (don't call him progressive; he hates that term), Burton is also one of the most passionate and colorful pols in the state—certainly in language, as he demonstrated in talking about the legislature's failure after Proposition 13 passed:

> Everybody said with Proposition 13, they're going to close this, they're going to close that, it's going to stifle local government—and they [the state legislature] bailed it out so that nothing bad happened right away. So the people just figured everybody was full of shit, and then by attrition [over ensuing

years], libraries and playgrounds and schools got fucked. But . . . if they
would have given them [voters] shock therapy . . . it might have been able to be
reversed.[25]

But that did not come close to happening. "Proposition 13" became part
of the national lexicon. People knew instantly what it symbolized: power of
the people. Within a year, seventeen other states faced similar measures, and
twelve were approved. Within two years, there were tax-cutting measures in
all but seven states in the nation. Idaho and Massachusetts cut and limited
property taxes; Colorado and New York enacted spending limits. By 1994,
every state had some sort of state or local spending limits, and by 2011 at least
twenty states had limits on property tax. In California, "baby 13" initiatives
were spawned to restrict tax collection even more.

Under Prop 13, all property taxes in 1978 were rolled back to the property's assessed value in 1975, with taxes on all property cut to 1 percent of
assessed value as of that base year. It capped the annual increase to 2 percent,
although when the property changed ownership, it could be reassessed to its
current value. This last provision created a corporate tax loophole big enough
to fly a fleet of private jets through, and the money saved by corporations due
to this loophole could finance such a fleet. The law also resulted in glaring
inequities: One neighbor who bought a house before 1978 would enjoy the
Proposition 13 tax rate, while a new neighbor in a similar home would have a
tax bill thousands of dollars higher.

Not content with confining the measure to property taxes, Proposition 13's
authors also set a requirement of a two-thirds majority vote for any "special"
taxes and permitted no other property or sales taxes to be levied on real property except for transfer taxes.

Up until the passage of Proposition 13, a property owner's tax bill could
include levies for local jurisdictions—city and county operations, the local
school board, "special district" services such as parks, flood control, and the
like. All of these entities established tax rates to fit their budgets and would
forward the figures to the county assessor's office. Proposition 13 ended all
that, resulting in a massive upheaval of the tax system. In 1979, a year after

the measure became law, property tax collections dropped 52 percent, from $10.3 billion to $4.9 billion. It was what the voters had wanted, but it was not necessarily good for the entire populace. There were also more nebulous consequences. Californians, who had taken pride in, and benefited from, the state's colossal projects undertaken during the administration of Pat Brown, such as freeways, bridges, and universities, had come to see their government as wasteful and untrustworthy, an opinion reinforced by the welfare bashing of Reagan, the ranting of Jarvis, and the "small is beautiful" philosophy espoused by the state's then governor, Jerry Brown.

Proposition 13 taught voters that through the initiative process, they could take matters into their own hands if necessary. Drunk with success, the citizenry went on a binge, approving a flurry of initiatives, most of them constitutional amendments, in the ensuing years. Between 1978 and 2014, California's state constitution was amended seventy-three times, compared with forty-seven amendments in the preceding sixty-five years. It became the third longest constitution in the world. Prop 13 was a boon to the special interests that have the most to gain from these new laws, as well as to the so-called "initiative industry" of consultants and signature gatherers—who often are paid per signature.

Many ballot initiatives improved the status quo; some were frivolous; and others were ill considered, such as those that mandated programs without providing a mechanism to fund them. But the tool worked well enough that politicians and activists of all stripes continued to find it useful. Eventually, even legislators and governors, including Jerry Brown as recently as November 2012, turned to the initiative process to get laws enacted when the legislature, immobilized by partisan politics, refused to act.

One law no politician has wanted to touch is Proposition 13 itself, often referred to as the "third rail"[26] of politics in California; tampering with it practically ensures political death to any politician.

But now may be a good time for some serious revision. Unfortunately, as the years have passed, two serious flaws have been exposed in its construction: First, it created an ever-widening disparity in property taxes paid by neighbors whose homes have the same value, depending on whether they bought it before or after the proposition's passage; second, it allowed corporations to exploit loopholes that cost the state billions of dollars in lost revenue.

Santa Clara County's assessor, Larry Stone, offered himself as an example of the tax-disparity issue, pointing out in a 2011 interview that his new neighbor in Sunnyvale, in the heart of Silicon Valley, paid $18,000 in annual property tax compared with Stone's $3,000 for a house he bought in 1975. "You couldn't invent a crazier system," Stone told *Bloomberg*'s Christopher Palmeri.[27] Then there was the much-publicized statement in 2003 by billionaire Warren Buffett, criticizing the assessment system and asserting that he only paid $2,300 in pre–Prop 13 taxes on a $4 million home in Orange County's Laguna Beach.[28] He bought it for $151,000 in 1971.[29]

In a dramatic example of a nonsensical consequence of Prop 13 that benefits those least in need, the San Francisco online news magazine *Bay Citizen* inaugurated its first issue on May 26, 2010, with a lead story about property tax inequities in that city's aptly named Gold Coast section of Pacific Heights. Writer Elizabeth Lesly Stevens researched tax records and found a sevenbedroom and seven-and-a-half-bathroom Gold Coast home purchased in the 1940s for $93,000 to illustrate this point.

The home was inherited in 1987 by the owner's daughter, who paid $7,722 in taxes in 2009.[30] She put the 6,800-square-foot home on the market for $55 million and, had it sold, the new owners would have paid $500,000 a year in taxes. A nearby neighbor bought his house in 2009 for $29 million; his property tax bill was $336,110. Other neighbors living in multimillion-dollar homes pay less in property taxes than a homebuyer who today buys a new home for $500,000 elsewhere in that city.

As for corporate interests and business owners, they quickly learned how to slip through loopholes in the law to escape paying a fair share of taxes. For example, if a corporation owning commercial property is sold or merged, but the property remains deeded to the corporation, the property does not have to be reassessed, even though the ownership of the corporation has changed. Also, corporations can avoid reassessment if a commercial-property change leaves no single new owner having a majority interest.

One example of this is the purchase by members of the Gallo wine-making family of about 1,500 acres of prime land in Napa and Sonoma, in the heart of California's wine country, around 2002. The purchasers were from the family of winemaker Louis M. Martini. In this case, all of the Gallo family members were minority owners of the new property, so no reassessment took place; the property was treated as though it had not changed ownership at all, although one hundred percent of it was under new ownership. A reassessment would have been in the tens of millions of dollars, according to John Tuteur, the Napa County assessor.

In another example, Texas billionaire Michael Dell, founder of the Dell computer company, and his wife used a partnership, a trust, and a limited liability corporation to buy shares in Ocean Avenue LLC, the corporation that owned the luxury Fairmont Miramar Hotel in the beach city of Santa Monica, spending $200 million ($662,000 per room) in 2006. Though the hotel's ownership changed hands, none of the three new owner entities possessed more than a 50 percent interest. Although Dell believed the assessment on the former property value of $85 million should carry over, the Los Angeles County Assessment Appeals Board disagreed and ruled that the new owners should pay the additional $1.3 million annual property tax. The corporation filed a Superior Court suit to overturn the decision, and the court's decision in favor of Dell was affirmed by the Court of Appeal. Dell was granted a tax refund of more than $314,000 and filed for $2.5 million in attorney fees.

Not foreseen when Prop 13 passed was the resulting gap, due largely to such loopholes, that would develop between individual homeowners and corporate property owners. The tax burden between the two was split about 50-50 statewide when Proposition 13 was enacted, but the numbers over time have shifted dramatically. As an example, apartment buildings and corporations in Los Angeles County in 1975 accounted for 60 percent of the tax rolls, with single-family homes comprising 40 percent. Today, those percentages are reversed, with homeowners in the county shouldering most of the tax burden, similar to what has happened statewide. The impact can be seen by translating these percentages into dollars: In 2014–15, Los Angeles County had $1.19 trillion of the entire state's $4.918 trillion in assessed property value; a fair increase in the tax burden of nonresidential corporate property owners would put upwards of $6 billion into state coffers to the benefit of all Californians.[31]

Kevin Starr, the prominent California historian and professor at the University of Southern California, captured the problem well in an interview with *Bloomberg*'s Christopher Palmeri: "Proposition 13 set up an unfair and dysfunctional two-tiered system of property taxes. It choked off a source of revenue, and the lack of that revenue has brought California to the edge."[32]

Antitax advocates and self-appointed "spokespeople" who make a living channeling Howard Jarvis include Grover Norquist and Jon Coupal, who heads the Howard Jarvis Tax Association. These two go for blood whenever someone hints at amending Proposition 13—to close corporate loopholes so folks like the superwealthy Gallo family and Michael Dell have to pay their fair share of taxes, for instance.

Would Jarvis, who died in 1986, have been satisfied to see this shift in the tax burden? Coupal believes so. "Protect Prop 13" is his organization's mantra, and if an advocate is inclined to advertise the cause, the slogan is available to be downloaded as a Web site banner or desktop wallpaper.

But Harvey Englander, a Democratic political consultant who worked closely with Jarvis for two years after the measure passed, believes Jarvis would have supported amending the measure today. As he told Palmeri: "H. J.'s goal was property-tax relief for homeowners or renters. He didn't love big corporations. He said, 'Someday Prop 13 will need to be updated.'"[33]

Despite the revered status in which conservative Republicans hold Howard Jarvis, he does not come close to fitting the mold of an ideologue Tea Party advocate, and those pushing that agenda miscast him. Jarvis, a Republican, formed a bond with Jerry Brown, a fellow pragmatist. He wrote in his memoir that he had voted for Brown for governor over Brown's Republican opponent, Attorney General Evelle Younger, in November 1978, five months after Prop 13's victory.[34]

The antitax crusader described a warm relationship with the young Brown, whom he first met on a Sunday morning in 1970 when he was home with his wife and Brown was on the Los Angeles Community College Board of Trustees and running for secretary of state. Brown called, asking if he could make an appointment to talk about taxes, estimating that he would only need an hour. Jarvis invited him to come on by.

"Pretty soon Jerry arrived and I said to him, 'Have you had breakfast?' He said he hadn't. So Estelle fixed him breakfast. Later on she fixed us lunch, and that night she fixed dinner for us. I spent all day telling Jerry everything I knew about taxes. I didn't care whether he was a Democrat, and Pat Brown's son. I would have spent that much time with anybody running for office on either ticket."[35]

In an interview, Brown recalled the meeting, noting that Jarvis and his wife lived close to his Laurel Canyon home and that he did drive over to meet with Jarvis that morning, though "I think he exaggerated" how long Brown stayed that day.[36]

Jarvis wrote that Brown was thinking of starting an initiative to abolish property taxes for low- and moderate-income homeowners, while Jarvis preferred to give everyone tax relief, regardless of their income. Brown thought the state could not afford to lose all that revenue, but he knew taxes were a big issue because "every other voter asked him about property taxes."[37]

Eight years after first meeting Jarvis, Brown was governor and campaigned against Proposition 13, referring to it as "a monster." Instead, he supported Proposition 8. While not favoring one economic stratum of homeowners over another, it at least would have given homeowners and renters some relief.

When Proposition 13 won handily, Brown did a turnaround and embraced it with such fervor that a *Los Angeles Times* poll three weeks after the election revealed that a majority of people thought the governor had supported it all along. Brown's critics saw his move as purely political, to boost his November reelection bid.

But Brown in our interview denied that motivation, saying that he had no choice: "How could I have subverted it? You can't. It's the law. It is the Constitution."[38] He also voiced respect for the huge pro-13 vote in what was the largest primary election turnout in the state's history.

Jarvis, fresh off the cover of *Time*'s June 19, 1978, issue, believed that Brown was sincere in his efforts to implement the new constitutional amendment. And he publicly gave Brown credit in speeches, even going so far as to make a television commercial for Brown's reelection. Gray Davis, former governor and Brown's chief of staff, recalled being present when the commercial was taped:

> We gave [the script] to Howard, the day of the commercial, and he looks like he's furiously making changes. And we go, "Oh my God, what is he going to do?" He crossed out [the first three] words: the first sentence [was] "Paul Gann and I wrote . . ."[39]

Jarvis wrote about the Brown commercial in his book, in which he praised Brown for carrying out the spirit of Prop 13 after its passage by imposing a hiring freeze on state agencies and then submitting a state budget.[40]

To state Republican leaders, Jarvis was something of a black sheep. To borrow from the title of Jarvis's memoir, they were mad as hell when they learned of the commercial for Brown and that Jarvis had also met with the state's senior senator in Washington, D.C., Democrat Alan Cranston. Jarvis, who had already made a commercial for Younger, expressed anger at his fellow Republican critics. Jarvis told them his interest was in implementing Prop 13, and he explained, "I can't implement this thing with people who are not in office. But so many conservatives are so narrow-minded that they don't understand that."[41]

Between the June 1978 victory and the election that November, Jarvis campaigned for candidates around the country, mostly Republicans but some Democrats—some running for the same office—if they supported the tax-cutting precepts of California's new amendment. The twenty candidates for whom he campaigned in California were all Republicans, and fourteen of them won.

In a final blow to his Republican critics, Jarvis took four pages in his memoir to explain and justify why he voted for Jerry Brown for governor that November. It came down to what Jarvis saw as Brown's efforts to make Prop 13 work and Jarvis's view that Younger did not have a commitment to the measure.[42]

Perhaps even more astounding was Jarvis's admission that if Jerry Brown and Ronald Reagan were to be their party's candidate for president the following year, 1980, "I'd have a hard time opposing either of them."[43]

Jarvis died in 1986, so whether he would have put up a fuss about altering the law synonymous with his name is anyone's speculation. But what is certain is that the sentiment of the populace has changed with the times, especially since the Great Recession.

Having borne the brunt of its ramifications, Californians have softened their antitax stridency and also their unwillingness to tamper with Prop 13. One month after the tax-increase initiative Proposition 30 passed, the Public Policy Institute of California released the results of a statewide survey revealing that voters, by a margin of 57 to 36 percent, would be willing to modify Prop 13 and support commercial properties being taxed according to their current market value.

Five months later, the state Democratic Party voted for a resolution to reassess nonresidential commercial property regularly. Then there was a California Field Poll in which 49 percent of voters said they generally support some changes in the law, while 34 percent wanted no changes. Significantly, fully 69 percent, including 71 percent of Democrats and 64 percent of Republicans, said they would support making it more difficult for commercial property owners to avoid reassessments. Only 17 percent of voters opposed equalizing the burden on commercial property owners and private homeowners.

The state legislature has attempted a couple of times to craft a measure to do this, but business interests successfully fought it. Pro-reform forces abandoned a plan to put a corporate reassessment initiative on the statewide ballot for November 2016 after Governor Brown told a national real estate group he would be reluctant to support a split roll tax, indicating the reason was because of its low potential to win. Reform proponents say they will keep trying to revise the law.

For many Californians old enough to remember the 1978 ballot fight, "Proposition 13" remains the easiest, most immediate answer to whatever ails California, whether the question is, How did the state's once vaunted education system sink to the bottom? or How did its roadways and bridges, once the envy of the nation, fall into such disrepair? The wholly irreverent John Burton, whose knowledge of California politics and governance is unrivaled, answers those kinds of questions without a second's thought or a smidgen of diplomacy: "What happened? Proposition 13; it's pretty fucking simple."[44]

3

Moonbeam to Laser Beam

t will emerge . . . over time, what kind of a person I am," Jerry Brown once told an interviewer. "Knowing yourself is a task for a life."[1] Since uttering those words forty years ago, he has learned a lot about himself, as have people following his life and career. From the day he gave his first State of the State speech in January 1975, when he seemed a bit unprepared, to seeing him in action today, it is clear he has mastered the art of governing. Watching him in the waning hours of the 2012 Proposition 30 election, when the media were predicting its demise, Brown displayed a remarkable self-assurance that can sometimes come across as arrogance. The man wears confidence like an old jacket; he's comfortable, even if it doesn't always fit the occasion.

This became obvious when I began following Brown's political career as a young reporter at the *Los Angeles Times,* where I was a government and politics junkie. In the span of a year, Brown had enjoyed a meteoric rise, holding his first elective office in 1969 as a member of the Los Angeles Community College Board of Trustees, a race in which he finished first in a field of 133 candidates. Becoming California's secretary of state less than a year later, in 1970, at age thirty-two, he revolutionized an office that had been moribund for much, if not all, of its existence. Just four years later, he was elected California's thirty-fourth governor, the youngest in more than one hundred years and only the sixth Democrat since the state's founding in 1850.

Some of his earliest actions as governor were confusing, as when his first budget eliminated the oil-depletion allowance, upsetting conservatives, and cut back on welfare assistance, dismaying liberals. But Californians quickly would come to know this governor for running a tight fiscal ship. By 1978, when he won his second term, he had established that for all his perceived flaws—opportunistic, distracted, unfocused—he was arguably the most interesting politico around: iconoclastic, irreverent to the point of disdain, especially when it came to the game of politics and its players, and sometimes downright eccentric. He could wield rhetoric like a rapier, and sounded impressive even when you could not always understand what he was saying. In his 2013 State of the State speech, for example, his declaration that his school-funding reform plan would be based on "subsidiarity" sent many reporters to their online dictionaries, a not uncommon occurrence when translating Brown.

When he became the thirty-ninth governor in 2010, California's oldest elected head of state, he acted quickly to make his mark, motivated by the companionship of advancing age—a persistent reminder that time is not to be wasted when there is much to be accomplished. He often navigated through political waters following a course from his earlier tenure that he once termed a "canoe theory of politics,"[2] which loosely translates to paddle a little to the right, then a little to the left, and glide down the middle.

He began his third term in 2011 by vetoing the first budget sent to him, by a Democratic-majority legislature, because he wanted deeper cuts. The veto of a budget was the first ever by a California governor, and it surprised legislative Republicans and infuriated Democrats. Brown took a firm stand: "California is facing a fiscal crisis, and very strong medicine must be taken. I don't want to see more billions of borrowing, legal maneuvers that are questionable, and a budget that will not stand the test of time."[3]

His move succeeded, aided in part by a constitutional amendment, Proposition 25, approved by voters in 2010. The amendment allowed budgets to be passed with a simple majority vote instead of the two-thirds majority formerly required. It also mandated legislators to lose pay for every day the budget went past its June 15 deadline for passage. Before Prop 25 was enacted and only one or two Republican votes were needed to attain a two-thirds vote in the Democratic majority legislature, budgets historically were late.

Before 2011, Republican lawmakers typically would hold the governor hostage so they could trade their vote for something they wanted, a good example not of how democracy is supposed to work but, rather, of how partisan politicians do.

For example, Governor Schwarzenegger's 2008 budget was finally passed 106 days late, when moderate Republican senator Abel Maldonado broke ranks and joined Democrats to get the two-thirds vote needed to pass the budget. He traded his vote by getting the Democrats and Schwarzenegger to place a constitutional amendment on the ballot to establish open primaries in California. It passed, and the top two candidates in a primary now advance to the general election regardless of whether they are from the same party.

As you will read later, Brown in 2012 won his most significant battle against legislative Republicans by taking his multibillion-dollar deficit-erasing tax increase proposal directly to the voters as a citizens' initiative. He chose this expensive and time-consuming route because he had promised voters during his 2010 election that he would not raise taxes without their approval, and he wanted them to extend a set of fees, initiated by Governor Schwarzenegger, that were about to expire. Three Republican votes were needed to join Democrats in moving the measure to the ballot. Not one Republican would do so. It was not because they thought a democratic vote by the people was bad government but because they had signed a no-tax pledge drafted by Republican activist Grover Norquist, who was known to target those who broke it. Brown did get the initiative on the ballot, and his final tax plan was a more ambitious gamble, a small sales tax increase and an increase in income taxes on the wealthy. Until the final days leading up to the vote, the outcome was a cliff-hanger. The measure, Proposition 30, passed, and California was pulled back from the fiscal abyss.

Under Brown's leadership, with legislative support and voters agreeing to pay more in taxes, the state erased the $26.6 billion deficit he inherited;[4] created a surplus of more than $8 billion by May 2015; and, that year, could put aside $2.8 billion in the state's new rainy-day fund, also a voter-approved constitutional amendment, for which Brown campaigned in the 2014 election.

The state also was able to pay the last $15 billion installment on loans from 2002 to cover budget deficits and to repay $1 billion borrowed from schools and community colleges and more than half a million dollars borrowed from local governments.[5] This gave Brown and the Democratic-controlled legislature flexibility to move the state forward.

By the end of 2014, when he was reelected and began his fourth and final term as governor, Jerry Brown was being touted in many national media stories for his success in turning around the state. But he wasn't always a hero to members of his party. In his last term, he would still be angering many liberals over the 2015 budget, this time for not restoring welfare cuts or increasing funding for the developmentally disabled, even though the state's finances were much more flush than in recent years.

Jerry Brown sees California as a national model, particularly in the areas of climate change and other environmental issues, gay rights, income inequality, and immigration reform. He brought Republicans to his side to work on and support measures to spur business growth and retention in the state and ended up garnering financial support from some prominent Republicans for his 2012 reelection campaign.

The Brown model is a progressive one. In 2013, he signed bills that allowed transgender teens to choose which school bathrooms to use, raised the state's minimum wage to $10 an hour by 2016 (and to $15 an hour by 2022), and mandated overtime pay for domestic workers, a group that includes a large number of undocumented immigrants.

Signing eight immigration-related bills that year, Brown pointedly noted, "While Washington waffles on immigration, California's forging ahead . . . I'm not waiting."[6]

Thanks to legislation passed by a Democratic-majority legislature and signed by Brown, the state's estimated two and a half million undocumented immigrants can now get a driver's license, be licensed to practice law, and work in election polling places. Brown signed a measure to allow undocumented immigrants to apply for professional state licenses to work as doctors, dentists, and nurses, as well as in a number of other professions.

He also signed the Trust Act, which limits local law enforcement agents from cooperating with the federal immigration service by holding for deportation undocumented immigrants charged with minor offenses. Undocumented immigrants would have to be charged with or convicted of a serious offense before they could be held for forty-eight hours and transferred to federal immigration authorities for possible deportation.

California's Latino population is nearly 40 percent,[7] the largest ethnic group in the state. By 2013 there were record deportations under the Obama administration's Secure Communities program. This had been very costly for cash-strapped municipalities. An August 2012 report from Justice Strategies, a nonprofit research organization working in the area of criminal justice and immigration reform, found that Los Angeles County alone was spending more than $26 million a year to hold undocumented immigrants who would be released if not for Immigration and Customs Enforcement (ICE) requests to hold them, and that taxpayers statewide were spending $65 million a year for immigrant ICE holds.

"We're not using our jails as a holding vat for the immigration service," Brown said, in signing the act.[8]

The California Dream Act allowed undocumented students, who are not eligible for federal financial aid, to apply for help from the state for their college education. This was followed by the Dream Loan Program, which makes available up to $9.2 million in loans through state colleges and universities for these students.[9]

The Dream measures shine a light on the national immigration landscape and the progress that can be made at the state level while Republicans maintain their limited willingness to help undocumented residents in the nation. Brown's Republican predecessor, Arnold Schwarzenegger—an immigrant himself—had vetoed three similar Dream Act bills passed by the Democratic-majority legislature the three previous years. This may have served to please the shrinking Republican base, but it once again strengthened Latino support for Democrats, which will be discussed in detail later.

While Texas governor Rick Perry sent a thousand National Guard troops to secure the border when thousands of unaccompanied, undocumented children were entering the United States through Texas in 2014, Brown committed $3 million in funding for legal-aid groups to represent those who came across the border into California and who faced deportation.

It would be easy to say that Brown is only acting out of the same political expediency that propels the Republican Party into strategizing how to confront the growing influence of Latino voters. But Brown claims a long history of empathy for many of the less fortunate, ranging from helping exploited and victimized Latinos to working with Mother Teresa at her Home for the Dying (now Home of the Pure Heart) in Kolkata, formerly Calcutta. He was shaped by the sixties, when he even briefly—though to varying degrees, sometimes marginally—protested the Vietnam War, the House Un-American Activities Committee, the death penalty, and civil rights abuses of blacks in the South and California's Latino farmworkers, with whom he had worked. (A very early protest came during Brown's three and a half years in a Jesuit seminary. Roger Rapoport writes that young Brown once challenged a superior's decision to stop serving morning coffee to the young priests in training, asking the superior, "Why not let coffee continue to be served so that the novices might be free to exercise their power to refuse to drink it?"[10])

Much of his participation seems to have been driven by pure intellectual curiosity, an interest in events and political actions of individuals more than a desire to get personally involved in such causes. Brown is a master at symbolic action, so it is sometimes difficult to tell the depth of his commitment, but, regardless of motivation, he unquestionably has an appetite for intellectual growth that has been satiated in part by studying Zen in Japan, hosting a long-running forum show on lefty listener-supported Pacifica radio station KPFA in Berkeley, and absorbing the dictums of his favorite philosophers and thinkers. And while he paddled rightward after he walked into the mayor's office in diverse Oakland, emphasizing downtown development over neighborhood renewal, his time in office there, where he continues to make his home, has exposed him at close range to the pain and suffering of America's urban, minority underclass.

One cannot fully understand Jerry Brown, or how his brand of politics offers a national model, without understanding its early foundation. The fiscally conservative but socially liberal political credo of Jerry Brown was forged by having been thrust early in his political career into the greatest ideological debate of the past four decades: On the one hand was the traditional liberalism of Franklin Delano Roosevelt, which underpinned the administrations of Brown's father, the Republican turned Democrat governor, Pat Brown; on the other was the emerging conservatism led by the Democrat turned Republican governor and president, Ronald Reagan.

This rivalry of these opposing ideologies represents modern America's ongoing battle for the soul of the nation. Jerry Brown experienced it up close and personal, as the son of the once victorious and popular liberal trounced by the new conservative in 1966. The lessons of that ideological battle shaped Jerry Brown's political essence and have been evident throughout his political life.

The liberalism that was deeply wounded with Pat Brown's failed attempt at a third term as governor was a product of a major expansion of the role of the federal government born of Roosevelt's Depression-era New Deal and carried into the first years of Lyndon Johnson's Great Society. Reagan's defeat of Pat Brown in the biggest state in the nation came as an enormous shock to the American liberal establishment drunk on its own success. That success had been based on the conceit that big government, big spending, and an alliance between business and trade unions had produced an affluent society that assured the happiness of an ever more prosperous and primarily white middle class, with enough left over to satiate the needs of racial minorities and immigrants.

But the shock of Pat Brown's loss was generated amid obvious signs that this era of abundance had not extended to people of color. A suddenly aroused protest movement sprang to life, composed of African Americans and Latinos, joined by radical and sympathetic whites, whose disorderly and at times violent behavior was deemed repugnant and threatening to public order by a white middle class that was seething with discontent. Pat Brown, who won his first term by more than one million votes in 1958, was irreparably hurt by the right turn of the electorate in the mid-1960s over several issues, including his seeming inability to control the campus turmoil at Berkeley in his second term. With white college radicals protesting the Vietnam War, racial discord exposed in the Watts riots, and African Americans and Latinos asserting themselves through the Black Panther and La Raza Unida movements founded that same decade, white suburbia was shaken.

The political neophyte Reagan made the campus protests the focus of his campaign against Brown. In a May 1966 campaign address at San Francisco's Cow Palace, he railed in language that resonated with voters repulsed by the student unrest: "There is a leadership gap, and a morality and decency gap, in Sacramento. And there is no better illustration of that than what has been perpetrated . . . at the University of California at Berkeley, where a small minority of beatniks, radicals and filthy speech advocates have brought such shame to . . . a great university."[11] The audience of 4,500 people cheered and stomped their feet in agreement.

It wasn't just campus chaos that had upset Californians. They were displeased when high courts overturned laws that had been overwhelmingly favored by voters. This all contributed to a growing sense that voters were less and less in control of their lives and that the social fabric around them was shredding.

One such controversial ruling overturned the voters' repeal of the state's antidiscrimination Rumford Fair Housing Act, named for its author, William Byron Rumford, the first African American legislator from Northern California. The measure was strong-armed through a reluctant legislature by Governor Pat Brown and signed by him in 1963. The law was aimed at ending racial discrimination in housing by making it illegal for landlords or property owners to refuse to rent or sell housing to people of color. It was inclusive, saying that no one could deny housing to anyone based on gender, ethnicity, religion, marital status, or physical disability, but it was clear that people of color had long been the main target of such redlining practices.[12]

Today, of course, the provisions outlined in such a law are the norm; back then, the new law did not sit well with a lot of Californians, either because of latent or blatant feelings of racism or a more benign libertarian perspective that espoused freedom of association, an attitude of, "You can't tell me who I can sell my house to."

Soon after its passage, an initiative to repeal the law was launched by the California Real Estate Association, joined by the arch-conservative John Birch Society and other conservative Republican groups, such as the California Republican Assembly. More than one million signatures were gathered to place Proposition 14 on the November 1964 ballot as a constitutional amendment. It won with 65 percent of the vote, but the issue did not end there; it was declared unconstitutional by the Supreme Court of California in May 1966 for violating the equal protection clause of the Fourteenth Amendment, the ruling that would be upheld by the U. S. Supreme Court the following year.

The California Poll released in September 1966, four months after the state supreme court's opinion and two months before the Brown-Reagan election, reported that the "so-called 'white backlash' . . . seems likely to play an important role in the coming California gubernatorial campaign":

"White backlash" is a coined term to describe white resistance to the drive of Negroes to obtain more equality in housing, jobs, and other opportunities in society. The effects of the backlash may mean fewer votes for candidates who are active in supporting the Negro civil rights movement. The greatest area of sensitivity on this issue today in California seems to be the question of open housing opportunities for Negroes.

Over the years California Poll surveys have demonstrated that most whites are willing to support, albeit grudgingly in some cases, efforts to equalize opportunities for Negroes in education, jobs, public transportation, and public accommodations. However, they seem to draw the line when it comes to passing laws to make it easier for Negroes to move into the block in which they live, and this is where the battle lines may be drawn in the coming gubernatorial campaign.[13]

Reagan was a strong proponent of Proposition 14, stating, "If an individual wants to discriminate against Negroes or others in selling or renting his home, he has a right to do so."[14]

The poll noted that candidate Reagan was a proponent of the repeal of Rumford, and 57 percent of those planning to vote for him wanted the measure repealed, while only 27 percent of Brown's supporters favored repeal, and the rest were undecided voters who were for keeping the act as it was passed by the legislature. These figures bore out in the gubernatorial race, in which Reagan won 58 percent of the vote to Brown's 42 percent, an indication that Brown picked up those who were undecided on Rumford.

The 1966 election was a stunning loss for Pat Brown, who was eclipsed by Reagan in all but two counties in the state. It was also a life lesson for his son, who witnessed the force of the conservative shift in voter sentiment. The defeated Pat Brown captured this historical snapshot in an odd little book he wrote, *Reagan and Reality: The Two Californias,* published in 1970. It reflected the despair caused by a man Brown had dismissed as a second-class actor, who was soon to be touted as a likely candidate for the United States presidency. It captured the mood of the country and the fate of the Democratic Party nationally, at that time:

> Another major underlying change in society partially accounted for Reagan's victory in California in 1966, and, I believe, Nixon's victory nationally in 1968. . . . For more than thirty years, the Democratic Party aligned itself with, and sought to advance the cause of the underdog in the nation—the poor, the oppressed minorities, the struggling worker, and the intellectuals who allied themselves with the disadvantaged.
>
> After decades of policies, programs, and budgets, the Democratic Party had helped to broaden affluence in the nation, particularly in California, and reduce, numerically, the biggest source of its political strength. Today there are fewer poor, the blacks and other minorities have made substantial advances socially, and the "struggling" worker has two cars in the garage and a boat in the driveway. . . .
>
> Democrats retain a substantial edge over Republicans in formal voter

registration . . . but the registration figures are becoming meaningless in the moment of truth when citizens move into the booth to vote their feelings and opinions. California and the nation are still blemished by pockets of poverty and groups of underdogs, but the increased militancy of the poor, the blacks, and their student allies has antagonized the majority of affluent, taxpaying voters. Politically, the American underdog is today passé. When his hair is long or worn in Afro style, he is, in the mind of the majority, downright repulsive.

. . . The result was evident to me in California in 1966 and nationally in 1968 and now: In terms of the surface attitudes and opinions of the people, the Democratic Party today is the *minority* party in California and the nation.[15]

When Reagan defeated his father, young Brown was associating with shaggy-haired Vietnam War protesters and unsuccessfully imploring his father to spare rapist Caryl Chessman from execution. Chessman was sentenced to death when found guilty of kidnapping (a capital offense at the time), a charge that was based on his moving his victims a distance from their cars. The governor wavered on his decision and was judged indecisive by voters.

The younger Brown also had a deep mistrust of bureaucratic solutions and seemed to basically accept Reagan's critique of the limits of big government's power to cure what ails us. In fact, beginning with his service on the Los Angeles Community College Board of Trustees in 1969, his service as secretary of state in 1970, and on through his first two terms as governor, the younger Brown worked to separate himself from his father and shed the trappings of his father's political style. As a college trustee, he cracked down on campus dissidents while generally following a liberal agenda for other school business. As secretary of state, he attacked campaign contribution practices that his father had allowed, and, as governor, he seemed more son of Reagan than son of Brown in his trimming of state programs, including, more than once, welfare aid.

But time and retrospection have a way of softening harsh edges. At a drop-in meeting in Brown's office in the California State Capitol building in January 2013, having just introduced his new budget, he spoke respectfully and admiringly of his father to my author husband and me. He proudly showed us a photo on his wall of his great-grandfather's sheep ranch in Williams, California. He was clearly still enjoying the heady success of the 2012 election two months earlier, which not only gave him his Proposition 30 tax increase but a two-thirds supermajority in both legislative houses.

Since Jerry Brown's sometimes soaring, sometimes ragged personal political journey to that moment tells us so much about where California has been in the past half century and where it is going, we will spend some time examining it.

In 1980, when Brown was two years into his second term as governor, our professional paths crossed when I moved to Sacramento to become the state capital bureau chief for the *Los Angeles Times* after serving as the assistant metro editor for government and politics, which included coverage of the capital. My husband, Robert Scheer, a national correspondent for the *Los Angeles Times,* had interviewed Brown for *Playboy* magazine four years earlier and had maintained a cordial relationship with the governor.

Brown felt comfortable enough to drop by our suburban Sacramento home unexpectedly one evening, when he was in the neighborhood for an event. He asked if we had anything to eat and headed for the refrigerator. It took me by surprise, but I was also amused. This was "Jerry" (as he is referred to throughout the state, even by those who don't personally know him); he was never predictable and his late-night foraging was well known. A staff member in the governor's office in 1978 told author Orville Schell: "Often when he is in the office all alone at night"—his fifteen-hour days were legendary—"he just wanders around the offices looking for candy or other snacks on people's desks as if he were a mouse or something. Sometimes staff members play games with him—they'll put candy and cheese out on the desks to see how many nights it will survive."[16]

The night he came to our home, he was with his conservative Republican chief of staff, the very colorful B. T. Collins, a double-amputee, Green Beret Vietnam veteran who was extraordinarily popular with just about everyone in the capital, including journalists and politicians on both sides of the aisle. He humanized Jerry. Shortly after their visit, a personal note arrived at my home addressed to my two-year-old son, along with a souvenir hat from the California Conservation Corps, which Collins had headed. The note was signed by Brown, but that was pure B. T.

Brown was a lame duck at the time, finishing his second term as governor, and he soon would pass the keys to the state to a much more conventional Republican attorney general, George Deukmejian, or to Los Angeles Democratic mayor Tom Bradley. As the governor headed out the front door of my home after his visit, he turned and said, "You people in the press corps are really going to miss me." I asked why, and he responded: "Because it's going to be very boring around here."

It is true that the staid former prosecutor Deukmejian, the victor, would never drop by unannounced and head for the kitchen. But Brown's cachet was much more than that. He created news, showed a healthy (and popular) irreverence for the trappings of the office, and was far different from other politicians. He loathed political fund-raisers and disdained the influence of money in politics and the machinations of those governing. He liked to throw curveballs.

His political career began after graduation from Yale Law School, when he left Northern California and headed south. Settling in one of the most heavily populated metropolitan regions in the country was a practical, calculated strategy. He had spent his childhood, youth, and undergraduate college years in the San Francisco Bay Area. A native San Franciscan, Brown was a familiar face there, having been trotted out for photos and public appearances since the age of five, when his father stepped into the political limelight. To win statewide office, he had to know the entire state and to become known, north to south.

Some aspects of Brown's life and career have been consistent from the beginning. He was and will always be a fiscal conservative who is liberal on social issues, while leaning right on criminal justice. He often comes across as self-assured, or arrogant, depending on one's point of view. This demeanor was evident when he ran for his first public office in 1969 and was elected to one of seven seats on the newly created Los Angeles Community College Board of Trustees.

He was just shy of his thirty-first birthday, with scant professional experience for the position. He had recently moved to Los Angeles, where he had landed a job as an attorney in the corporate law office of Tuttle and Taylor in Century City.

This fairly obscure post nevertheless managed to attract 133 candidates in the primary, of which only fourteen made it to the general election; seven would emerge victorious. The candidates were men and women, whites, African Americans, Latinos, and Asians. The *Los Angeles Times* endorsed seventeen of the 133 candidates, and Brown was one of them.

Where the newspaper cited the chosen candidates' careers in education, law, or the corporate executive ranks, the Brown endorsement noted his experience as a member of the California Narcotic Rehabilitation Advisory Council and a consultant to the Chile-California Program (an economic development program for which Brown served as a private investment consultant in Santiago, where he stopped on a five-month trip to Central and South America).

Was this the right stuff to run a college system? It really did not matter. Brown was smart and connected and had that key factor in electoral politics— name recognition, thanks to a father who had completed sixteen years in statewide office, eight as California's attorney general, followed by eight as governor.

But Brown Jr. had something else going for him: with his Jesuit training, education in the classics, and the vast historical and literary references that popped out of his head at opportune moments, he stood out from the pack. He was an articulate speaker with a deep well of knowledge and a striking way of expressing it. Of course, he had also learned more than a little bit about politicking from his father.

He started his campaign by noting the antiquated accounting practices of the community college district and promoting technological advances to save taxpayer money; the message resonated with constituents. He also talked about the state's providing more financial support, suggesting an oil severance tax—a levy on oil and gas producers, which he would end up promoting unsuccessfully for many years. (By 2016, California remained the only major oil-producing state without such a tax.)

Brown had no trouble winning the primary election, placing first among his thirteen fellow contenders for the general election runoff, with sixty-one thousand votes more than the second-place winner, Mike Antonovich, a conservative Republican who would go on to serve in the state assembly and, later, as a Los Angeles County supervisor for thirty-six years, to be termed out in 2016. Three months after the primary, Brown topped the queue in the general election with 67 percent of the vote. Antonovich and Brown would end up clashing, offsetting each other's votes throughout their time on the community college board, where five conservative votes to two liberal tallies were common.

Inevitably, the identifying phrase "the son of former governor Edmund G. Brown Sr." became an appendage placed by reporters somewhere in the vicinity of Brown Jr.'s name in any story. He had to establish himself and his own identity. He learned, possibly from observing Ronald Reagan's magnetism—Reagan charmed the masses as a protelevision presence, having done many commercials for General Electric—and Brown applied that behavior to his new position as a community college board trustee. He was a masterful performer of that dance politicians conduct with the media, leading them around and occasionally sweeping them off their feet with words tailor-made for front-page headlines or TV sound bites. Little he did escaped media attention.

One of his first actions of note was hardly progressive, but it catered to the people who had embraced Governor Reagan's fiery promise to crack down on campus dissidents. With Antonovich, Brown cowrote a successful motion, within three weeks of taking office, to ban out-of-district community college transfers for protesters convicted of crimes related to campus disturbances within the previous three years.

Just a few months later, he announced his run for secretary of state. Remembering how effectively Reagan used Pat Brown's handling of student protests against his father in the 1966 gubernatorial election, Jerry Brown attempted to inoculate himself against charges of being soft. He proposed an aerial force to fly over campuses experiencing student protests, calling for jets to be equipped with such crowd-control devices as pellet guns, tranquilizer guns, and water cannons.

The absurd proposal went nowhere, but Brown's opportunism played well in the media and garnered plenty of free attention. And, of course, it mostly helped attract conservatives. Moderates and liberals, however, must have been a bit confused given Brown's earlier request as a college board member that flags be flown on the college campuses at half-staff in solidarity with the student protesters killed by the National Guard at Kent State. The board's conservative majority rejected that, as Brown most certainly assumed they would. But "paddle left, paddle right" was the pattern that would persist over the next four decades.

At the same meeting in which the dissident student transfer issue was discussed, the board made national headlines for firing Los Angeles Valley College teacher Deena Metzger for reading in class the poem "Jehovah's Child." She said she wrote it as part of a lesson relating to Supreme Court decisions on literature and pornography. Another teacher, Leslie Hoag, who also assigned the poem to her class, was fired as well. One national columnist called the poem "an incredible mass of obscenity fairly reeking with pornography and blasphemy," which is how the five conservatives on the board saw it.[17] One line, for example, read, "In Christ's name kindness is sucking the cock of a turned cheek—Jesus style—Jehovah would have bitten it off."[18]

Attorney Brown argued against the firing, saying that he loathed the idea of spending taxpayer funds on defending a case sure to be overturned on First Amendment grounds. He viewed the incident as constitutionally protected free speech and an exercise of academic freedom, and he would cite it as such in public statements.

But then, although he voiced strong opinions on the Metzger case and the measure banning the transfer of student dissidents, he left the board meeting before a vote was taken on either issue, citing urgent business at his law firm. The vote to fire Metzger was 5-1, with Brown absent. As he had predicted, the teacher did sue and win; the state supreme court ruled that both teachers be reinstated with back pay, and Brown earned a reputation as an advocate of freedom of expression.

Brown later played what would become his hallmark card, hyperfrugality, attacking the board majority for spending taxpayer money on itself. Brown and his fellow board members worked together at the school district headquarters, sitting at metal desks with plain chairs and one two-drawer metal file cabinet each. That suited the Brown of simple pleasures just fine, but not the majority of his colleagues: They voted to appropriate $75,000 for "administrative" purposes, which included $4,900 to swap out those spartan furnishings with new desks, executive chairs, and file cabinets. There was another $46,800 to add two secretaries at salaries of $900 a month each and partitions that would provide separate private office space for each of the seven board members.

Brown objected to $23,300 for personnel and office facilities for the communications office, which, he told the *Los Angeles Times*, was for "press agents to toot our own horn."[19] He called the entire appropriations measure self-serving and said he would challenge "every attempt to spend the taxpayers' money for any purpose not directly related to educating those students who want an education."[20]

Nice grist for a reporter's mill, and the public was sure to like it. At the time the college board voted on the appropriations measure, 3,800 students were expected to be turned away from the county's eight campuses in fall 1969. An additional 5,500 students could not attend summer classes because they could not get the ones they needed, due to reduced course offerings. Multiply those numbers by the number of family members—and potential voters—who shared the frustration of the turned-away students, and you end up with many Angelenos who would likely appreciate Brown's gesture of self-sacrifice.

Of course, he did not actually have to do without the renovations, since the board voted 5-2 to spend the money, but it was Brown, not the others, who got the favorable publicity for an issue that otherwise would have been a barely noticed routine expenditure. So while Brown lost that battle, he won the media war, earning not only a lengthy story in the biggest newspaper in California but also a headshot photo that took up almost one-quarter of the two-column story space. Other media outlets flocked to cover the story, and Brown's reputation as someone who was watching out for the taxpayer was born. (This careful attention to saving taxpayer money, accompanied by media attention, would be a consistent weapon in his political arsenal, even if it sometimes smacked of frivolous micromanaging. In his first "small is beautiful, less is more" gubernatorial term, he ordered an end to giving free briefcases to state workers; nearly three decades later, he went after their cell phones and government cars.)

The simple fact was this: If Jerry Brown the trustee called a press conference, the media came. He was adept at spewing quotable comments as well as barbs at his critics on the board, all the while roping in constituencies that would be valuable when he ran for statewide office. He tried to get school cafeterias to serve only lettuce picked by members of the United Farm Workers Union, shoring up his Latino and prolabor bases. He told editors of Los Angeles's black-owned newspaper, the *Sentinel*, to launch a movement to change the name of LA Southwest Community College, which was located in a predominantly black community of Los Angeles, to Martin Luther King Jr. Community College.

He made this last statement after failing to convince the college board to permit annual memorial services on King's January 15 birthday, which, of course, later became an annual federal holiday. The *Los Angeles Times* story on the board discussion reported that Brown's nemesis, Antonovich, "said that to honor Dr. King would be to honor someone who advocated civil disobedience. [Antonovich] likened King's actions to those of [Robert F. Kennedy's assassin] Sirhan Sirhan when it comes to taking the law into one's own hands."[21] These meetings were anything but boring for a community college beat reporter, at least as long as Brown was holding court.

Brown was elected to a four-year term, but he was ready to bail. It wasn't so much that he was almost always on the losing end of vote tallies as it was that being an elected trustee was a springboard to higher office. Thus, when he found a higher office with no incumbent, why wait? And why waste valuable time running to represent a district seat and spending years in the state assembly or senate? He wasn't about to climb that ladder. He was ready to catapult from a local community college board to statewide office, and he cleverly went for one that was so obscure that, if his plan worked, there was nowhere to go but up.

In 1970, when Jerry Brown announced that he was running for secretary of state, the office was perceived as a dull position with absolutely no buzz. Few knew what the secretary of state did. They might know that someone named Jordan had been in the post for most of the twentieth century, because Republican Frank C. Jordan won the seat in 1910 and was on the statewide ballot every four years. He died in office in 1940, and in 1942 his Republican son Frank M. Jordan ran and won, serving until 1970, when he also died in office at the age of eighty-one. One of Frank Junior's most notable acts was to suggest that blue and gold be made the official colors of the state of California, and so they were.

Despite their lackluster record, Frank M.'s widow, Alberta, wanted to keep the job in the family—it might have helped if her name had been Frank—but she lost the Republican primary to James Flournoy, who coincidentally had the same last name as Houston Flournoy, the Republican running that year for state controller. Even though James was black and Houston was white, their shared last name caused confusion nonetheless. And then there was young Edmund G. Brown Jr., now thirty-one, whom some voters might have confused with Edmund G. Brown Sr., running for an office that never made news.

If you've been paying attention, you know what happened next: Brown Junior made news. The secretary of state, among other duties, maintains the state's archives, commissions notaries public, records trademarks, maintains business filings, affixes the Great Seal on legislation and other documents with the governor's signature, and—here it gets interesting—serves as the state's chief elections officer. Brown saw that golden ring and seized it.

He announced that if he got elected, he would not certify any election if candidates failed to report all of their campaign contributions—and, of course, that included Democrats. It seems that for nearly six decades, the Frank Jordans had been allowing candidates to list only the names of contributors and a grand total of all donations. Also, an attorney general's opinion, issued by Jerry Brown's father when he was in that post, allowed campaign contributors to be listed by first initial and surname without the individual sums each person donated, a practice Jerry Brown did not hesitate to pronounce "absurd." He made clear that such limited information would no longer be adequate if he were elected, contending that money from special interests and lobbyists was "inherently corrupting."[22]

To demonstrate how lacking in transparency this practice was, Brown read to the media a list of campaign-report entries filed with the secretary of state's office, where candidates included as sources of contributions such entries as "Trans. Fin," "Victory Committee," "Friends," "cocktail party," "All others," "various friends and acquaintances," and "Perry," to name a few. Once in office, Brown vowed, he would make a copy of every check donated to him and give the information to the media.

About a month before the primary election, Brown reported $48,408 in contributions and loans to his campaign, going out of his way to list the donors and amounts they gave for all contributions, not just those over $500, as the law at the time required. The Los Angeles Times published the story, including the names of well-known donors.

Brown beat James Flournoy by three hundred thousand votes and took the oath of office in January 1971, the only Democrat to win statewide office in that election. Three weeks later, lest anyone think his crusade against anonymous donors was just campaign rhetoric, he announced that he would file a $250,000 lawsuit against anonymous opponents of a November 1971 ballot measure, Proposition 18, that would have permitted use of gasoline tax monies to help fund rapid transit and antismog projects. He moved ahead with the suit, personally arguing one contested point before the state supreme court: corporations and organizations that contributed for or against statewide ballot measures should have to identify themselves.

The high court agreed with Brown. In just a few days, Standard Oil of California, Gulf Oil Corp., and others, who had given $95,000 among them, identified themselves as the formerly anonymous corporations. Obviously, they had a vested interest in keeping people in their cars and the cars at the gas pump. (The attorney general's crusade would evolve into the landmark Proposition 9 Political Reform Act, which will be detailed later.)

The revelation was a victory for Brown and for public disclosure advocates. As usual, with all the media attention, Brown came away as an anticorruption hawk. After decades of nothing to report from the secretary of state's office, Brown was lighting the place up. He revealed himself as a crusader for election reform, fulfilling a campaign promise to keep the good guys honest, much to the public's liking. The new secretary of state was as obsessed then as he would be in 2012 as governor, ferreting out the true sources of millions of dollars in campaign donations against Proposition 30.

Like the proverbial dog with a bone, he would not let go. At a news conference on September 16, 1971, he threatened to prosecute candidates from the 1970 primary and general election campaigns who failed to comply with the state election code regarding the source of contributions. The *Los Angeles Times* reporter covering the story called Brown's move "unprecedented."[23] All candidates were notified of the filing requirements before the primary and general elections and again immediately after them. Not submitting the general statement is a misdemeanor, while not reporting the details of contributions over $500 is a felony if one is aware of the law. They were all certainly made aware.

Brown sent certified letters to 134 violators, warning them of his intention to prosecute. He was an equal-opportunity campaign-finance cop: forty-seven were Democrats and forty-four were Republicans. They included ousted U.S. senator and former actor George Murphy and his opponent in the Republican primary, as well as the millionaire industrialist Norton Simon, a friend and major donor to Brown's father. Also warned were a former head of the state Democratic Party, judges, and others. The rest were members of the so-called fringe parties: twenty-three conservative American Independents, thirteen liberal Peace and Freedom Party members, and eight who ran for nonpartisan offices. Some Republican critics slammed Brown for playing favorites, but the targets of his attack, more than half of whom were Democrats, made that claim untenable.

Of course, since he had notified all subject candidates, Brown could have waited—being told they faced from six months to five years of imprisonment might have been all the incentive they needed to comply. But Brown liked the press conference strategy to garner maximum public attention. His critics called him out for being a publicity seeker, but it seemed like whining because Brown was right: the law was clear. He merely was enforcing it for the first time, after decades in which his Republican predecessors ignored the law.

His actions did not endear him to legislators of either party. Democrat lawmakers were sufficiently unhappy with him to cut his secretary of state budget to the extent that he had to give up his more swank offices in Century City and move to a relatively dreary state building in downtown Los Angeles and cut two staff members he could no longer pay.

In the end, however, Brown made his point. A comment by *Los Angeles Times* reporter William Endicott in September 1971 expressed what few in public office would admit: "Voters have a right to know where candidates raise their campaign funds. Without adequate reporting, special interest groups would have a free license to virtually buy and sell elections. Our campaigns would be conducted behind a cloak of financial secrecy."[24]

This phase of Brown's political life highlights another pattern. People often underestimate the casual, seemingly flighty Brown. But he can be astonishingly dogged, particularly once he sees an opening to make a change or a splash—preferably both. And for all the "Governor Moonbeam" jibes he endured after trying to get California into the space race, he often proved far ahead of his time, as he did in his push for transparency in elections.

In any event, an intrigued media extensively covered Brown's four years as secretary of state, quite a difference from his predecessors in that post. Brown and his longtime media adviser and former journalist Tom Quinn, who had been with him through his tenure on the community college board, were both skilled at working the media. Some issues and debates served a dual purpose; they were legitimate, and they seemed calculated to appeal to constituencies whose votes would prove useful in future elections.

Brown's positions on issues most often distinguished him from his Republican colleagues and critics. One centered on implementing the Twenty-Sixth Amendment to the U.S. Constitution, giving the right to vote to anyone age eighteen or older. The national push for allowing eighteen-year-olds to vote had its seeds in the anti–Vietnam War movement, when protesters adopted the slogan "old enough to fight, old enough to vote"—first heard when Congress lowered the draft age to eighteen during World War II. It was a hot button issue during Brown's youth, and it would be difficult not to have visions of newly enfranchised voters queuing up as Democrats come Election Day 1972.

The Twenty-Sixth Amendment was adopted on July 1, 1971, one day after Ohio's vote to approve it provided ratification by three-quarters of the states, including California. When it came to registering for the vote, a question was raised about whether college students could register using their temporary address near their campuses, or whether they would have to register using their permanent address, in most cases where they lived with their parents. That, of course, could be hundreds or even a few thousand miles away.

In Washington, D.C., the Republican attorney general, John Mitchell, clearly trying to drive down a youth vote, urged the nation's secretaries of state to ban college students from registering at their college addresses. California's Republican attorney general, Evelle Younger, adopted the same position, ruling that college students under the age of twenty-one would have to register in their home state.

Elections, falling as they do on the first Tuesday in November and in June, would have forced students who permanently lived in California to leave their out-of-state campuses to vote. College students from other states going to school in California would not be permitted to vote for or against California laws and office holders. Brown and the Democrats grasped this and jumped at the chance to advocate for thousands of students, or, put another way, tens of thousands of potential voters.

Brown took the issue to the state supreme court, which ruled that people between eighteen and twenty-one could register to vote at their own address rather than their parents'. Brown could not resist tweaking the president and U.S. attorney general. He wrote to Nixon, urging him to seek Mitchell's resignation for his "partisan political ploy," a move that got Brown wide media coverage. He recognized the potential of the youth vote. Voter registration ranks swelled immediately; California added 84,705 voters between eighteen and twenty-one to its ranks by the day after the Twenty-Sixth Amendment was ratified, and Brown predicted that number would grow close to 100,000. Those were votes he could use in his bid for governor three years hence.

In April 1973, Brown took his push for campaign finance reform to the ballot box, joining forces with two citizen lobby organizations to launch an initiative for the June 1974 primary election ballot. Public interest had heated up with all of Brown's talk about corruption, vote buying, the undue influence of lobbyists who throw money at politicians, and the conflict of interest that often results. Two nonprofit organizations—the People's Lobby, founded in the 1960s by Joyce and Ed Koupal, and the liberal advocacy organization Common Cause, founded by Republican John Gardner—were fired up about campaign financing and joined Brown's route of direct democracy, using the initiative process to change the system.

Deputy Secretary of State Dan Lowenstein and Bob Stern, also on Brown's staff, did the heavy lifting in writing the initiative, which qualified as Proposition 9, the Political Reform Act, on the California ballot. One of Brown's major contributions, whether conscious or not, had been to rile up the electorate with his continual talk of corruption in politics and need for reform. This led voters to welcome strict regulations to staunch the flow of lobbying dollars and the wining and dining of officeholders.

Much of that was a page out of the Gipper's playbook. Governor Ronald Reagan, who took office in 1966 as an outsider—and indeed he was, by one measure, since he had never served in public office—disparaged incumbents such as Jerry's father, Pat, and other career politicians to convince people to vote for a political novice.

Yet shared tactics aside, the two men inevitably clashed. They were elected simultaneously in 1970: Jerry Brown as secretary of state and Reagan as a second-term governor. In December 1973, Brown could not resist going after Reagan for wasting taxpayer money on a state-leased executive jet costing $152,500 in the two months during the energy crisis, which was caused by the Arab oil embargo. Earlier in the year, Brown charged, taxpayers paid for trips for Reagan "to attend testimonial dinners honoring Frank Sinatra and Bob Hope."[25] (Brown got rid of the jet when he became governor and today, as then, uses Southwest Airlines—Pacific Southwest Airlines in the 1970s—for flights throughout California.)

Reagan would later attack Brown's gubernatorial campaign ads as "thoroughly dishonest"[26] and also criticized Brown for supporting public employees' right to strike. In his final State of the State address, Reagan pointedly suggested that the secretary of state's position be made nonpartisan.

Despite this parting shot, Proposition 9 and Jerry Brown both won in the primary election in June 1974, though the political reform measure proved even more popular than the young candidate for governor, securing more votes than the three Democratic contenders combined. The Republican primary election victor, Houston Flournoy, had campaigned against Prop 9 but awoke the morning after the election a wiser man, internalizing the 69.9 percent of yes votes for Prop 9 and declaring he would abide by the new law's spending rules for the general election in November, even though the reform act would not take effect until January 1975.

To enforce the new constitutional amendment, the law established the Fair Political Practices Commission with the power to issue subpoenas, fines, and injunctions. The initiative's main author, the thirty-one-year-old attorney Lowenstein, was rewarded for his efforts by being named the inaugural chair of the five-member commission. He was a logical choice, since he knew the hundred-plus-page document intimately.

Politics as usual ceased after Proposition 9, at least for the moment, forcing candidates and campaign committees to undergo a sobering change of life-style. They had to disclose contributions and expenditures that the FPPC could audit and comply with limits on how much could be spent on their campaigns, calculated by a formula based on the state's voting-age population (nine cents per vote for the governor's race, for example).

Public officials had to disclose any personal income or assets that might present a conflict of interest in matters that came before them in their official capacities. Major changes were demanded by the strict reform measures, which curtailed the free spending of lobbyists, and put severe restrictions on entertaining, gifts, and campaign donations. There was, for example, a ten-dollar-a-month limit placed on how much a lobbyist could spend on a single public official, an amount that would cover "two hamburgers and a Coke," as Brown had noted.[27]

Within two years, however, the courts would intervene. In its 1976 *Buckley v. Valeo* decision, the U.S. Supreme Court ruled that mandatory spending limits were unconstitutional and placed a limit on free speech unless they were tied to incentives such as voluntary public funding. Following that precedent, California courts struck down Proposition 9's spending limits. Other provisions of the act prohibiting lobbyists from making direct contributions to candidates and requiring monthly reports to the secretary of state by lobbyists detailing their transactions with public officials and their families were struck down.

There was a significant provision that remained, banning anonymous and third-party contributions (which Jerry Brown targeted in the 2012 Proposition 30 campaign). This distinguishes California as tougher on these sorts of deceptions than federal law, which allows nonprofit political action committees to keep donors' identities confidential. The courts let stand the ten-dollar-per-month limit that a lobbyist could spend on a single public official, though today, due to inflation, it's only enough for a Happy Meal at McDonald's.

Just as proponents of reform measures feared, striking these provisions resulted in record spending in later years, with one state assembly campaign for an office that paid $99,000 annually totaling more than $6.3 million to wage.

Worse, though, was the fact that the door was again wide open to escapades by lobbyists and their enablers, the most powerful legislators among them.

An excellent example is the famous "napkin deal" of 1987, where lobbyists and lawyers for four often-warring factions of physicians, manufacturers, trial lawyers, and insurance companies—all major political donors—secretly gathered over the course of days to make radical anticonsumer changes to the civil liability law. In return, they agreed to cease their independent and costly battles through initiatives and legislation for five years.

Insurance companies facing increased regulation from the legislature won a reprieve from that threat, as well as protection from lawsuits; physicians won a promise that they would not lose protections they had received that limited damages in malpractice suits and got a higher standard of proof that plaintiffs had to meet to collect damages; trial lawyers agreed to stop fighting reform measures in return for an increase in fees from malpractice judgments; and manufacturers won restrictions in product liability law, which banned consumers from suing tobacco companies. The biggest stakeholder—the public—was not represented.

They did this without scrutiny from the public, consumer advocates, or legislators but with the complicity of the leaders of the legislature—Assembly Speaker Willie Brown and Senate Judiciary Committee Chairman Bill Lockyer—who had outlined the plan on a cloth napkin in an upstairs room at Frank Fat's, a capital hangout (where the napkin later was framed and hung on a restaurant wall). Brown jammed the measure through the legislature by not allowing debate, and Governor George Deukmejian signed it into law.

Writer Paul Glastris captured the maneuver perfectly in an article for the *Washington Monthly*: "There's an elegant sleaziness here if you peel back the layers. Here are the doctors (protectors of our health) joining lawyers (defenders of the wronged) to protect tobacco companies (makers of the most deadly product on the market) by taking away from malpractice victims part of the damages courts extract from doctors and giving it to the lawyers."[28]

There was a comeuppance in the end: Consumer advocates were so peeved at being left out of the process that the following year they sponsored—and voters approved—Proposition 103, which contained regulations and rate rollbacks on the insurance industry. In 1997, the legislature repealed the provisions of the Napkin Deal. Finally, in 2002, a ruling by the California Supreme Court eliminated all immunity from lawsuits previously enjoyed by the tobacco industry.

Getting back to Proposition 9, its most immediate result was that it firmly established Jerry Brown's popularity with voters. At the end of 1974, five months after the measure was approved, Brown rode its slipstream into the governor's office; it did not hurt that he had the same name as his father. Considering that election to a governor's position generally takes years of preparation, Jerry Brown's trip from the secretary of state's office to the governor's digs required relatively little effort for a huge payoff.

He was one of three significant Democratic primary candidates but the only one with statewide name recognition. And he was the only credible candidate known in both of the state's major population centers, north and south.

His four years as secretary of state starring in the role of political reformer put him in good standing for the top job. Here was campaign cop Brown facing his main primary election opponent, Assembly Speaker Bob Moretti, who supervised the playground where legislators engaged with lobbyists in the very games Proposition 9 was designed to curtail; the contrast was not lost on voters.

Brown easily beat Moretti and his other June primary opponents. Back in 1974, the media helped popularize Brown, cementing his public image as a squeaky-clean reformer, the one willing to blow the whistle on how the political game was played. In fact, it was remarkable how he managed to appear the outsider, the new face in the crowd, even though he had been steeped in politics his whole life, learning by watching his father. It seems probable that a man who spent a long stretch preparing to be a priest actually did loathe the often amoral behavior of the professional politician, or perhaps the elitism that comes from that station in life. He could not, of course, claim to remain a political virgin entirely, having had to ask for money to fund his many campaigns over the years.

Brown, pushing himself as a tightfisted moderate, actually wasn't that different on the issues from his Republican opponent, Flournoy. But there were two hot topics on which they clashed: capital punishment and decriminalizing marijuana. On both, Brown, often a hard-liner on public safety, took the liberal side, fighting against executions and supporting a reduction in the ten-year prison sentence for marijuana possession. Flournoy likely was not helped by what happened just three months before the election, when President Richard Nixon resigned from office in the Watergate scandal, hurting Republicans in the fallout.

Brown had been ahead by a wide margin earlier in the race, but as Election Day drew near, his lead diminished. He won by just under 180,000 votes, 2.9 percent, the closest California gubernatorial election in fifty years. All statewide offices went to Democrats except for one: Attorney General Evelle Younger was reelected. He would run for governor against Brown four years later.

The fact that this race was so different from his two previous runaway victories was sobering for Brown. At a raucous victory night celebration in the ballroom of the Beverly Hilton Hotel, he showed he was shaken. Journalist Richard Reeves reported that as Brown's father, Pat, who had secured thousands of dollars from donors for the campaign, was completing admiring remarks about his son, Brown Junior turned to his father in a low voice that was picked up by nearby microphones: "I almost lost because of you; people remembered you as such a big spender."[29]

It seems unlikely that that was the reason for his small margin of victory, and he tried to make light of the comment when he realized people had heard it. But his statement indicated his belief that his father's liberal reputation might prove an albatross for his own career.

After a grueling campaign, most candidates take a relaxing vacation to decompress, but Brown headed to the Zen retreat at Tassajara Hot Springs in Monterey County with his friend and adviser Jacques Barzaghi. The governor-elect was always comfortable in solitude and practicing Zen; at the Jesuit seminary, he had disciplined himself to accept and embrace the long periods of silence that were part of that life. Some people comprehend his meditative nature, and others cannot grasp it, thinking him odd, or that it is an act or self-improvement scheme. Perhaps ironically, he has never been a politician to mix God and politics in his speeches or persona, yet he has done more formal spiritual exploration than most Americans, much less politicians.

But it was his politics that now brought him to the main stage of state government. The youngest governor in the country and the youngest elected in California in fifty years gave the shortest inauguration address, just a tad over one thousand words delivered in about nine minutes on a cold, gloomy day, January 6, 1975, followed by a meal in a Chinese restaurant in Sacramento. (His second inaugural dinner, in 1979, was at his Capitol office, "a dinner catered by a cheap Chinese restaurant located in a rundown shopping mall," columnist George Skelton wrote.)[30] Quite unlike his style today, Brown began rather awkwardly: "I probably won't come again to this rostrum for a while. As a matter of fact, I wasn't sure I was going to make it. My father thought I wasn't going to make it, either. But here I am."[31]

He told his audience, "I just want to tell you what's on my mind." First, he bemoaned the low turnout in the election, noting that "more than half the people who could have voted refused, apparently believing that what we do here has so little impact on their lives that they need not pass judgment on it. In other words, the biggest vote of all in November was a vote of no confidence. So our first order of business is to regain the trust and confidence of the people we serve."[32]

He then made clear that he would use the power of his new office to bring the predominantly Latino farmworkers in California's rich agricultural fields under the protection of the state's labor laws. He had worked with these laborers as a volunteer during his student days at the University of California, Berkeley, taking student volunteers to pick strawberries in the fields near Stockton and researching farm-labor law. That was the basis for what he proposed in his inaugural address: making unemployment benefits available to farmworkers and giving them the right to a secret ballot in labor-organizing efforts. He also said he would work to bring collective bargaining rights to public employees, a position that was toxic to Republicans, who saw it as irresponsible.

Indicating that he would run a tight fiscal ship, Brown said he was committed to not seeking a tax increase. This was a rough period for the economy. The OPEC oil embargo of 1973 led to soaring oil prices and sparked a recession and rising unemployment. The first few months of the Brown administration would see California lose 140,000 jobs. Pledging no new taxes offered no relief to offset decreasing state revenues and higher costs for health and welfare.

He signaled in his inaugural address that all branches of government and all departments would have to tighten their fiscal belts as they slimmed down expenditures, and in an announcement that might have surprised his staff, he pledged to cut his own office budget by 7 percent. He also proposed to eliminate certain tax benefits to the oil and insurance industries.

The first speech of the novice governor ended almost as soon as it began with this final thought, much of which is still relevant today: "The rising cost of energy, the depletion of our resources, the threat to the environment, the uncertainty of our economy and monetary system, the lack of faith in government, the drift in political and moral leadership—is not the work of one person, it is the work of all of us working together. I ask your help. We have a lot of work to do. Let's get to it. Thank you very much."[33]

He lost no time in imprinting his carefully curated frugal image on the office. He sold the armored Cadillac limousine Reagan had used, choosing to ride in a blue Plymouth Satellite instead (though it was that year's model and not an old used car, as myth has it). He refused to move into the $1.2 million governor's mansion fifteen miles away from the capital that was being constructed with private funds on the wishes of the outgoing first lady Nancy Reagan, who declared the old Victorian governor's residence in the city of Sacramento "a firetrap."

"It was not a firetrap," Brown could not resist correcting in our interview nearly forty years later.[34] He later returned to the mansion in December 2015 after $4.1 million in renovations, funded by proceeds from the sale of the governor's residence the Reagans had built in nearby Carmichael. Brown and his wife, Anne Gust, moved from their loft apartment near the Capitol. Their accommodations no doubt had been an upgrade from Brown's modest $250-a-month, sixth-floor apartment that served as his Sacramento home during his first term. It had been a short walk from his office and furnished with a few things from the governor's mansion and other state apartments; bedsheets and towels were provided by the state's psychiatric hospital in Napa.

The media lapped it up, and the people loved it, but it was the real thing: the genuinely ascetic, no-frills Brown who has not changed over the years. One of our interviews in 2013 began at Oakland International Airport, where we were meeting to fly to Los Angeles. He walked through the terminal unaccompanied by security or staff, seemingly impervious to the startled people tapping their companions and pointing at him, surprised to see their governor as just another lone traveler.

Asceticism came naturally to the former priest in training, whose reading the British philosopher-economist E. F. Schumacher, author of *Small Is Beautiful: Economics as if People Mattered,* reinforced his apparently natural instincts toward simplicity and frugality.

Once in office, Brown came through on his promise to tighten the fiscal belt. In 1975, he demanded zero-based budgets from department and agency heads with no increases over the previous budget and required justification for any new initiatives, a stance not entirely popular with his fellow Democrats. He terminated hundreds of state workers, cut some state programs, including welfare aid, and did not attempt to raise taxes. His first budget increased state spending just under 5 percent, compared with Reagan's average annual increase of 12 percent.[35]

Brown defended his tightfistedness in a 1975 television interview with ABC reporter Dick Shoemaker. Asked about not giving more funding to the University of California (a perennial issue), Brown noted, "People always say money, give us more resources, give us more planning, more experts. Well, I would only say: the Vietnam War. The other side had less resources, less planning, less experts, less PhDs, and they won."[36]

The best summation of Brown's spending philosophy was provided by the governor himself, in a 1976 interview with CBS reporter Murray Fromson, when Brown explained his tightfistedness: "It's not because I'm conservative; it's because I'm cheap."[37]

Whatever the reason, it earned him a surprising fan—his predecessor, Ronald Reagan, who was running for president. In an interview for the July 1975 issue of the monthly Libertarian magazine *Reason,* editor Manuel Klausner asked Reagan for an assessment of Brown, six months into his administration. "How do you think he is doing so far?" Klausner asked.

Reagan responded by stating the obvious: "Well, he is an enigma." Then he added, "I am overjoyed, of course, at his budget approach. And I just assume that that probably stems from his Jesuit training—that that has him thinking in terms of property and economy. I think he's going to find that some of his own appointees are not sympathetic to his budgetary approach. They've got their own constituencies and pretty soon they're going to be wanting to do things for those constituents and that's going to call for spending and then he's going to find that he might be battling the legislature on one idea and his own appointments on the other."[38]

Jesse Walker, managing editor of *Reason,* wrote, "In Brown's first year in office, Reagan's director of programs and policies joked that his old boss 'thinks Jerry Brown has gone too far to the right.'"[39]

He did have a large staff turnover. He was unconventional to the point of seeming quirky, and some of his nettlesome habits and behaviors became the fodder of news stories by the same press corps that had given him positive coverage over the previous five years. He arrived late to meetings, sometimes two hours tardy to his own staff gatherings, whose frequency diminished along with his attention span for such office traditions; he took a long time to make appointments to positions, taking six months to fill his first judicial openings; he had a freakishly long workday—twelve to eighteen hours was not a rarity—and he expected his staff to be just as devoted to their jobs. Seventy- to eighty-hour workweeks were not uncommon. Bachelor Brown, who didn't have a family waiting for him at home, had no problem making work his life.

He was infamously fascinated with space exploration, earning the moniker "Governor Moonbeam" from famed Chicago columnist Mike Royko, who liked to make fun of those way-out-there Californians.[40] Royko came to like Brown and regretted coining the term; he eventually asked people to put it to rest, but the term pops up to this day, as when *New York Times* columnist Maureen Dowd quipped that "the former Governor Moonbeam is now Governor Laser Beam" in a 2011 column.[41]

As governor, Brown literally changed the face of government in California, becoming the first head of the state to appoint to important positions people who reflected California's population. People of color and women were appointed to commissions, his cabinet and staff, regulatory licensing bodies, departments, and agencies. They were named judges throughout the state's courtrooms, justices of the state supreme court, and regents of the University of California.

Brown created the country's first energy-efficient standards and led the nation in the development of solar and wind energy, just as he is setting a model with his climate change efforts today. He also created 1.9 million new jobs and took steps to protect the environment.

On the down side, he did not provide enough funding for some environmental programs, and his spartan budgets left some departments and services underfunded and understaffed. He started his second term, in 1978, having defeated his Republican opponent, Attorney General Evelle Younger, by 1.5 million votes, the largest margin in that race in the state's history. But he had to implement Proposition 13, which he might have avoided had he pushed the legislature to act earlier on a viable alternative.

His runs for the presidency twice while in office—in 1976, two years into his first term, and in 1980, two years into his second term—turned off some voters in his home state. Though he did not come close to being nominated by his party, he did win five states in the first effort. But in 1980, challenging Jimmy Carter's renomination, he lost badly. Perhaps the best thing about that campaign was his slogan: "Protect the Earth, serve the people, and explore the universe."

He did get to explore the world, if not the universe, after he left the governor's office in 1982 and unsuccessfully ran for the U.S. Senate, losing to Pete

Wilson. After the campaign, he set off to Mexico for six months to study Spanish; to Japan, to study Zen Buddhism; to Kolkata (then Calcutta) to work alongside Mother Teresa; and to Bangladesh to serve as a CARE ambassador during the catastrophic floods of 1987. Cynics suggested that these forays were politically motivated. But he seemed to sincerely view them as a spiritual journey of sorts, as he explained in a 1996 *Salon* interview with his former director of the Office of Research, Fred Branfman. In describing his work in Kolkata, he contrasted politics, where the game is climbing to the top, with working with the poorest of the poor, and "to see them as no different than yourself, and their needs as important as your needs." In serving them, Brown said, "you are attaining as great a state of being as you can."[42]

However, in nurturing his spiritual side, Brown did not give up on politics. He returned to California and in 1989 became head of the Democratic Party of California for two years before making a third run for the presidency, in 1992. His biggest challenger was Bill Clinton. Brown managed to win narrow victories in Maine, Colorado, Nevada, Alaska, Vermont, Utah, and Connecticut, but he placed second in Michigan and lost Wisconsin to Clinton, 34 percent to 37 percent. He had announced that he would take no contributions except from individuals, and the maximum he would accept was one hundred dollars. As a result, his finances were severely limited, and he dropped out. He did end up with the second-largest number of delegates to the convention, 596 to Clinton's 3,372, but he hated the triviality of content that consumed the campaign and the difficulty of trying to move the conversation from unimportant "sound bites and diversionary distractions" to talking about such issues as the influence of money in politics. As he told Branfman in the 1996 interview, "Well, when you try to change the rules, when you are assaulting the citadel . . . you become the skunk at the garden party and you say, 'Wait a minute, guys . . . we ought to talk about how this process works.' And what's really behind it."[43]

It has been said that he developed a dislike for the Clintons—or certainly their brand of "Democrat" as part of the Democratic Leadership Council. Brown noted the DLC "has among its membership tobacco lobbyists, who are in the business of killing people."[44]

Brown was asked about the choice between Clinton and his Republican challenger Bob Dole in the upcoming election. He answered, "Essentially, what we're faced with is the evil of two lessers." Both candidates, he said, "are moving the country in the wrong direction, but they are doing so at a different pace."[45] He noted "Clinton has reneged on his commitment to revitalize American cities, he has a slavish adherence to global business, and he's failed to deal with raising the family income—and all this has been wrapped in such schmooze that a number of groups that should be more active are lulled to sleep."[46]

But the voters rejected Brown for Clinton, who became president. Those ideological disagreements Brown had with Reagan and Clinton over the proper role of government regulations would surface with a vengeance in 2000, when Brown's former chief of staff Gray Davis, who had been elected governor two years earlier, would see his career sabotaged and the state crash in one of the most devastating crises in its history, enabled in part by the Enron Loophole, tucked away in a law signed by Clinton that freed Enron from regulation of its energy trading on electronic commodity markets.

4

The Enron Assault

The obsession for deregulation is basic to conservative doctrine, whether concerning environmental rules, financial regulation, or any number of other government-mandated policies that are seen as stifling to business interests and profits. When Democrats also jumped on board the fast train to energy deregulation in California in the late 1990s, the result was disastrous, though useful in helping curtail efforts for energy deregulation elsewhere in the nation. It pays to revisit the California experiment to help explain why regulation is not a dirty word in the Golden State and why other states should heed the warning about the course they travel toward unfettered deregulation.

The scenes that took place in California in 2000 and 2001, replayed over the course of many months, could have been from a Hollywood movie: Technicians from the energy provider Enron, greedy for profit, gleefully conspire to fraudulently shut down the Las Vegas generating plant to drive up prices when California's power grid operator has ordered rolling blackouts for two consecutive days. Half a million people are left without electricity for hours, in their homes, schools, and offices. In this opening scene, an Enron trader identified as Bill Williams lays out a plan to a Las Vegas energy official identified by his first name, Rich:

[Phones dialing/ringing]

Bill: *Hey, Rich. This is Bill up at Enron . . . I'm givin' you a call; ah, we got some issues for tomorrow.*

Rich: *Okay.*

Bill: *You ready for some issues? . . .*

Rich: *All right, shoot, I've got a pen and paper.*

Bill: *All right, man. I'm . . . this is gonna be a word of mouth kind of thing . . . tonight . . . we want you guys to get a little creative and come up with a reason to go down.*

Rich: *Okay.*

Bill: *Anything you want to do over there? Any . . . cleaning, anything like that?*

Rich: *Yeah. Yeah. There's some stuff we could be doin' tonight. . . .*

Bill: *That's good . . . It's supposed to be, ah, you know, kinda one of those things.*

Rich: *Okay, so we're just comin' down for some maintenance, like a forced outage type thing?*

Bill: *Right.*

Rich: *And that's cool?*

Bill: *Hopefully* [They laugh and discuss a new schedule Rich received, then Bill tells him to ignore it and continues with a new plan.] *. . . So, you're checking a switch on the steam turbine.*

Rich: *Yeah, and whatever adjustment he makes tonight is probably not gonna work, so we're probably gonna have to check it tomorrow afternoon again.*

Bill: *I think that's a good plan, Rich.*

Rich: *All right.*

Bill: *I knew I could count on you.*

Rich: *No problem . . . I'm sure you'll have a good time. All right. So, I gotcha covered for tomorrow.*

Bill: *Thanks a lot, Rich.*

Rich: *All right, I won't even put that in the book.*

Bill: [laughs][1, 2]

Twelve years later, far removed from the governor's residence and the devastating electricity crisis that destroyed his political career and led to his recall from office, Gray Davis vividly remembered that forced outage on January 17, 2001, as if it were yesterday. We were sitting in the elegant conference room on the twenty-second floor of the prestigious Century City law firm Loeb & Loeb, where the former governor is "of counsel," beholding a stunning view overlooking the expanse of the Los Angeles Country Club golf course. We spoke of Davis's accomplishments as governor—1999–2003, notably in education and environmental protection, after having served as Jerry Brown's chief of staff from 1974 to 1981. But he was most animated talking about that day in January, when he declared a state of emergency that lasted until November 13, 2003, shortly before he left office:

"There's automobile accidents [from nonfunctioning traffic signals]. People are stuck in elevators. I mean, [Enron] just purposely tried to shaft California. . . . We always suspected something was wrong, but I never believed that Enron would purposely shut down a power plant, which is a crime. But it was clear that's exactly what they were doing to drive up prices."[3]

The smoking gun for this concocted incident and many others like it would be found in phone conversations tape-recorded in 2000 and 2001 between energy brokers, power plant operators, and electricity-grid managers. Transcripts of the recordings, which exposed the depths to which the energy traders had sunk, were released in June 2004 and February 2005 by the Snohomish County Public Utility District in Everett, Washington, in a lawsuit against Enron.

The plant being discussed in the above transcript served more than two million customers in Northern California. Enron's motive for the shutdown was to drive down supply, thus driving up—astronomically—the price it could charge for electricity on spot markets, sometimes by a factor of twenty. A pattern of such chicanery was so successful that it drove wholesale electricity prices for the state up 800 percent from April 2000 to December 2000.

By declaring a state of emergency, Davis authorized the state, through the Department of Water Resources, to purchase electricity to protect the health, safety, and economic interests of Californians and to forestall bankruptcy of the state's energy utilities. In an early example of government bailing out "too big to fail" companies, two days later Davis signed emergency legislation authorizing the Water Resources Board to spend up to $400 million of taxpayer money—enough for just two days—to buy power for the two biggest utilities.

By the end of the crisis, that would seem like pocket change, as California filed lawsuits seeking tens of billions of dollars in losses caused by market manipulations by Houston-based Enron and other energy companies. The roots of this embarrassing economic and political disaster, triggered by radical deregulation of an essential public resource, marked perhaps the high-water mark of California's flirtation with what is being called here the Texas model; perhaps not coincidentally, many of the key beneficiaries of the state's misery were based in the Lone Star State.

"The boys from Texas," as California historian Kevin Starr referred to them, were a motley group of energy producers and distributors who, along with a few from outside the Lone Star State, brought California to its knees, as if it were a Third World country. At the head of this pack was the since disgraced and bankrupted Enron, whose officials, most notably its chairman, Kenneth Lay, rained campaign dollars by the millions upon politicians of both parties to do its bidding and change regulatory laws that would directly enrich Enron, under the guise of benefiting residential and large business consumers by opening up markets to competition.

Presidents Clinton and Bush, the latter a Texas boy himself, both catered to Lay, while federal and state government actions enabled Enron to manipulate the energy market in a way that would change the course of California history, lead to the first recall of a California governor, and plunge the state into fiscal calamity for some time to come. Clinton enabled deregulation in the financial world, which led to the Great Recession and economic meltdown of 2008. His efforts apparently aiming for national deregulation of energy at the behest of Lay might have been accomplished except for the unmitigated disaster that was occurring with energy deregulation in California, which forced members of Congress to think twice about foisting similar scenarios on the entire nation.

Davis recalled in our interview that when he sought federal help for the crisis, first from President Clinton and then from his successor, George W. Bush, he received the same answer. "Both President Bush and President Clinton told me to go see Ken Lay. They both said it. The same solution: 'Go see Ken Lay.'"[4]

A Democrat who was awarded the Bronze Star for service in the Vietnam War, Davis was recalled and replaced by actor Arnold Schwarzenegger largely because he appeared ineffective in preventing the skyrocketing utility bills and blackouts that had plagued the state's residents since the crisis began. Yet what allowed Enron and friends to basically extort the state was a law passed unanimously by the legislature and signed into law by Republican governor Pete Wilson in 1996, a year before Davis took office. It had been supported and facilitated by California's own Public Utilities Commission, the agency that was created to protect consumers but has been cozy with utility companies over the years.

It was a bipartisan screwup, to be sure: key state senate supporters were Democrat Steve Peace, of San Diego, nicknamed "the father of deregulation," and Republican Jim Brulte, of San Bernardino, who wrote the Electric Utility Industry Restructuring Act. (In his earlier life, Peace had been a film director, his most memorable offering being the cult horror classic *Attack of the Killer Tomatoes.*) The law became effective January 1, 1997, with full implementation slated for March 1998. Hailed at the time by the *San Jose Mercury News* as "the boldest piece of utility legislation in state history,"[5] it proved instead to be one of the state's greatest errors in judgment ever, costing thousands of jobs and endangering lives, and it would serve as a cautionary tale to head off or limit deregulation efforts in the rest of the nation.

The door to energy deregulation actually had been opened by the feds a half decade earlier with congressional passage of the 1992 Energy Policy Act, signed into law by President George H. W. Bush. The expansive and complex legislation consisted of twenty-seven titles a college political science class would need a semester to master. In brief, it was designed to lessen dependence on imported energy, promote energy conservation, and establish incentives for renewable clean energy.

Its mandates were wide-ranging, from requiring low-flush toilets to establishing radiation standards at the Yucca Mountain nuclear waste repository. But it also provided entrée into the electricity market for independent power companies by authorizing the Federal Energy Regulatory Commission to give them access to the nationwide grid while exempting them from restrictions by which regulated utilities had to abide. Implementation was left to the states.

Enron, a Houston-based energy powerhouse that started as a gas marketing company, had become a big player in lobbying for federal deregulation beginning in 1990, even though it did not even have any significant generation or transmission capacity. But it saw an opportunity to gain new markets and expand business by selling power using the transmission grids owned by giant utilities. Other independent energy producers, consumer groups that believed competition would lead to lower utility bills, and some conservative free market advocates joined Enron in its lobbying efforts.

The Energy Policy Act put the Houston company and others like it in a position to compete with regulated utilities—but not in the energy-hungry market of California, where competition was not permitted under the longstanding monopoly system. The new Energy Policy Act could not nullify the law in California; rather, state law would have to change.

A combination of economic factors in the Golden State abetted the desire for deregulation. In 1994, two years before the passage of deregulation, California was exiting a recession in which nearly 750,000 jobs had been lost in the three preceding years.[6] In addition, average electricity prices had risen to be the sixth highest in the nation. Only residents of Alaska, Hawaii, New York, New Jersey, and New England paid more for electric power. Major California companies, hit with utility bills that were as much as three times higher than what they would have to pay in other states, had been threatening to move out of California; the last thing the state needed was to lose more jobs, something that had to have been much on the mind of Governor Pete Wilson.

Large consumers wanted to be able to buy electricity in bulk in a competitive market from suppliers other than the three big utility monopolies that controlled most of the state's electricity distribution—San Diego Gas & Electric (SDG&E), in the far south; Southern California Edison (SoCal Edison), in the midcentral and southern parts of the state north of San Diego County; and Pacific Gas and Electric (PG&E), in the north and central regions, including the San Francisco Bay Area.

Local monopolies had been established with the 1935 passage of the federal Public Utility Holding Company Act (PUHCA), enacted to regulate utilities and to break up the large trusts that had owned and operated the utilities since the 1920s. The law established the utility companies as local regulated monopolies that were guaranteed a profit in exchange for serving an entire community.

It was this law that Enron tirelessly lobbied to repeal, its calls for energy deregulation having won the endorsements of both the Clinton and Bush administrations. At a meeting of the Coalition of Northeastern Governors in Vermont in December 1996, Enron CEO Jeffrey Skilling (who later would be sent to prison for his role in the company's collapse) implored with some urgency, "Every day we delay [electricity deregulation], we're costing consumers a lot of money. It can be done quickly. The key is to get legislation done fast."[7]

At that time, California's new deregulated law was but three months old, and Enron was just preparing to upend the entire system in the Golden State. Enron would engage in major manipulation of the energy markets and cause a crisis that produced the greatest number of blackouts since World War II and generated billions of dollars in surcharges to West Coast residents and businesses in 2000 and 2001. California was virgin territory for the plunderers from Texas, representing the most lucrative energy market in the country.

Before deregulation, California's three large, private, regional utility companies provided bundled services for electricity, including generation, transmission, and distribution, to three-quarters of the state's residents, about twenty-seven million consumers. All three utilities or their forebears dated back more than one hundred years, and all were investor-owned entities that for most of their history served their clients efficiently, with serious disruptions in service pretty much limited to the antics of Mother Nature—an earthquake here, a firestorm there.

Another one-quarter of Californians were provided electricity by municipally owned and operated utilities that were exempt from deregulation. These included the Los Angeles County cities of Los Angeles, Pasadena, Glendale, and Burbank—plus Sacramento, Lodi, Palo Alto, and Santa Clara in the north and Riverside and Anaheim in the south. Like the big three, they were regulated by the state's Public Utilities Commission, whose predecessor was established in 1848 to regulate the state's powerful railroad industry and later came to regulate privately owned water, telecommunications, and passenger-transportation companies.

Governor Wilson was hearing the drumbeat for deregulation from the business community and his PUC appointees, who tended to be conservative business types. He came to believe that utility reform was needed. He also wanted to see employment increase and the California economy rebound on his watch, and he believed competition in the delivery of energy would help boost both goals.

A retrospective examination of the walk-up to deregulation offers a glimpse into how laws are made and how those who benefit can work the system, even if it takes years to achieve their goals, as well as how the most well-meaning intentions can go awfully awry. A 2001 report by the Center for Public Integrity noted that the "disastrous" California deregulation law of 1996 "precipitated what has been described as the most costly public policy miscalculation ever by state lawmakers."[8]

By the mid-1990s, the pro-deregulation forces were organizing to get what they wanted. The large industrial customers that had been threatening to leave the state formed Californians for Competitive Electricity (CCE) to lobby for deregulation. The CCE was composed of the California Manufacturers Association, one of the most influential special interest groups in Sacramento; the California Large Energy Consumers Association, primarily a coalition of cement companies and steel manufacturers; the California League of Food Processors; and the California Independent Energy Producers. They represented big bucks, with the manufacturers' association alone dropping $1.7 million in lobbying dollars in the state capital in 1995 and 1996.

More money was to be had from the utility companies. For years they had donated to officeholders to forestall any discussion that would fuel the debate for public power, but now they supported deregulation on the assumption that they would make more money. The same 2001 Center for Public Integrity report noted that California's three large utility companies spent $69 million between 1994 and 2000 on political spending and lobbying, most of that on promoting deregulation, both to get the law passed and to keep it in force.[9]

The five members of the state Public Utilities Commission, appointed by the governor, took the first major step in deregulation, issuing in 1993 a two-hundred-page report, followed by another report the following year, both making the case for deregulation. In December 1995, the PUC, having decided that the state's longtime energy regulatory system had become "fragmented, outdated, arcane and unjustifiably complex," voted three to two to open the state's electricity industry to competition, effective January 1, 1998.[10]

The utilities wanted to enshrine deregulation into law. That would require passage in the legislature and the signature of Governor Wilson. Everyone set to work. By the time it was over, the three utilities would spend $4.3 million on lobbying efforts and drop $1 million into campaign caches.[11] From 1994 until he left office early in 1999, the three large utility companies or their parent companies gave $171,000 to Wilson and $277,000 to Steve Peace, the San Diego Democrat who, as chair of the Senate Energy Committee, would navigate the measure through the sea of lawmakers and lobbyists right to the governor's desk.

In a frenzy to get deregulation enacted, Peace held many meetings, sometimes several concurrently, over eighteen days in August 1996, managing the fray late into the night on occasion. "The Steve Peace Death March" is how Republican Bill Leonard, a former senator, described the process to the *Los Angeles Times*'s Nancy Vogel.[12]

Imagine the stakes for all parties: Lobbyists for the utilities and energy companies—private, public, and municipally regulated—were in the battle, as well as lobbyists for labor, environmental, and consumer groups. There were heated disagreements, begrudged compromises, disappointments, and big victories. Indeed, there seemed to be something for everyone. The three utilities got approval to recover their billions of dollars in "stranded costs"; environmentalists received a $500,000 annual subsidy for renewable and alternative energy projects; labor got a multimillion-dollar program to retrain utility workers; the municipal utilities were granted the right to retain their independence; large public and industrial users such as the University of California and Bay Area Rapid Transit District got $200 million in price breaks; and consumer advocates got a 10 percent rate cut and temporary rate freeze for residential customers and small businesses.

The deregulation measure passed both houses of the legislature without a single nay vote. When Governor Wilson signed the landmark law on September 23, 1996, he observed, "We've pulled the plug on another outdated monopoly and replaced it with the promise of a new era of competition."[13]

One key aspect of deregulation was to encourage the big utility players to sell off their generating plants in order to promote competition, which, after all, was one of the main selling points of the new law: If ownership of the generating plants was diffuse, no one owner could influence prices and gouge consumers because there would be so many competitors. The concept looked good on paper, and it was love at first site for the utilities. They saw easy gobs of money, and energy companies from across the country lusted for a lucrative new place to do business after decades of being locked out. There were bidding wars and swift sales, and in the end $3 billion went into the hands of California's three major utilities, with the biggest winners of generating plants being Duke Energy, of Charlotte, North Carolina; Dynegy Inc., of Houston; AES Corporation, of Arlington, Virginia; Mirant Corporation, of Atlanta; and Reliant Energy, of Dallas.

Experts would later say that such a grand sell-off of generating plants with no agreement on price caps for a set period of time was extremely short-sighted and risky. Los Angeles legislator Roderick Wright said it well, telling the *Los Angeles Times*'s Vogel: "To sell the power plants was stupid. To sell the power plants without contracting for the electricity borders on criminal . . . and the price of rent is going to be whatever the new guy paid for your power plant plus the price of electricity."[14]

Key elements of the deregulation legislation went into practice on March 31, 1998, accompanied by an $87 million advertising campaign—the cost being passed on to ratepayers—explaining the new system to the state's residents. That same year, concerned consumer advocates sponsored a 1998 ballot measure, Proposition 90, to overturn deregulation, but industry interests spent $40 million in a campaign against the measure, and it failed.

The law established two new entities that were necessary to make the new system work: the nonprofit California Independent System Operator (Cal-ISO), headquartered near the state capital in Sacramento, and the California Power Exchange (PX), which operated out of two offices in Los Angeles County. There was also an Electricity Oversight Board that would monitor the entire operation.

Cal-ISO would operate the high-voltage-transmission power grid serving most of the state and be responsible for managing congestion on the system, as well as for balancing generation needs and the load on the system. The PX was created to operate two markets to buy and sell electricity, in an auction-style procedure, for delivery the same day (day-of market) or next day (day-ahead market). The idea was that under the deregulation plan, 95 percent of the power needed by customers in areas under the control of Cal-ISO would be bought and sold through the PX.

The "real time" energy market essentially allowed for Cal-ISO to buy power to continuously supply to the grid in an amount equal to the amount of electricity being demanded by consumers. In case of a plant outage or some other such disruption in the delivery of power, or to correct an imbalance between supply and demand, which could result in a blackout, Cal-ISO could call upon producers to provide electricity through an auction market run one day and one hour ahead of the actual consumption of electricity.

Under the deregulation law, the big three utilities that still had generating plants they had not divested in 1998 could not use the output from those plants for their own use but rather were required to sell it to Cal-ISO and PX markets and then buy all of their energy from those same Cal-ISO and PX markets, a seemingly cumbersome exercise designed to promote competition.

A typical sale and purchase of electricity would go like this: Sellers would submit bids to the Cal-ISO and PX markets, noting the amount of electricity and capacity they wished to sell and the price they were asking. The auction operator would rank the bids from the lowest to highest price and then select the bids it needed to meet energy demands. The bid selected by the highest-priced unit set a "market clearing price" that all buyers paid and all sellers received.

That's how it was supposed to work, anyway. It did not take long before it all came crashing down.

It was a painful irony that the first consumers to run into trouble were in San Diego County, whose legislator, Steve Peace, played the starring role in the deregulation drama. When the law passed, consumers had been protected with a rate freeze to be in effect until March 2002, or until the utilities paid back their "investments," or "stranded costs," whichever came first. For some, payoff of their investments occurred much earlier than 2002, thanks to the sell-off of their generating facilities. For $365 million, San Diego Gas & Electric was able to unload a nearly fifty-year-old generating plant in the coastal city of Carlsbad—an ugly eyesore of a facility that detracted from the beauty of the nearby Pacific Ocean and its lovely beach—along with nearly twenty combustion turbines from all around the county. The sales price, paid by Houston's Dynegy and NRG Energy, based in Minneapolis, amounted to four times the value of the property, and its sale helped retire the San Diego utility's debt.

Gone was the debt, but gone also was the price freeze. In June 1999, SDG&E sought and got permission from the PUC to charge market rates for its electricity, and for the first time on July 1, 1999, less than a year and a half into deregulation, homeowner and small business customers from San Diego County and the south part of Orange County had to pay prices set not by a regulated utility but by a free market.

At first, the cost was not significantly different. For the first ten months, an average monthly utility bill that had been $50.60 before the price freeze lifted rose slightly to average only $3 a month higher. But when the first heat wave hit in May 2000, air conditioners kicked in, and so did higher prices for electricity. San Diegans saw their utility bills begin to climb, and soon they tripled.

The average price of residential electricity increased 413 percent from the third quarter of 1999 to the third quarter of 2000. The utility bill in some homes approached the cost of the rent payment. The burden led to businesses raising their prices, laying off employees, or folding. Schools, hospitals, and other public agencies were hit hard. The legislature stepped in to impose price caps, but by then the average monthly electric bill for San Diego customers was $120.

B ack in the nation's capital, in-house lobbying stepped up for Enron, which had spent nearly $1.7 million in 1999, in addition to the $710,000 the company paid to lobbying firms that year. Some of that money was spent working with Texas Republican senator Phil Gramm, including personal contact from Ken Lay,[15] to get a federal deregulation bill through Congress;[16] some of it was spent meeting with regulators and staff at the Commodity Futures Trading Commission (CFTC), Department of the Treasury, and the Federal Reserve.

The heads of those agencies—the CFTC chair, William Rainer; Treasury secretary Larry Summers; Federal Reserve chair Alan Greenspan; and Securities and Exchange Commission chair Arthur Levitt—were members of the President's Working Group on Financial Markets, whose job was to make recommendations for regulatory policies relating to commodity trading. Enron reported in its lobbying disclosure form to have lobbied the working group members.

In November, the working group unanimously recommended against deregulating energy trading, cautioning that it could lead to price manipulation, but the efforts of Enron and Gramm continued. The following year, 2000, Enron spent more than $1.7 million in in-house lobbying expenses and another $890,000 on outside lobbying fees.[17] Enron again reported contacting the CFTC, the Federal Reserve, and the Department of the Treasury. During the decade ending in 2002, Enron gave members of Congress—75 percent of them Republican—$5.8 million, making it the largest corporate campaign donor from the energy/natural resources industry.[18]

The case of Enron is a textbook example of how business gets done in the nation's capital when corporations with millions of dollars to spend intersect with government officials and members of Congress who grant them unfettered access to work the system, however long it takes to get what they want.

Gramm and his wife, Wendy, could be Exhibit A. Several years earlier, at the tail end of the Bush administration, Gramm's efforts on behalf of Enron were aided by Wendy, who had been appointed in 1988 by President Reagan to head the CFTC. Her actions ended up significantly hurting California by enabling the manipulation by Enron that crippled the state. Just one week after Clinton's November 1992 presidential election victory, with her term about to end, Wendy Gramm initiated a rules change requested by Enron that prohibited the government from regulating energy commodity contracts and "swaps." This directly benefited Enron, which had been moving billions of dollars in derivatives contracts and which, under the new rule, no longer had to disclose information to the government about these actions.

Normally such a rules change would take a year or more of study and debate, but Wendy Gramm sped up the process and brought it to a vote before the commission on January 14, 1993, six days before Clinton's inauguration, with only three of the five commissioners present. (Two seats were vacant.) All were George H. W. Bush appointees, and they voted two to one for the new rule. Sheila Bair, taking the position that deregulation of energy futures contracts "sets a dangerous precedent," cast the nay vote.

Six days later, Wendy Gramm resigned her post; five weeks later, she swung open the golden door and walked onto the board of directors of Enron, where she became a member of the audit committee. Enron would pay her between $915,000 and $1.85 million in salary, board attendance fees, sales of stock options, and dividends from 1993 to 2001.

Enron was the largest corporate contributor to Phil Gramm between 1989 and 2001, his last year in the Senate, giving him nearly $100,000. In

2000, Enron and its employees enriched the campaign coffers of George W. Bush by $110,000 and $300,000 to the Inaugural Committee after his election. Enron, including its employees, was Bush's largest single contributor over the years.

The consequences of Wendy Gramm's closing act as CFTC chair were significant and almost immediate for Enron. From 1991 to 1992, revenues in Enron Gas Services, the division of the company that at the time operated futures contracts, increased by 10 percent ($4.7 billion), while they increased 30 percent ($6.1 billion) from 1992 to 1993, most notably in the recently unregulated futures contracts known as "pre–risk management activities." Enron was heavily pushing its deregulation agenda, and its efforts, while expensive, paid off big-time, especially in California.

In May 2000, Phil Gramm took a field trip to Chicago with his entire Senate Banking Committee to discuss Enron's top priority—commodity-trading deregulation—with Rainer, Levitt, and others. Less than a month later he introduced the Commodity Futures Modernization Act of 2000, which specifically excluded energy trading companies like Enron from regulation; the bill made no progress in the Senate, however, and Gramm and Enron were forced to bide their time.

Meanwhile, a combination of factors created havoc in California. Sparse rainfall in the Pacific Northwest, whose thunderous rivers fed the turbines, led to a decrease in hydroelectric capacity of suppliers; the price of natural gas, the fuel that fired most electrical generators in the state, increased dramatically between December 1999 and December 2000; generators went offline for maintenance; population growth and increased demand in Phoenix, Las Vegas, Portland, and Seattle siphoned energy from the 20 percent of electricity California had been importing for its use; and the job growth that California so needed had finally kicked in at 3 percent a year, creating greater demand for power.

Add to all of this the fact that no new generating plants had been built in the state in ten years, in part because of environmental issues, including the public's disdain for nuclear power, and in part because no power firm would risk such a huge investment without knowing how deregulation was going to play out. Certain underdeveloped power transmission paths also proved to be bottlenecks, highlighting the need for investment in the state's infrastructure.

By May 2000, all of these factors led to the period enshrined in history as "the California energy crisis." The market was intended to create not only competition for a bevy of new players but also lower costs for consumers, but instead, it had created an opportunity for master manipulators to rip off consumers, plunge the utilities into near bankruptcy, cost the state tens of billions of dollars, and subject nearly every man, woman, and child in California to rolling blackouts not experienced since the days of World War II, when the reasons for what was happening were at least comprehensible.

Back at Cal-ISO, managing the grid was a challenge. Unlike other commodities, electricity cannot be stored or drawn from reserves but must be generated and distributed constantly. Therefore, the electrons being pumped into the transmission wires have to match precisely the rate of consumption off the grid by all manner of electrical devices, from air conditioners to toasters, computers to neon signs. The grid managed by Cal-ISO could handle neither a surge of electricity with no end source available to consume it nor a sudden heavy draw with no electricity available. Either scenario, throwing supply and demand out of equilibrium, would destabilize the system to the point of blackouts. To prevent blackouts, Cal-ISO operators could make emergency purchases at whatever price necessary, bypassing the competitive pricing set by the power exchange. Thus power producers had a financial incentive to sell in an emergency situation through Cal-ISO rather than through the power exchange.

For example, during a summer heat wave with temperatures of more than 100 degrees for several days, power producers got paid seventy-five cents per kilowatt-hour to wait on standby in case Cal-ISO needed more power, and another seventy-five cents per kilowatt-hour to provide it if necessary. The cost to the power provider to generate that one kilowatt-hour of electricity was fifteen cents, making for a tidy profit. While at its inception it was believed that Cal-ISO would account for purchasing only 5 percent of the electricity used, at peak times it was running closer to 30 percent of sales, diminishing the competitive-pricing intent of the law.

In the very hot summer of 1999, Cal-ISO operators scrambled from Canada to Arizona for extra power to avert blackouts. Those purchases in the summer of 1999 cost $1 million; a year later, they totaled more than $100 million. The power exchange, with prices changing constantly, turned out to be a more volatile and expensive way to purchase power than long-term contracts would have been. And utilities, complaining that it cost billions of dollars more to go through the power exchange, would have preferred such contracts.

On May 22, 2000, on another scorching day, heavy electricity usage put the grid on overload, and Cal-ISO declared the first stage 2 power alert when reserves dropped to 5 percent. When the temperature in San Francisco hit 105 degrees on June 14 and several plants were closed for "maintenance" purposes, California suffered its largest planned blackout since World War II. Rolling local blackouts targeted 97,000 PG&E customers, a method the company used in hopes of averting a massive, statewide, uncontrolled blackout. That summer, prices spiked.

In the six months between May and November 2000, power suppliers reaped an estimated $505 million in additional profits for the stock market, while consumers saw their electric bills increase by $10.9 billion more than those of the summer of 1999. Reliant Energy of Houston alone saw its wholesale energy division profits skyrocket 600 percent in the third quarter of 2000, with California accounting for $100 million of the $276 million increase. The average prices were 37 percent to 187 percent higher than they should have been in a flawless competitive market.

One SoCal Edison senior vice president rhetorically asked the *Los Angeles Times*'s Nancy Vogel: "Why are prices on a Sunday in 1999 seven times lower than prices on a Sunday in 2000? Same load [demand], no plants are out or anything like that. What would do that? . . . As demand started going up, the marketers figured out a way that they could exercise market power."[19]

That also seemed obvious to the governor, legislators, the utilities, and many others. On August 2, 2000, Governor Davis called for an investigation into "possible price manipulation in the wholesale electricity marketplace," while the state attorney general, Bill Lockyer, announced that his office was investigating the sharp price increases in San Diego as part of a larger inquiry into deregulation problems.[20]

In the end, it would be the audio tapes and transcripts of the Enron conversations that exposed the energy giant's callous disregard for the people of California and a conspiracy to game the system. The tapes, released June 14, 2004, and transcripts were part of more than 100,000 pages of documents submitted as evidence in a $122 million lawsuit Enron filed against Washington's Snohomish Public Utilities District seeking payment for delivery of electricity.

The tapes sound like a Hollywood parody of amoral greed, and in nearly all of them Enron traders are heard laughing. In one crass example on August 5, 2000, two unidentified Enron traders celebrated when a forest fire shut down a major transmission line into California, cutting power supplies and forcing an increase in prices:

[Phone rings]
Person 1: *Yeah.*
Person 2: *The magical word of the day is "burn, baby, burn."*
Person 1: *What's happening?*
Person 2: *There's a fire under the core line; it's been derated from 45 to 2100.*
Person 1: *Really?*
Person 2: *Yup.*
Person 1: *Burn, baby, burn . . .*
Person 2: *Just wanted you to know.*
Together: *Burn, baby, burn.*
Person 1: *That's a beautiful saying . . .*
Person 2: *(Laughs) So, I'll tell you—*
Person 1: *Cool, wow.*[21]

Very rarely, a trader voiced concerns about the morality or legality of what the traders were doing. "I'm just trying to be an honest camper so I only go to jail once," trader John Lavorato tells Enron's West Coast trading czar, Tim Belden, on August 4, 2000. "Fuck, this isn't a joke. I'm a little—nobody else seems to be concerned anymore about it, except for me."[22]

Four days later, Belden made some flattering statements about a respected coworker, Jeffrey Richter. "He just fucks California," Belden says on the transcript. "He steals money from California to the tune of about a million—" At which point he was interrupted by a more circumspect colleague, urging him to "rephrase" his comment. "Okay, he, um, he arbitrages the California market to the tune of a million bucks or two a day," Belden spins.

Both Belden and Richter later pleaded guilty to charges relating to their roles in manipulating electricity markets for Enron. It was found that they and other traders had given colorful nicknames to the myriad fraudulent "games" they employed, including "Deathstar," "Fat Boy," "Ricochet," and "Get Shorty." One gimmick involved faking congestion, then getting paid extra to relieve it, while another, known as "Wheel-Out," meant Enron got paid for scheduling electricity over a line it knew to be out of service or at capacity.

Perhaps the most infamous of dozens of damning conversations, however, was the much-reported "Grandma Millie" discussion. Bob Badeer, a trader at Enron's west power desk in Portland, Oregon, where the November 30, 2000, conversations were recorded, and Kevin McGowan, in Enron's central office in Houston, gave the nation an epic sound bite when discussing how California officials were demanding refunds for price gouging by electricity-generating companies.

> **Kevin:** *So the rumor's true? They're fuckin' takin' all the money back from you*
> *guys? All that money you guys stole from those poor grandmothers in*
> *California?*
>
> **Bob:** *Yeah, Grandma Millie, man. But she's the one who couldn't figure out*
> *how to fuckin' vote on the butterfly ballot* [a reference to the election

problems in Florida that paralyzed the Gore-Bush presidential election tabulation].

Kevin: *Yeah, now she wants her fuckin' money back for all the power you've charged right up—jammed right up her ass for a fuckin' $250 a megawatt hour.*

While Enron's traders were mocking them, Californians felt helpless, their anger and anxiety evident in statewide polls. A *Los Angeles Times* poll in October 2000 had nearly half the population—47 percent—disapproving of the legislature's passage of deregulation four years earlier, while only 32 percent approved. A poll that same month by the Public Policy Institute of California showed half of Californians believed the escalating energy prices would hurt the state's economy "a great deal" in the coming year.[23] As the situation worsened in the following months, so too did the voters' antipathy toward Governor Gray Davis and the legislature.

Nor could Californians take advantage of the idea that they could choose their energy supplier, consumer choice being one of the hallmarks of competition. The Public Utilities Commission had sold the public on increased competition from hundreds of potential power suppliers, which, it was assumed, would lead to lower costs.

By December 2000, fewer than ten companies were offering California consumers electricity service, although about three hundred initially had shown an interest. Less than 2 percent of nine million residential customers had chosen a new provider, while around 5 percent of small businesses and 13 percent of major industrial users and other large institutional users had switched.

Given the disclosure of the Enron traders' hateful words, it became more unlikely that Californians would want to trust the concept of deregulation again, at least not anytime soon. Again, the Kevin and Bob show, talking about a California businessman who came into the Enron office in Houston:

Kevin: *He's like, "Yeah, you know, I'm in California now and my small consulting business, my energy costs have gone from $100 to $500 a month.*

It's unbelievable, I don't know what to do." I just turned from my desk; I
just looked at him, I said, "Move!"

[Laughter]

Kevin: *The guy was like horrified. I go, look, don't take it the wrong way.*
Move. It isn't getting fixed anytime soon.

Bob: *You know man . . . that's the best thing [inaudible] about it. That's so*
beautiful.

Kevin: *Oh, best thing that could happen is fuckin' an earthquake, let that thing*
float out to the Pacific and [give] 'em fuckin' candles.

Bob: *I know. Those guys—just cut 'em off.*

Kevin: *They're so fucked, and they're so like totally—*

Bob: *They are so fucked.*[24]

By December 2000, five new power plants were under construction or approved, and another twelve were being considered by the state. On December
7, 2000, with supplies low, dipping to less than 3 percent, and some power
plants not operating, Cal-ISO declared the first statewide stage 3 power alert.
To avert rolling blackouts throughout the state, two large state and federal
water pumps were stopped temporarily to save energy, which allowed the
blackouts to halt.

A dramatic and quite significant shift in the energy marketplace in the
country's largest state had taken place: The electricity producers, who had had
the foresight to buy up the aging generating plants for many times what they
were worth, were suddenly in the catbird seat, their combined profits up
75 percent in the summer of 2000 over the previous summer. Also sitting
pretty was the Los Angeles Department of Water and Power, a municipally
owned agency that not only was exempt from deregulation but also was selling much-needed excess electricity through 1999 and 2000, making $200 mil-
lion in eighteen months. Its general manager, S. David Freeman, who would
go on to become Governor Gray Davis's energy czar, told the *Los Angeles
Times,* "A blind pig could make money in this market."[25]

Enron was raking in the profits, but that was far from true for the three
big utilities. Having sold their generating plants, they now were at the mercy

of mostly out-of-state owners of those very plants, and these "too big to fail" giant utilities were going bankrupt. They desperately wanted price caps, but the new deregulation law had shifted oversight from the PUC in Sacramento to the Federal Energy Regulatory Commission (FERC) in Washington, D.C., whose chairman had been appointed by President George Bush on the recommendation of Bush's friend and campaign donor, Enron's "Kenny Boy" Lay.

An increasingly beleaguered and furious Governor Gray Davis, facing an angry populace as well as desperate utility executives and shareholders, traveled to Washington in December 2000 for a meeting with members of the Clinton administration, in its waning days, seeking relief for his state. He had vivid memories of that meeting, as he recalled in the interview in his Century City law office:

> I'm in the Treasury secretary's boardroom with just about ten days left in Clinton's administration. And [Energy Secretary Bill] Richardson is there, and [Treasury Secretary Lawrence] Summers is there; Ken Lay is there; [Secretary of State] Warren Christopher is there; [SoCal Edison CEO] John Bryson's there. I mean, it's everybody—every major utility owner in California, and every major energy supplier. . . . There [were] probably thirty people representing utilities and energy suppliers. [They said] "You have to raise rates, Governor." I have two Republicans and two Democrats [from the legislature] with me. They all said, "No, we're not going to raise rates." They all said no, I mean, this whole energy scheme was Enron's idea; it's not working, and we're not going to punish the consumer.[26]

Davis may not have realized it at the time, but the deck was already stacked against him. Summers, whose office was used for the meeting, had a close relationship with Lay; supported the so-called Enron loophole in the Commodity Futures Modernization Act exempting Enron from regulation;

and favored Enron's goal of energy deregulation in all states. Lay offered Summers a position on the Enron board of directors, which Summers declined when he assumed the presidency at Harvard; Lay also hired Linda Robertson, an assistant Treasury secretary, as a lobbyist for Enron on Summers's recommendation. The list goes on.[27]

As Kurt Eichenwald details in his book *Conspiracy of Fools,* Alan Greenspan, the Federal Reserve chairman at the time, sat at the head of the table during the meeting and listened as Davis stated the obvious: "The thing is, if deregulation fails in California, it will fail in the United States."[28] Greenspan and Summers lectured Davis on the point Libertarians and laissez-faire economists would later argue: The energy crisis was an example not of deregulation per se but of the dangers of incomplete deregulation:

"Truthfully, Governor, California hasn't deregulated," Greenspan said. "The state simply replaced one form of regulation with another. It's become a system of central planning run amok."

Summers joined in: "You have a fixed price set by the state for selling electricity to the public. But you have a variable, floating price when you buy electricity."

Greenspan cautioned, "That's not sustainable," adding that "the first step is that prices for consumers are going to have to go up."[29]

After Davis presented evidence that energy suppliers were manipulating the market, Greenspan and Summers argued on behalf of the energy producers, and Summers opposed Davis's request for government intervention with price controls, saying, "Governor, this is classic supply and demand. The only way to fix this is ultimately by allowing retail prices to go wherever they have to go."[30] According to Eichenwald, Davis warned the pair that this was a political problem that could be resolved by the people of California, who can change laws and policy through the initiative process; in other words, they could undo deregulation as easily as it had been implemented. Eichenwald writes that, two days later, Ken Lay showed up at the governor's office in Los

Angeles and suggested that Davis put all the blame for the state's "serious problems" on his predecessor, Pete Wilson, and, mimicking Summers and Greenspan, suggested raising prices.[31]

By his actions, Summers seemed to be keeping a commitment he had made to Ken Lay. When Summers was about to take office as head of Treasury, he received a "Dear Larry" letter of congratulations from Lay, and he responded on May 25, 1999, to "Ken," writing, "I'll keep my eye on power deregulation and energy-market infrastructure issues."[32] Helping Governor Davis and the people of California did not appear to be on his "to do" list.

Later, moderate economists would use California's energy crisis to support the idea that capitalism functions best with moderating restraints and rules maintained by government. After all, Enron, despite its short-term profits, would soon be bankrupt, and the attention California's pain garnered would certainly limit the spread of electricity-deregulation schemes that favored speculators.

Clinton himself, just less than a year earlier, on July 10, 1998, had introduced in the Senate the Comprehensive Electricity Competition Act, a national energy deregulation plan that would have opened the $200 billion national electricity market to competition. In a statement, Clinton said the competition would save consumers $20 billion a year. He may have been thinking of his friendly relationship with Ken Lay, but he could not have been appreciating what was happening in California.

Within a short while, Davis and California got good news and bad news: On December 13, 2000, Energy Secretary Richardson issued an unusual executive order demanding that out-of-state power suppliers had to sell electricity at the standard "just and reasonable" rate to California. They had been refusing to sell because they had good reason to believe that the utilities teetering on the brink of bankruptcy would not be able to pay them.

Two days later, the bad news came: FERC rejected wholesale price caps to rein in the generators and instead encouraged the utilities to enter into long-term contracts with the power generators to avoid the high wholesale prices available through the power exchange. A flexible rate cap of $150 per megawatt-hour was approved, although the utilities could charge more if they could prove it was warranted. On this day in 1999, California had paid $45 per megawatt-hour, but in 2000 it was paying $1,400 per megawatt-hour.

The same day FERC rejected the wholesale price caps, Enron's most valuable point person in the Senate, Phil Gramm, pulled a fast one. On December 14, after Congress had reconvened in a lame duck session just days after the U.S. Supreme Court's ruling ensuring George W. Bush's election as president, Gramm introduced the same bill he had introduced in June, but with a different number, with Representative Thomas Ewing doing the same in the House; Gramm got his legislation attached to the appropriations bill, over which Congress and Clinton had been tussling for weeks. Congress passed the bill on December 15, 2000.

An enthusiastic Clinton signed the measure on December 21, shortly before he left the White House. Now Enron could operate an electricity auction by bypassing regulated trading auctions, without transparency or government examination of any sort. The significant measure, which would play out in a dark way in California, had undergone no debate or committee hearing in the Senate, thanks to Gramm's machinations.

It is amazing, in hindsight, how little clout the Democratic governor of the country's most populous state had with the popular president of his own party sitting in the White House. For Clinton, who had become a convert to deregulation in high finance as well, California's concerns were apparently parochial or transitory. If he believed the crisis was already over, he couldn't have been more wrong.

Back in California, the future was looking bleak for the utilities. By January 2001, they could not hold on much longer. SoCal Edison and PG&E told the state Public Utilities Commission that they were close to bankruptcy because they were restricted by rate caps and therefore could not pass on to consumers the spiking wholesale rates they were paying for electricity. At one point that month, Duke had charged $3,380 per megawatt-hour, a dramatic increase above the $76 a megawatt-hour they said they had charged throughout 2000. The PUC approved emergency temporary rate increases of 7 percent to 15 percent, but it was not enough.

On January 16, SoCal Edison announced that it would not be able to pay

$596 million it owed creditors, while PG&E was also close to defaulting on payments. The credit ratings of both companies were downgraded to low junk status. A commodity that had been taken for granted under a system that had worked for more than one hundred years was now the topic of conversations across the state. A statewide poll by the Public Policy Institute of California that month had three in four residents saying the cost and supply of energy was a "big problem."

On January 11, Cal-ISO called a stage 3 alert that endured for thirty-two days. Within a few days, the situation would grow more dire, due to greater market manipulation by Enron, which had become common practice. The impact of the 2000 Gramm measure, combined with California's energy deregulation, enabled Enron to manipulate the power market in the West to a greater extent than ever before beginning December 21, 2000, the day Enron was permitted to operate an unregulated trading auction by its subsidiary EnronOnline.

Before that date, although electricity prices were high in California, there had only been one stage 3 emergency, or "rolling blackout," as it was called, from the time the energy crisis began in May 2000 to December 21, 2000. That emergency was called on December 7 and lasted two hours. But from December 21 until the crisis was ended, when California's power market was reregulated in June 2001, there were thirty-eight stage 3 emergencies in California; stage 2 emergencies increased 81 percent from 2000 to 2001; and there were nearly 30 percent more stage 1 emergencies declared during that time.

A December 2001 report by Public Citizen on Enron's influence over government noted the impact of Enron's lobbying efforts and influence with Gramm: "The correlation is clear: Phil Gramm's commodities deregulation law allowed Enron to control electricity in California, pocket billions in extra revenues and force millions of California residents to go hundreds of hours without electricity and pay outrageous prices."[33]

Three days later, President Bush was sworn into office and his new Energy secretary, Spencer Abraham, on January 23 granted what he said would be the last extension of Richardson's emergency order directing power wholesalers to sell to California, a move that clearly helped Bush friend "Kenny Boy" Lay and Enron.

This lends some credence to one theory as to why Enron was shafting California and Davis. In our interview, Davis said he believed Republicans were convinced that he was going to run for president, so they wanted to see him fail in order to doom such a possibility.[34]

On February 1, the state legislature approved another $10 billion buying plan to further help the giant utilities, agreeing to sign long-term contracts with generators at prices lower than on the open market. The state was spending between $40 million and $50 million a day buying power on the spot market. Five days later, the Bush administration announced that the emergency order requiring wholesalers to sell to California would not be renewed.

But just hours before the order was to expire, a federal judge in Sacramento, Frank Damrell, granted a temporary restraining order forcing a major producer, Reliant Energy, to continue to sell to California. It was "the only thing that saved us," Davis recalled.[35]

Despite the state's efforts, SoCal Edison and PG&E had taken on such huge debt that they defaulted on payments to the Power Exchange and Cal-ISO. In January 2001, the Power Exchange ceased trading on its markets. PG&E filed for bankruptcy in April 2001, and SoCal Edison came close to doing the same.

On the other hand, Enron's profits skyrocketed. In the first six months of 2001, Enron Whole Services posted revenues of nearly $97 billion, an increase of 350 percent over the same six-month period in 2000. In 1999, the entire year's revenues were $35.5 billion, a record revenue gain at the time.

From January to October 2001, the state spent $10 billion buying electricity on a short-term basis from energy suppliers, including Enron. According to a lawsuit filed by the state against Enron on June 14, 2004, power buyers spent about $27 billion each in 2000 and 2001 for wholesale power, compared with $7 billion in 1999. The Public Utilities Commission passed on those costs to consumers. The suit was filed about four years after the energy crisis began, and Californians were still paying among the highest rates in the nation for electricity.

The state finally got relief from FERC in April 2001, when the commission agreed to allow a cap on wholesale prices during stage 1 or higher emergencies when reserves fell below 7 percent. A month later, the state Public Utilities Commission and California Edison filed charges of price-fixing against El Paso, which owns the largest natural gas pipeline serving Southern California. The high price of natural gas had driven up the cost of electricity generated by gas-fired plants and added an estimated $3.7 billion to the costs of the energy crisis. Also in May, Cal-ISO submitted a plan for a revised market to FERC, calling for extended price caps.

Then a bombshell hit. On May 6, FERC released internal Enron documents revealing that Enron traders had created phony congestion on the California power grid. By the end of that month, Attorney General Lockyer filed suit against Enron and eleven other energy providers. In June 2001, with the California crisis now a prominent national scandal, FERC extended California's price caps to spot-market sales in California and ten other western states. At that point, Enron could no longer operate, and since it had chosen not to purchase any of the utility plants, it could not even fall back on producing electricity, which other distributors could. Enron eventually went bankrupt, and the $1.52 billion settlement with California agencies and private utilities reached on July 16, 2005, could not be paid in full.

Ken Lay and other Enron executives were convicted of criminal charges unrelated to their activities in California. Lay died of a heart attack while his case was on federal appeal. The "Big Five" accounting firm Arthur Andersen also was convicted of criminal charges (later overturned) related to its lack of oversight of its client Enron, and voluntarily surrendered its CPA license, leading to its collapse.

In July 2001, 80 percent of California residents believed the crisis would hurt the state's economy for the next few years, and 65 percent said that rather than leave matters to the legislature to resolve, the voters should intervene and take to the initiative process to set energy policy. The legislature and governor took a huge hit in terms of how they were thought to be doing their jobs. At the start of 2002, only 39 percent of residents approved of Governor Davis's handling of the matter. Among likely voters, only 32 percent thought he was doing a good job, including fewer than half of Democrats (46 percent) and independents (42 percent), and only 24 percent of Republicans.

While he was able to win reelection in 2002 against a weak Republican opponent, ultimately the damage done to Davis proved irreparable. On October 7, 2003, less than a year after beginning his second term, an election was held to recall him and simultaneously elect his successor from among 135 candidates who filed papers to run. One was future Internet entrepreneur Arianna Huffington, several were political figures, and others could have starred in Looney Tunes cartoons. The biggest name that stood out in a wide but weak field was Republican Arnold Schwarzenegger, superstar and political outsider, who was elected. While it had allowed Republicans to recapture the governor's office and cast a new star in their political firmament, for true believers in the deregulated Texas model, the Enron crisis actually proved to be a pyrrhic victory.

It wasn't supposed to be this way. When the Texas congressman Thomas "Dereg" DeLay, majority whip in the House and longtime friend of Enron, set out his "free-market vision" for the electricity industry at a Heritage Foundation lecture, he had boasted that it would bring "electricity into the competitive world [and] will unleash new products, greater efficiencies, business synergies, and entrepreneurial success stories" creating "new industries, new entrepreneurs, and new jobs."[36]

California's experience was clearly the opposite. Perhaps sensing that things had gotten out of hand and were boomeranging, deregulation stalwart Phil Gramm early on tried to spin it as an example of how liberal California was getting everything wrong.

"As they suffer the consequences of their own feckless policies, political leaders in California blame power companies, deregulation, and everyone but themselves," the Texas politician opined. "And the inevitable call is now being heard for a federal bailout. I intend to do everything in my power to require those who valued environmental extremism and interstate protectionism more than common sense and market freedom to solve their electricity crisis without short-circuiting taxpayers in other states."[37]

Not heeding the lessons of California, the state legislature in Gramm's home state deregulated the energy market there in 2001, effective January 1, 2002, during the same time California was buckling under deregulation. While other states saw the California experiment as a red flag and slowed down, stopped, or reversed their energy deregulation efforts, Texas plunged ahead.[38]

While profitable for Texas power companies, the system did not work for all Texans. A March 2014 report from the Texas Coalition for Public Power found that from implementation through 2013, "Texans in deregulated areas have consistently paid more for power than Texans outside deregulation. All told, Texans living in deregulated areas would have saved more than $22 billion in lower residential electricity bills since 2002 had they paid the same average prices as Texans living outside deregulation,"[39] such as Austin, with its municipally owned utility.

The report noted that ten years before implementation of deregulation, the average residential prices Texans paid were 6.4 percent below the national average, while in the first ten years under deregulation, they paid prices that were 8.5 percent above the national average. Also, the Texas Public Utilities Commission uncovered that in the first year of deregulation, "six companies netted $29 million in improper revenues for engaging in activities similar to the illegal activities that Enron used in California."[40]

For many Californians, the lesson was quite clear. The reckless behavior of Enron and its assault on the state's economy made the case against free market radicalism and for sound regulation. And while the rest of the nation may have experienced schadenfreude from the plight of Californians, whom they imagined all lived the high life on bluffs overlooking the Pacific, for residents of the state, all signs pointed in a different direction: pragmatism over ideology.

When the once supremely popular "governator" Schwarzenegger would overreach with a special election centered on a quartet of far-ranging reform initiatives supported by free-market ideologues, he was dealt a devastating political defeat from which he never fully recovered. The message was clear: no more experiments. It was the end of the unregulated free-market illusion that Reagan had done so much to propagate for many Californians. Enron's stealth attack on the California economy was the last Californians wanted to hear about the Reagan revolution. In this particular fight, California won the round. The failure of deregulatory fetishism in California, which has continued to be championed in Texas, would define the competition between the two states over which is a better model for the nation.

5

A Tale of Two States

*If you don't support the death penalty and citizens
packing a pistol, don't come to Texas. If you don't like
medicinal marijuana and gay marriage,
don't move to California.*

—RICK PERRY, *FED UP!*

T he rivalry between Jerry Brown and Rick Perry provided plenty of journalistic fodder over the years and served to distinguish the two—and
the states they governed—as polar opposites on key issues and policies.
Sometimes the banter was downright personal. Perry so often bashed California on his frequent trips to poach businesses that residents of both states
were startled when Perry told a *New York Times Magazine* interviewer, over
lunch at a Los Angeles restaurant, how much he likes the Golden State.
"Perry told me that he loves California, vacations in San Diego annually,
visits the state about six times a year and might even move here in January
[2014] when he's done with his fourteen-year stint running Texas," wrote
Mark Leibovich.[1]

It calls to mind the lyric we Californians understand fully: *"How ya gonna
keep 'em down on the farm, after they've seen Paree?"*

As might have been expected, Perry's California crush showed up on the
Internet and Texas media, prompting a spokesman to clarify: the governor
had been asked what state *other* than Texas would Perry like to live in and
quoted from a partial transcript of the interview, in which Perry responded,

"I would live in California if I could afford it. Why wouldn't you want to live out here? Seriously?"[2]

Perhaps he did not realize what a kerfuffle it would cause at home, or maybe he was focused too intently on the folks he was in Los Angeles to address—Jewish Republicans—and trying to convince the writer he was a member of the tribe. Leibovich wrote that while waiting to eat his Reuben sandwich at the renowned Nate 'n Al Deli in Beverly Hills, Perry "took a moment to appreciate his surroundings. 'I'm more Jewish than you think I am,' he told me [possibly rehearsing his speech for campaign dollars]. 'I read the part of the Bible that said the Jews are God's chosen people.' He boasted that he has been going to Israel since 1992."[3] Perry was the gift that kept on giving. Writer Julie Wiener nailed it in a Jewish blog item headlined "Rick Perry, the Jew," busting him for "clearly scoring all the Jewish points he can, short of discovering a Jewish ancestor or actually converting."[4]

Despite Perry's frequent visits to California, he rarely has anything nice to say about the state. In fact, his backers paid for advertisements so he could slam California's "bad for business" climate and try to poach companies to move to Texas. The Texas versus California grudge match, manufactured in large part by the media and politicians, is primarily symbolic but nevertheless brings to light real differences in the way America's two most populous states are facing the present and future and provokes the question of which might better serve as a cultural and economic model for the nation.

The two big players propelling those models have been the conservative Perry, who used his governorship of Texas twice in seeking the presidency, and the pragmatic liberal Brown. Perry's presidential aspirations are in the ashcan of history, but his views are embraced by other prominent Republicans, including his successor, Greg Abbott, and governors Scott Walker, Sam Brownback, Bobby Jindal, and Rick Scott, among other conservatives. These governors and Brown are political polar opposites on climate change, immigration, the environment, workers' rights, tax structure, gay marriage, and just about any other topic.

Perry's envy for the Golden State extended beyond its physical attributes. Not only does California have the largest population in the country, with

39 million people (Texas has 27 million), it also receives more venture-capital investment—$25 billion more in 2015—than all other states combined, leaving its Silicon Valley clone, Austin, scrambling for crumbs. If it were a country, California would qualify for admission to the Group of Eight—the largest industrialized economies in the world—with its standing as the seventh largest and a gross state product (GSP) in 2015 of $2.464 trillion. Texas would rank fourteenth with a gross state product of $1.5 trillion.[5]

Perry worked diligently as governor to move his state up the ranks in these areas, by visiting populous states and trying to recruit businesses and people to move to Texas. California was his most frequent target. His "hunting trips" heated up when he was stumping for president of the United States, pressing his claim that he could replicate the Texas oasis of conservative prosperity for the entire nation if he were president. He flamed out in the 2016 primary, but it was not for lack of trying.

By mid-2014, Perry had traveled across the country to five other big states—all not coincidentally led by Democratic governors—including New York, Illinois, Maryland, Connecticut, and Missouri—where he customized his "miracle" pitch to each. His trips cost a Texas marketing and promotion group, TexasOne, more than $1 million in media ads—$1 million in New York alone.

A thirty-second radio spot broadcast in California got big bang for Perry, not so much for its content but for the California governor's off-color response. It hit the airwaves in the state's six most populous media markets, with Perry saying, "Building a business is tough. But I hear building a business in California is next to impossible. . . . I have a message for California businesses. Come check out Texas . . . and see why our low taxes, sensible regulations, and fair legal system are just the thing to get your business moving—to Texas."[6]

Brown found himself surrounded after an event the next day by a half dozen reporters, with microphones and a few TV cameras, asking about Perry's ad. He seemed a bit perplexed by their interest. "It's not a serious story," he said. "You take a little radio ad, and all you guys run like lapdogs to report it. It's a nowhere. It's not even a burp. It's barely a fart."[7] Smiles could not be suppressed.

What had been little reported amid all the bluster was that the results of all these recruiting efforts were pretty much all hat and no cattle, as they say in Texas.

As Director Kish Rajan of Brown's Office of Business and Development— GO-Biz—later opined on Perry's trips and that ad: "I can understand why Rick Perry is interested in California. We were the national jobs leader for most of the last year [2013] with 257,000 new private sector jobs."[8] He cited a September 2010 Public Policy Institute of California study of business relocations and homegrown jobs in California over fourteen years,[9] reporting that "during the two years of the highest departures in the study, California lost just .05 percent of the state's total establishments. At that rate, it would take twenty years to lose just 1 percent of our businesses to relocation."[10]

Rajan also referred to a study titled "The Job Creation Shell Game" that makes clear the hype that goes into stories about Texas stealing jobs from California, or from any other state. In addition to revealing that Texas was the third-biggest jobs exporter to California, the study by the public policy group Good Jobs First found:

> For the first seven years of the Perry administration (2003 to 2009 . . .) Texas had a net gain of 28,375 relocated jobs (inbound jobs minus outbound). That is only 0.23 percent of the state's 12.2 million jobs at the start of that time period, for an average annual rate of just 0.03 percent jobs gained. Even if the state's numbers have picked up a bit in the recovery, twice that rate would still be an extremely small impact.
>
> Put another way, these results suggest Texas officials should spend 99.97 percent of their economic development time and money on everything besides chasing other states' jobs.[11]

Regardless of the math, Perry had been able to build a case in the media for his presidential bid by capitalizing on what has come to be labeled in the media as the "Texas miracle." The "miracle," for which Perry took credit, consists of a number of factors that brought national media attention to the governor and his state. These include cruising through the Great Recession relatively unscathed, escaping the brunt of the mortgage foreclosure meltdown, posting an impressive jobs-creation record for many consecutive months, and, as Perry and his fellow travelers tell it, helping businesses grow by following a strict conservative blueprint virtually free of "oppressive taxes,"[12] "onerous" regulations, and "frivolous" litigation.

It wasn't just the right wing blogosphere and talk radio that drove the "miracle" bandwagon but also mainstream media, including *Forbes,* the *Wall Street Journal, New York Times, Los Angeles Times,* and *USA Today.* Because Texas is a model for a state that follows the fundamentalist bible of economic conservatism, it is important to examine the state's evolution and the credibility of its narrative if it is to be considered a legitimate model for the nation.

Let's consider two factors that comprise the "miracle:" the foreclosure meltdown and jobs. Perry constantly celebrates his state's "freedom" from regulations. But it was precisely tough antipredatory lending laws and restrictions on mortgage equity withdrawals that saved Texans from the worst of the foreclosure crisis that hit the rest of the nation. In early 2010, the foreclosure rate among homeowners with subprime loans in Texas was less than any state except Alaska. For the first half of 2011, California had the third-highest foreclosure rate in the country, and Texas had the sixth-lowest, with less than 6 percent in foreclosure or close to it.

Texas's strong consumer protection laws long predate Perry, going way back in the state's history. In fact, when Texas formed as a state in 1845, its constitution banned state-chartered banks and forbade private lenders from hawking mortgages to homesteaders, thanks to a law enacted after a traumatizing period in 1838 when many homesteaders lost their property to foreclosure due to a bank panic. The prohibition of banks was omitted in the 1869 constitution but seven years later was reinstated in the constitution of 1876. Finally in 1904, voters approved a constitutional amendment permitting the state to charter banks.

But there were enough consumer laws on the books to protect Texans from any nefarious banking practices that could lead to the loss of one's home. For example, Texas law bans prepayment penalties, balloon loans, and negative amortization loans. There are strict regulations on refinancing and home equity loans—the kind that proved disastrous in other parts of the country. Texas has only permitted home equity loans since late 1997. Foreclosures in Texas have to be ordered by a court, not the lender, and the borrower is not liable for money damages beyond sacrificing his or her home.

In California, housing prices climbed steeply before the crash, more than 130 percent from 2000 to 2006, with a buildup of equity. When the housing market collapsed and home values plummeted, tens of thousands of California homeowners suddenly found themselves owing more on their homes than they were worth; they were "underwater" on their mortgages, and banks foreclosed on homes when owners could not pay.

In Texas, by contrast, home values only grew by about 30 percent. Fewer homeowners took money out of their home's equity than in any other state, and they borrowed less when they did, thanks in large part to the state's consumer protection laws.

The recession of 2008 was devastating to California's economy. There were substantial job losses, attributable in large part to the collapse of the real estate industry during the mortgage meltdown. The nation's economic problems were magnified in California, particularly in that industry. The ripple effect was dramatic—home construction, real estate, home furnishings, landscaping, and other related industries all suffered. California lost the greatest number of private sector jobs—855,200—in the country from January 2008 to January 2012, while Texas enjoyed the nation's largest gain—139,800 jobs, largely due to its booming oil industry, according to Bureau of Labor Statistics figures.[13]

The two states had nearly identical unemployment rates from 2000 to 2006, but California's spiraled upward along with the housing meltdown. By August 2011, California unemployment was the third highest in the nation, at 12.1 percent, while in Texas, 8.5 percent of the workforce was unemployed. That same month, Perry was boasting in speeches that Texas had created 40 percent of the jobs in the nation over the past year, which was true (it was actually even higher—47 percent). But he failed to mention another truth. As pointed out that month by the respected FactCheck.org project at the Annenberg Public Policy Center:

> While Texas has created jobs, the state hasn't created enough of them to keep pace with a rising population and labor force. In fact . . . unemployment got worse in Texas—going from 7.7 percent in June 2009 to 8.4 percent in July 2011. . . . And Texas's unemployment rate—while still below the national average—is now higher than that of 26 states.[14]

Texas job gains had been spurred by a booming oil industry, which saw the state's domestic oil production share increase to 40 percent, from 25 percent over the previous five years. Meanwhile, California had steady job growth through 2013, and by June 2014 the state had finally recovered all of the jobs lost during the recession. As California bounced back from that period, the real estate industry rebounded, and so did tourism and other service industries.

With the passage in November 2012 of Jerry Brown's Proposition 30 tax increase initiative, which provided more money for schools, there were education hires after years of layoffs. The *Los Angeles Times* reported that between 2011 and 2014, California has been among the top ten states in job growth, with only North Dakota, Utah, Texas, Colorado, and Nevada having greater rates of employment growth. By December 2015, California's unemployment rate had fallen to 5.8 percent, while Texas stood at 4.7 percent.

But Texas had experienced some serious trouble. Crude oil prices peaked in June 2008, when the high price of $145 per barrel was realized, having climbed steadily from $92.97 in January of that year. By June 2011, the price stood at around $110 a barrel. According to Dallas Federal Reserve Bank research, an increase in oil prices is generally accompanied by job growth that is stronger than that of the nation as a whole, with a 10 percent increase in oil prices resulting in a 0.3 percent increase in employment and a 0.5 percent increase in the GDP of Texas.

In addition, taxes on oil helped bloat the state's budget reserves, which grew to more than $9 billion in 2010, six times what it had been when Perry first came into office. In 2014, prices were still hovering around $90 a barrel, spurring jobs creation in the oil sector as well as in related industries, such as petrochemicals and refining. But by January 2015, when Texas was producing more than three million barrels of oil a day, close to 12 percent of the state's 2012 GDP, the price of crude oil had plummeted to about $48 a barrel.

Economist Brian Kelsey, founder of the Austin economics research firm Civic Analytics, told *Austin American-Statesman* reporter Claudia Grisales in December 2014 that the state could lose 212,000 jobs and $13.5 billion in total earnings if revenue from oil and gas fell 20 percent.[15] Grisales also reported that "Michael Feroli, JPMorgan Chase's chief U.S. economist, made an even more dire prediction in a [December 18, 2014] note to clients. He compared the current situation in Texas to the 1986 state recession, which happened after oil prices dropped by about 50 percent in a six-month period. 'As we weigh the evidence, we think Texas will, at the least, have a rough 2015 ahead, and is at risk of slipping into a regional recession,' Feroli wrote."[16]

Lower prices had cost thousands of Texas oil and gas jobs in the fall of 2014 into March 2015, when Texas lost 25,400 jobs, the most jobs lost in any state in the country, while California gained 39,800, the most gains in the country that month.[17] By February 29, 2016, the crude oil barrel price was $33.75.[18]

Perry's "miracle" claims were challenged more than once, including in his last speech as governor on January 15, 2015, by the ever-diligent FactCheck .org, which posted this five days later:

> Rick Perry, in his last official speech as Texas governor, mixed and matched jobs data to embellish the state's job gains.
>
> Perry claimed Texas had created 1.4 million jobs since December 2007 while the rest of the United States lost 400,000 jobs. Actually, according to the job-growth measure used by most economists, the rest of the country *gained* more than 500,000 jobs.
>
> In the same speech, Perry used the standard job-growth measure to claim that Texas had "created almost one-third of all the nation's new jobs"

since he took office. And he claimed that his state had created 441,000 jobs in the past year—again, using the standard job-growth measure. But if he had stuck with the jobs data he used to compare Texas's growth since 2007 to the rest of the nation's, he would have had to cite a number that's more than 100,000 jobs *lower* than the one he used.[19]

Over the past several years, a few journalists and researchers uncovered other myths in the Texas-miracle narrative, though they lacked the attention the mainstream media gave to the "miracle." One issue arose over the much-heralded Texas Enterprise Fund (TEF), created by the Texas legislature in 2003 at Perry's urging to provide millions of dollars in grants to companies chosen by the governor, lieutenant governor, and speaker of the house to expand or relocate to Texas. Several California companies have been among the recipients.

For example, Apple received $21 million after it acquired a 100-employee supplier to the iPad in the Austin area and later announced it would expand in Austin, which added its own subsidies to total $30 million for the move. The TEF Web site[20] indicated that Apple projected having 10,685 jobs there. Caterpillar was given two grants totaling $9.675 million (and later also built a 400,000-square-foot distribution center in Kern County, California). Chevron was given $12 million for moving a division with 800 employees to Houston in 2013. The solar-products manufacturer SunPower Corp. was given $2.5 million to relocate to Texas and employ 450 people, while the online auction site eBay, the recipient of a $2.8 million grant, announced an expansion of its Austin office and the creation of more than 1,000 jobs.

The fund claims to have awarded more than $555 million in grants from its inception through the 2014–15 fiscal year ending August 31, 2015, with $427.4 million of the grant money dispersed and $43.5 million returned for various reasons by August 2014. The grantees committed to a total capital investment of almost $24 billion and creating 230,346 "direct, indirect, and induced jobs forecasted by third-party economic impact analysis."[21]

The numbers are impressive. But a series of investigative stories over the years raised serious questions about the way the fund was being operated and the grants distributed and monitored. One of the earliest stories, "Slush Fun," by Dave Mann, ran in the *Texas Observer* on March 11, 2010. It detailed how nearly 37 percent of grant recipients returned the favor with political contributions to Perry or the Republican Governors Association, which Perry headed in 2008.[22] A detailed report published six months later by the watchdog group Texans for Public Justice, dubbed the TEF a "phantom jobs fund."[23]

The study analyzed fifty grants to companies that espoused job creation goals in the previous two years. Of those, only eleven were performing, while the percentage of terminated, amended, and nonperforming projects jumped from 42 percent in 2008 to 66 percent at the end of 2009. About two-thirds of the analyzed groups had failed to meet their job creation goals, had to lower the number of jobs they had committed to create, or had their contracts canceled by the state.

One of the underperformers was Countrywide Financial, of Calabasas, California, which received $20 million in 2004. In a press release, Perry called it the "crowning jewel" of the program. Countrywide failed in 2008, a facilitator and then victim of the mortgage meltdown, and was taken over by Bank of America, which paid back only $8.5 million of the grant.[24]

Texans for Public Justice followed up the *Texas Observer*'s "Slush Fun" story with another report in October 2011, which revealed that contributions from TEF grantees to Perry and the governors association were continuing. The report cited the *Texas Observer* article and added:

> This report finds that 43 companies that landed a total of $333 million in TEF awards contributed almost $7 million to Perry's campaign and the Perry-affiliated Republican Governors Association (RGA). TEF companies sometimes made corporate contributions directly to the RGA, while company PACs, owners or executives gave to both the RGA and to Perry's campaign (which cannot accept corporate funds). These contributions included $1,652,159 to Perry's gubernatorial campaigns and $5,331,701 to the RGA. The 43 TEF recipients that contributed to Perry and/or the RGA represent about half of the 90 companies that received TEF awards but received 76 percent of all TEF-awarded funds.[25]

Mark Maremont of the *Wall Street Journal* elevated an examination of the TEF into a national forum in his detailed story under the headline "Behind Perry's Job Success, Numbers Draw New Scrutiny." He exposed yet another chink in the "miracle" facade. Maremont unearthed more details of this inconvenient truth: Many of the jobs being claimed in the stories of success never in fact had materialized, or the numbers were bolstered by job gains that were tangential to the projects for which they were intended.[26]

Maremont focused in one instance on a $50 million grant in 2005 to Texas A&M, Perry's alma mater, to establish the Texas Institute for Genomic Medicine. It was the largest grant awarded by the fund. In a report to the Texas legislature in 2011, Perry credited the institute with producing 12,000 additional jobs, way over the 5,000 that were promised by 2015. But according to the institute's director, Maremont reported, only ten people were working in its new building in October 2011.

When the reporter asked a Perry spokeswoman to explain the difference in numbers, she said the job totals were provided by the grant recipients and had not been "verified."

One explanation Maremont reported was that a biotech firm in the Houston area that had agreed to produce about 1,600 of the project's jobs employs just 220 people total in the state, after having cut nearly 400 jobs in Texas.

Maremont explained the discrepancies between jobs promised, jobs claimed, and the reality: "To reach their estimate of 12,000-plus jobs . . . officials included every position added in Texas since 2005 in fields sometimes related only tangentially to biotechnology, according to state officials and documents provided by Texas A&M. They include jobs in things like dental equipment, fertilizer manufacturing, and medical imaging."[27] This also was the case with other grants.

One might wonder why so many years passed before the state of Texas itself investigated the TEF, given that taxpayer money was the oil that kept the TEF machine running. It took legislation by the Texas state senator Wendy Davis, the 2014 Democratic nominee for governor, to order a formal review of the fund. Finally, in September 2014, just four months before Perry was to leave office, the Texas State Auditor's Office released a scathing report.

It was highly critical of the overseers of the TEF for, among other things, distributing $222 million—nearly half of what was awarded—to universities and other entities that never submitted an application or gave an estimate of the number of jobs they would fill, which supposedly had been requirements for receiving the money. Compliance was so weak that the auditor could not substantiate many jobs and investments that were credited to the fund.[28]

"Critics have complained that the Texas Enterprise Fund was a loosely controlled treasure trove for Perry to dole out state money to favored projects," wrote *Dallas Morning News* reporter Christy Hoppe.[29] "The audit did little to dispel that."[30] Nearly everything about the process came under fire, including the recouping of money when projects failed.

The Texas legislature had declined to make any TEF grants in the 2013–14 fiscal year.[31] However, in January 2015, within ten days of being inaugurated to succeed Perry, Governor Greg Abbott, a former Texas attorney general, indicated that the TEF would survive with reforms, but he quickly set about abolishing another of Perry's pet programs, the Texas Emerging Technology Fund.

Perry had also credited that project with contributing to the state's job growth. But the program, which gave away $200 million for start-up businesses, was befouled by bankruptcies, lack of transparency, and accusations of political influence, such as favoring some Perry campaign donors with millions of dollars in investment funds for questionable start-ups, a practice that earned a *Wall Street Journal* headline, "Rick Perry's 'Crony Capitalism' Problem."[32]

The TEF did benefit many large corporations, but whether they always benefited Texas taxpayers is questionable. Take, for example, one of the program's highest-profile grants, its third largest, for $40 million to Toyota. The automaker agreed to move its headquarters from Los Angeles County's South Bay city of El Segundo to the Dallas suburb of Plano and take its employees along for the ride. The announcement received national media attention. Indeed, it was a huge victory for Perry and a big blow to Governor Brown, who got the news from Toyota only three days before the media announcement on April 28, 2014.

Once again, spinmeister Perry took to the stage to brag about the move, singing his one-note song about the automaker being attracted by Texas's "employer-friendly combination of low taxes, fair courts, smart regulations, and world-class workforce."[33]

But the Texas workforce was not an attraction to Toyota, which made clear its preference to transfer its 3,000-member workforce from California. As for being "world class," it should be noted that Texas ranks fiftieth among all states in the percentage of population that graduated high school, forty-fourth in its projected high school graduation rate, forty-sixth in average SAT scores, and thirtieth in the percentage of adults with at least a bachelor's degree. California ranks fourteenth in the last category.[34]

Following Perry's remarks, Toyota's North American chief executive, Jim Lentz, pointed out to the *Los Angeles Times* that the company already has a manufacturing plant in San Antonio producing Tacoma and Tundra trucks and wanted to consolidate its operations.[35]

"It may seem like a juicy story to have this confrontation between California and Texas, but that was not the case,"[36] Lentz told *Times* reporters Jerry Hirsch and Tim Logan, saying the main reason for the move was not financial incentives from the state or local tax breaks in Plano, which he considered a "minor factor," but rather that Toyota had "brainpower" in three states (a plant in San Antonio, sales and marketing in California, and engineering and production staff in Erlanger, Kentucky) and wanted to move its headquarters near the manufacturing base in the South. "Geography is the reason not to have our headquarters in California," he said.[37]

As for the claim that onerous regulations and high taxes in California repelled Toyota, the automaker said Toyota was leaving 2,300 employees in California at a motor-racing division in Costa Mesa, a design studio in Newport Beach, a parts factory in Long Beach, and port facilities. "We're not pulling out of California," Lentz told the *Times*.[38]

While Perry hammered away at his message that California is bad for business, Governor Brown and bipartisan supporters in California's state legislature worked to change that perception. The creation of GO-Biz, the governor's Office of Business and Development, was a key to the new strategy. GO-Biz was established in 2012 to focus on creating jobs and spurring economic development by streamlining the permit and regulatory processes, a longtime complaint of owners of businesses of all sizes.

On October 4, 2013, Brown signed eighteen measures billed as strengthening the state's business climate, including among other incentives sales tax exemptions on all manufacturing equipment and research and development equipment for biotech, and also tax credits on hiring and wages for employers who create jobs and hire certain categories of the unemployed.

The probusiness measures had bipartisan support in the legislature, a rarity when Brown came into office in 2010. Again with bipartisan support, the state created a $750 million business development program with tax incentives to attract new out-of-state companies and retain others that were considering moving out. Unlike the TEF, which awarded grants upon a promise of creating jobs, California entices with tax exemptions, including up to the first $200 million for manufacturing equipment.

In 2014, Brown, with bipartisan support, approved a deal heavily lobbied for by the entertainment industry to help keep television and movie productions and jobs in California by more than tripling funding for the industry's tax credit program to $330 million a year, allowing many more projects to qualify. The deal jettisoned an unpopular lottery system that had been used to allocate funds and now will dole out credits based on how many jobs will be created.

It was expected that the new plan would stem runaway production to Canada and the United Kingdom, as well as other states, including Louisiana, New York, and Georgia. The new legislation was projected to employ tens of thousands of industry workers over time. Los Angeles alone experienced a 10 percent increase in location filming in 2014. Although the increase was mostly due to television shows and the shooting of TV commercials, large-budget film activity was expected to pick up in 2015 after a change in funding rules allowed films with budgets over $75 million to qualify for subsidies. In 2014, more than a dozen films made in the Los Angeles area got the tax credit, including *American Sniper, The Gambler, Jersey Boys,* and *Nightcrawler,* while on-location television production in 2014 increased 12 percent over the previous year. In 2016, $53.9 million in tax credits was awarded to projects set to employ more than 2,540 cast and crew members.

In June 2014, GO-Biz released the names of thirty-one California companies to receive the first $30 million through a new program called California Competes. The initial recipients of California Competes incentives have committed to creating 6,000 positions for workers and to invest more than $2 million to expand operations. The program has been replenished with $150 million for the fiscal year that began July 1, 2014, and $200.9 million for 2015–16. Several of the grantees are companies that have moved or were considering moving some operations to Texas but were enticed to stay in California.[39]

Among those receiving initial awards were Samsung Semiconductor ($6 million), Petco Animal Supplies ($2.6 million), and Amazon Fulfillment Services ($1.575 million),[40] which seem to be pitting California and Texas against one another. Petco, headquartered in San Diego, opened a satellite support center in San Antonio in 2011, while Amazon built 3.3 million square feet of space in three fulfillment centers in Texas in 2013. It has four such centers in California. Samsung Semiconductor was considering moving to Austin, where it established an office in 2005 with a $10.8 million TEF grant, but the city of San Jose provided $7 million in incentives in 2014 to expand there instead, and Samsung wanted to stay in the real capital of the tech world.[41]

Brown's popularity among tech executives was evident in April 2016, when a majority of respondents to the Silicon Valley Leadership Group's annual CEO survey gave him a high score for creating a business-friendly environment. The 178 respondents named housing costs, traffic congestion, and the cost of recruiting and retaining employees as top challenges, ahead of business taxes and regulations.[42]

Austin, which adopted the name Silicon Hills in the 1990s, is a major center of high-tech companies. Like Northern California, Austin is a liberal enclave, teeming with Democrats, a city whose residents are the base of a strong environmental movement, in contrast to Perry and conservative legislative Republicans, who, like their brethren in Congress, mock the truth of climate change.

If there is any place in Texas where Silicon Valley residents would feel most comfortable, it is Austin. It is also where much of the venture capital destined for Texas ends up. But any Texas boast that the Lone Star State comes close to California in venture capital receipts is ludicrous.

In 2000, for example, California was credited with 42 percent ($39.3 billion) of the nation's venture capital dollars. Over the following ten years, the total of venture capital investment in the United States was $372 billion, of which $167 billion went to California companies. In 2010, the state continued to be the national leader, capturing $12 billion, while runners-up Massachusetts and New York were far behind, with less than $2.5 billion.

This pattern had been consistent for more than a decade, with California continuing to far outpace all other states. In 2015, California companies received $33.7 billion in venture capital, or more than 57 percent of the total $58.8 billion in U.S. venture capital investment, the highest figure since 2001.[42] This investment in 1,773 deals—more than 40 percent of the total.[43]

In mid-June 2014, governors Brown and Perry were in a bare-knuckled competition for a big prize: Elon Musk, CEO of Tesla Motors, who pushed Brown and state legislators to the limit to try to make a deal. The big winner would be Musk. The automaker's headquarters are in Palo Alto, home to Stanford University, and there is a manufacturing plant in Fremont, just across the southern tip of the bay from Palo Alto. Tesla was looking for a location for a new $5 billion battery "giga factory" that eventually would employ an estimated 6,500 workers. California and Texas were in the running, along with Arizona, Nevada, and New Mexico.

On a trip to California for a series of Republican fund-raisers, Perry took a high-profile drive in an electric Tesla Model S sedan, arriving at the state capital to be greeted by a throng of journalists, notebooks in hand, with television and still cameras grabbing the photo op. Perry stepped from the car looking more California than Texas, sporting stylish sunglasses and a black polo shirt under a black sports coat, gray muted-print slacks, and black shoes. He could have been stepping right out of a Tesla commercial.

Brown labored hard to court Musk, working with legislators of both parties to come up with incentives—a $420 million tax credit over fifteen years—and considering granting waivers to the state's stringent California Environmental Quality Act (CEQA, pronounced "*see*-qua") to build the plant. That angered Brown's environmental supporters, as did discussion of possibly limiting lawsuits that would be inevitably brought by environmental activists. Tesla's Musk had made clear that any delay in approval would ensure that Tesla would build its factory with its 6,500 jobs in another state. The fact that such a "green" company as the electric automaker might balk over these strict laws was not lost on environmental advocates.

Brown, Republican and Democratic legislators, and Tesla representatives worked through the end of the 2013–14 legislative session without a final vote on the thirty-five-page proposal, but its sponsoring senators continued to work on a resolution. It was all for naught, as Tesla soon announced that it had chosen Nevada for its giga factory, for $1.25 billion in tax and other incentives over twenty years. In the end, Brown said the price tag Tesla placed on the deal was too high for California.

A legal fight between Brown and environmentalists over gutting the decades-old CEQA never materialized, but the fact that diluting the law was even considered was alarming to environmentalists. It remains a hot button issue with developers and other business leaders, who have complained about constraints and delays due to environmental regulations placed on development and expansion of their businesses, while the lack of such regulations in Texas is pitched as an asset in trying to attract businesses from California.

At the same time, in contrast to Texas, California has been a model for the nation in setting high environmental standards, imposed by both the legislature and the voters through the initiative process. Two landmark measures were CEQA, which was signed into law by Governor Reagan, and the California Coastal Zone Initiative, enshrined in the constitution by California voters in 1972, resulting in the creation of the California Coastal Commission.

Like many conservatives, Perry contends that environmental and other regulations have no place in a state where creating jobs and expanding business are the top priorities. Perry has emphasized that one reason companies leave California for Texas is so that they have a place to expand, unfettered by state environmental, zoning, and worker-friendly regulations that are viewed by him and others as onerous to businesses. (It should be noted that many such regulations, such as the Endangered Species Act, and a host of civil rights and health and safety protections, are federal and thus apply to both states.)

Others argue that the benefits of a healthy environment are better for business, not to mention the state's residents, especially in the long run. The Port of Los Angeles is an example of this. Much of an investment of $1 billion in capital improvements there was accelerated by stakeholders agreeing to "green" plans and practices that the port claims will result directly or indirectly in one million jobs and reduction in toxic emissions. One port commissioner said in an interview that she and her colleagues took to heart the mantra of former Los Angeles mayor Antonio Villaraigosa, "Go green to get green," and it has paid off.[44]

On the other hand, according to *Texas on the Brink*, a Texas legislative report, Texas leads the nation in carbon dioxide emissions, volatile organic compounds and cancer-causing carcinogens released into the air, toxic chemicals released into the water, and hazardous waste generated.[45] Texas also dumps more carbon pollution into the atmosphere than any other state, more than California and Pennsylvania combined. It ranks seventh in the nation in the number of hazardous waste sites on the National Priority List.

During his first term, Perry signed legislation to speed construction of eleven new coal plants in Texas, while the Environmental Protection Agency under the Obama administration proposed new air-pollution standards for oil and gas operations. On July 6, 2011, the EPA finalized the Cross-State Air Pollution Rule, which requires twenty-eight states to improve air quality by reducing power plant emissions that contribute to ozone and fine-particle pollution in other states.[46]

When the EPA rejected as inadequate Texas's plan for implementing the federal Clean Air Act, Perry issued a statement: "The EPA's irresponsible and heavy-handed action not only undermines Texas's successful clean air programs, but threatens thousands of Texas jobs, families, businesses and communities throughout our state," and he claimed that "Texas's air quality program has outperformed federal programs in virtually every category."[47] Perry led the move to undermine the EPA's right to limit greenhouse gas pollution, using his governor's Web site to slam Obama's environmental efforts that would derail a program Perry claimed had cleaned up the air over Texas.

Evidence, however, indicates that Texas air is anything but clean, yet the governor's Web site boasted that "Texas is a national leader in reducing emissions and known pollutants."[48] Perry casts the environmental war as a states' rights issue, perhaps being unwilling to accept that air pollution does not stop at the state border, a rather silly notion to maintain. In any case, on April 29, 2014, the U.S. Supreme Court, in a 6-2 opinion, upheld the Cross-State Air Pollution Rule.[49]

Perry also does not buy into another potential environmental hazard that runs head-on into business interests: fracking. (Brown has his own troubles over fracking in California that will be discussed in chapter 7.) Part of the earlier boom in Texas oil was generated by the drilling technique that injects chemical-infused water into shale layer to force out previously untapped pockets of natural gas. Fracking has made some Texans rich, while scaring the wits out of environmentalists who fear contamination of groundwater and air quality, as well as the mishandling of chemically contaminated waste.

Unsurprisingly, Perry rejects the health concerns. "You have this [Obama] administration talking about stopping hydraulic fracking, trying to scare people, and saying that hydraulic fracking somehow or other is going to damage the groundwater, and so we've got to stop this," he said, denying there was significant risk.[50]

Chief Executive magazine, which consistently ranks Texas the best state in the nation in which to do business, agrees with Perry about the need to give the nod to business over the environment. The magazine ranks California dead last, singling out as "job killers" its environmental regulations, including so-called green laws, such as the state's carbon emission restrictions and the mandate that manufacturers seek alternatives to toxic chemicals.

Perry is not unlike many conservative Republicans who refuse to believe the scientific evidence of climate change. In his book he says that global warming is "all one contrived phony mess that is falling apart under its own weight."[51] And in the 2012 Republican presidential candidates' debate, he said, "Well, I do agree that there is—the science is not settled on this. The idea that we would put Americans' economy at jeopardy based on scientific theory that's not settled yet, to me, is just nonsense."[52] Perry's successor, Abbott, is in that camp as well, and it was Abbott, as Texas attorney general, who sued the EPA over the Cross-State Air Pollution Rule.

Perry and Abbott fit the mold of Republican conservatives who loathe government regulations as the biggest threat to an individual's "freedom." In August 2014, Perry suggested Obama issue a "moratorium on regulations across this country because his regulations, his EPA regulations, are killing jobs all across America."[53]

He went further in an interview with WHO radio in Iowa in September 2011, in which he talked about terminating all regulations.[54] He does not elaborate on whether he would ask the Food and Drug Administration to stop testing and then approving or nixing new drugs, or whether he would stop the EPA from monitoring toxic chemicals in drinking water, or the Federal Aviation Administration from preventing air crashes. Nor do the media ask him to explain how the country would function in his vision of a United States with zero regulations.

Like Perry, Republican conservatives, including the 2016 presidential candidates, believe that there are two visions for America. Perry expressed it well at the Conservative Political Action Conference on March 7, 2014. "There's the vision common in blue states, where the state plays an increasing role in the lives of its citizens . . . then there's the vision common to American, red America [sic], if you will, the red state American vision, where the freedom of the individual comes first, the reach of government is limited,"[55] Perry said.

An example of the blue state vision would be California's embracing the Affordable Care Act and in its first year signing up 1.4 million in the state health exchange, Covered California, and enrolling low-income people for an expansion of Medi-Cal, the state-federal health program for the poor. The total exceeded three million Californians in its launch year.[56]

Red state Texas veered onto a far different course. When the U.S. Supreme Court allowed states to opt out of the Affordable Care Act's Medicaid expansion, which covers the lowest-income adult citizens, Perry, his successor Abbott, and more than a dozen other Republican governors did opt out—even though the federal government picks up the entire tab for three years and covers no less than 90 percent of the cost after that.

National Public Radio reported Texas hospitals lost $5.5 billion in 2014 for treating uninsured patients, much of which would have been reimbursed by the federal government; that reimbursement would total an estimated $100 billion over the next decade if Texas participated in the Medicaid expansion, and tens of thousands of jobs would be created.[57]

The Lone Star State has the highest rate of uninsured residents in the country, more than six million people, of whom 60 percent are Hispanic,[58] and the highest percent of nonelderly uninsured.[59] An expansion of Medicaid for the poor in Texas would cover an estimated 1 million uninsured Texans whose income is too low to be eligible for the health insurance exchange subsidy. But the Republican-majority statehouse and governor's office would rather deny Texas citizens health care than participate in a federal program they want to see eliminated.

In a speech in April 2014, Perry called it a "fool's errand" to add "more than a million Texans into this broken system."[60] Disagreeing was Bill Hammond, CEO of the Texas Association of Business, who said if Texas "participated in Medicaid expansion, it would save Texas businesses billions of dollars a year."[61]

The red state–blue state competition extends into other quality of life issues. Blue state California enacts and enforces environmental laws and those that protect workers' health and welfare and that provide a living wage, though with the rising costs of housing, that is more difficult to achieve for the working poor. Red state Texas has the largest number of employees in the country—more than 450,000, or 3.6 percent of its workforce—working at the federal minimum wage, which is $7.25 per hour.[62]

The minimum wage in California is $10 an hour (and will increase to $15 by 2022) and the state has only 0.5 percent working at minimum wage. In the past decade, Texas added more new residents—4.3 million—than any other state, with Hispanic minorities accounting for 65 percent of that population increase, according to U.S. Census figures. Many of these workers accept low wages and provide the cheap labor that attracts new business moving to the state. According to the aforementioned legislative report *Texas on the Brink,* Texas has the highest percentage in the nation of children in poverty.

In other quality-of-life areas, Jerry Brown signed legislation at the end of the 2014 legislative session requiring employers to provide their workers with a minimum of three days of sick leave; Texas has no laws requiring private employers to give leave of any kind to employees unless they are covered under federal laws. California was ahead of President Obama, who proposed in his 2015 State of the Union speech that Congress pass a law enabling employees to earn up to seven days a year of sick time.

In 2015, Brown signed one of the toughest pay-equity laws in the country, mandating that women, who, according to the U.S. Census, earn a median 84 cents for every $1 a man earns for the same job, will receive equal pay for similar work, not just the same work. For example, a female housekeeper who cleans rooms in a hotel would compare with a male janitor who cleans the lobby and banquet hall.[63] The law had the support of the Chamber of Commerce and all Democrat and nearly all Republican legislators in California.

In one of our interviews, Governor Brown summed up some key differences between the two states:

> Relatively speaking to Texas and to a number of states, California has strong hour and wages laws; strong environmental protections; protections against bias; protection of women; protection of workers; . . . protection against discrimination of various kinds. So whether looking at human rights or looking at the environment, or specific labor protections or land use, or air pollution rules, or water quality, trying to maintain a high quality of life, California over many decades has dealt with problems in a serious way.
>
> And people who come from states that haven't had the same commitment obviously will encounter both taxes and rules that they will find more burdensome than they would find in certain other places, be they Arizona or Mississippi or North Dakota. That's all true, but I don't see that a race to the bottom is a good idea, and I don't take the norm of California, nor does the legislature, and I don't think the people of California take as our norm, other

states that have less of a concern about these nonmarket issues, just like we don't take China or Mexico or, you know, the Ukraine as our standard here.[64]

In other words, argues Brown, why would California want to out-Texas Texas? To do so would be to deny the state's track record of attracting tens of millions from around the country and world in just a few decades. Sometimes it is for education in the renowned University of California system, sometimes for jobs, but there also are quality-of-life issues on which the state is still golden, such as tolerance. Perry ran for governor on a homophobic party platform and tells gays to leave Texas if they don't like it.

"Texans made a decision about marriage and if there's a state that has more lenient views than Texas, then maybe that's a better place for them to live,"[65] Perry told NBC in 2005, in response to gay veterans protesting the state's constitutional ban on gay marriage. And in June 2014, a Commonwealth Club of San Francisco lecture audience murmured loudly when he compared being gay to alcoholism:

"I wrote a book called *On My Honor,* and I [wrote] that people make choices in life, and whether or not you feel compelled to follow a particular lifestyle or not, you have the ability to decide not to do that. I made the point of talking about alcoholism, and I may have the genetic coding that I'm inclined to be an alcoholic, but I have the desire not to do that, and I look at the homosexual issue the same way," Perry told the surprised audience.[66]

Apparently not everyone in Texas agrees with Perry on gay rights. A number of cities in Texas have passed civil rights statutes, including Houston, Austin, Fort Worth, El Paso, San Antonio, Dallas, and Plano. Plano's ordinance, banning discrimination based on sexual orientation and gender identity in employment, housing, and public accommodations, passed in December 2014, prompted moves by four Republican state legislators to nullify the local laws and ban local governments from adopting similar antidiscrimination laws. The Houston city council passed an equal-rights law in 2014, but it was overturned by voters in November 2015.

Evidently, at least part of Texas is beginning to feel a little too much like California, which has unsettled Perry's successor enough for him to speak out about the state's "California-ization." In a speech in February 2015 to the conservative Texas Public Policy Foundation, newbie governor Greg Abbott sounded a warning: "The truth is, Texas is being California-ized with [plastic] bag bans, fracking bans, tree-cutting bans. We're forming a patchwork quilt of bans and rules and regulations that is eroding the Texas model. . . . Unchecked overregulation by cities will turn the Texas miracle into the California nightmare. This is a form of collectivism."[67]

Both states have a growing Hispanic population that includes a large number of undocumented immigrants, which presents an issue in both states that provides a final illustration of two distinctly different approaches. In California, Brown's response to the huge influx of undocumented and unaccompanied children who crossed the border in the summer of 2014 was to sign a measure to provide the children with $3 million in funding for legal representation to enable them to stay in the United States.[68] Perry sent one thousand National Guard troops to the Texas-Mexico border in a show of force.[69]

In our interview, Brown summed up the key difference between Texas and California: "We have a government that is reflecting the configuration of values and ideas that are operative in California in the twenty-first century and before," said Brown. "So that's just the way it is."[70]

But it wasn't always; Texas has not always been so inhospitable to undocumented people, nor has California always been so welcoming.

6

Diversity Trumps

The setting was a presidential primary debate. Two candidates were asked a simple question: Should parents of undocumented schoolchildren in Texas have to pay for their public education, or should the students be allowed to continue their education for free?

Candidate number 1: "I would like to see something done about the illegal alien problem that would be so sensitive and so understanding about labor needs and human needs that that problem wouldn't come up. But today, if those people are here, I would reluctantly say I think they would get whatever it is that the society is giving to their neighbors. But the problem has to be solved . . . Because, as we have kind of made illegal some kinds of labor that I'd like to see legal, we're doing two things: We're creating a whole society of really honorable, decent, family loving people that are in violation of the law and secondly we're exacerbating relations with Mexico. . . . If they're living here I don't want to see . . . six and eight year old kids being made . . . totally uneducated and made to feel that they're living . . . outside the law. . . . Let's address the fundamentals. These are good people, strong people. Part of my family is . . . Mexican."[1]

Candidate number 2: "The time has come that the United States and our neighbors, particularly our neighbor to the south, should have a better understanding and a better relationship than we've ever had. And I think we haven't been sensitive enough to our size and our power. They have a problem of

40-50 percent unemployment. Now this cannot continue without the possibility of . . . trouble below the border, and we could have a hostile and strange neighbor on our border. Rather than talk about putting up a fence, why don't we work out some recognition of our mutual problems and make it possible for them to come here legally with a work permit, and then while they're working and earning here they pay taxes here and when they want to go back they can go back and they can cross, and open the border both ways, by understanding their problems. This [working in the United States] is the only safety valve they have from that unemployment that probably keeps the lid from blowing off down there. I think we could have a fine relationship."[2]

One might assume these are Democrats. But here you have the April 24, 1980, debate between George H. W. Bush (candidate number 1) and his primary opponent, Ronald Reagan—the man who is something of a deity to the swarm of 2016 Republican presidential hopefuls who showed up at his presidential library in Simi Valley for their own debate in September 2015. None displayed the tolerance Reagan or Bush expressed that night in 1980 for undocumented immigrants. An exception, of course, was Jeb Bush, who is married to the "Mexican" Bush cited as "part of my family."

Contrast Reagan's call for an open border with Donald Trump's tarring of border-immigrants as rapists and murderers, desire to deport the estimated eleven million unauthorized residents, and plan to deny the birthright of U.S. citizen children of undocumented immigrants (which is unconstitutional). His attacks on Muslims were equally harsh. Others in the Republican rabble piled on when they saw Trump's popularity with voters growing.

What a fantastic setup for the Democratic Party. As you will see clearly demonstrated in this chapter with what happened in California in the mid-1990s, this does not bode well for the future of the Republican Party. The anti-immigrant rhetoric espoused by Republican governor Pete Wilson when he was seeking reelection in 1994 drove a stake through the heart of the Republican Party in California and beyond, and the damage reverberates today.

Even Republicans in California today do not agree with Trump's immigrant policies. A strong majority of 75 percent of Californians—including

53 percent of Republicans—believe undocumented immigrants benefit their state and should be allowed to live and work here under certain conditions, according to a statewide survey released October 1, 2015, by the Public Policy Institute of California.[3]

The PPIC survey showed that in addition to the 53 percent of Republicans, 83 percent of Democrats and 70 percent of people who consider themselves independent favor allowing undocumented immigrants to seek legal status. The breakdown along racial and ethnic lines was also strong, with Asians (76 percent), blacks (68 percent), Latinos (92 percent), and whites (63 percent) all heavily supportive of their undocumented family members, neighbors, friends, and even strangers. Californians are not alone in this: Nationally, 60 percent approve of a path to legal status, according to a July 2015 ABC–*Washington Post* poll.[4]

Although California now enjoys a reputation for its inclusionary policies and way of life, its history is tainted by stories of callous and sometimes brutal discrimination against its ethnic minority populations. Any boasting about multicultural California, which is discussed in this chapter, has to be leavened with remembrances of this grim history.

In the mid-1860s, more than one thousand Chinese railroad workers, constructing the western end of the Transcontinental Railroad through the Sierra Nevada, died in treacherous conditions. Survivors were left to live in abject poverty, under discriminatory laws, becoming victims of racial violence.

One of the most shameful periods for California—as well as the nation—involved anti-Japanese hysteria following the bombing of Pearl Harbor in 1941, which led to the internment of 110,000 West Coast residents of Japanese heritage. Among them were 93,000 Californians,[5] the vast majority citizens of the United States. They lost their homes, farms, stores, and possessions, not to mention their faith in humanity, when they were sent off to prison camps where temperatures could range from more than 100 degrees to freezing, depending on the season.

Antonin Scalia, the late conservative U.S. Supreme Court justice, told students at the University of Hawaii's law school in February 2014 that the nation's highest court was wrong to uphold the internment of Japanese Americans during World War II and spoke words in Latin that translate: "In times of war, the laws fall silent."[6]

On other occasions, racial and ethnic tensions, primarily in Los Angeles, exploded. The 1943 anti-Latino zoot suit riots during World War II, for example, involved attacks on Los Angeles Latinos by white servicemen stationed in Southern California. Other examples include the 1965 racial riots in Watts and rioting that followed the Rodney King verdict in April 1992.

California, of course, was not the only state with racial tensions or a racist past, but it has proved itself a model for how to assimilate new cultures. This came after the 1990s saw the last gasps of Anglo supremacy through a series of three statewide ballot initiatives designed to retain it. Those laws would fail in that mission and, particularly with the anti-immigration Proposition 187, would help bring about the demise of the Republican Party in California.

The inflammatory anti-immigrant rhetoric of Trump and his followers in the 2016 Republican presidential primary campaign and resulting ethnic tension were reminiscent of California under the Republican governor Pete Wilson after he thoroughly embraced Proposition 187 in 1994. In that case, as with Trump, such rhetoric was seen as a path to being elected. But as Wilson learned, the anti-immigrant tactic would have a lasting and disastrous impact on his political party in California and foreshadow a similar fate for Republicans nationally.

I n the summer and fall of 1994, debate swirled around the harsh, sweeping ballot measure that would end the rights to basic public health and education services for millions of undocumented Californians. The state was a tempest of rage and hurt as the measure sailed toward passage, lashed onward by Governor Wilson, who was fighting for his political life in his reelection campaign.

Some of the biggest street protests in the state's history ensued, with participants, including many students, defiantly brandishing Mexican flags and directly challenging the narrative that foreign-born children were an economic or cultural drain. After decades of political moderation and bipartisanship began collapsing in the tumultuous 1960s, California seemed to have reached a nadir of fractious division.

While white nativists and minority radicals rallied their troops in ever more passionate and earnest adversarial displays, two Mexican American satirists took a more nuanced approach, though not everyone got the joke. Long before Stephen Colbert's humorous reactionary Comedy Central persona came into being, Southern Californians Lalo Alcaraz and Esteban Zul formed a pseudo front organization, Hispanics Against Liberal Takeover—Halto— led by Alcaraz posing as phony conservative media personality Daniel D. Portado (get it—"deport-ado"?), who would argue for the "self-deportation" of those in the state illegally. It took a long while for some to realize this was satire, and some never did. In 1996, on National Public Radio's *This American Life*, "D. Portado" would play his role for a seemingly unknowing Ira Glass: "Well, I am here to help everyone get out. I hope to look forward to the day where I will stand at the border and say, 'Will the last Mexican out of California please turn out the lights?' That will be me."[7]

Back in 1994, out of the blue it seemed, supporters of the so-called "Save Our State" initiative had been handed a handsome, eloquent Latino supporter of their radical anti-immigrant position. Alcaraz/Portado appeared on Spanish-language media powerhouse Telemundo to make the case for "self-deportation centers," with Zul playing his wary bodyguard. "Neither the participants nor the producers were aware of our true identity," Zul later told the *Chicago Reader*. "It was the longest half-hour of my life."[8]

It did not take long for the most ardent supporter of Prop 187, Governor Wilson, to join the Halto chorus. As he opined in a postelection interview with *New York Times* conservative columnist William Safire, who was opposed to Prop 187: "If it's clear to you that you cannot be employed, and that you and your family are ineligible for services, you will self-deport."[9]

The "self-deportation" idea would be roundly mocked eighteen years later when proffered by Mitt Romney in a presidential debate.[10] Daniel D. Portado returned to the issue to leverage some serious satire out of Romney's gaffe. The fallout from Romney's self-deportation remark was still reverberating in

2013, when the Republican National Committee chairman Reince Priebus referred to it as "horrific."[11]

But in California, in 1994, the anti-immigrant tidal wave Wilson was riding was real. The governor, who early in the race had been badly trailing Jerry Brown's sister, former state treasurer Kathleen Brown, had thrown in all his chips on the hot-button immigration issue, just as Donald Trump would two decades later. Once a moderate San Diego mayor and U.S. senator, Wilson stoked a surge of xenophobia that was markedly uncharacteristic of his political past, joining the cause of a portion of the electorate that was much older and whiter than the state's overall fast-changing demographic.

The concept of making life so difficult for immigrants they'll leave became a sentiment that has gained momentum in recent years, led in part by Republican secretary of state Kris Kobach of Kansas, who helped draft the Arizona law that required state and local law enforcement officials to check the immigration status of people they stopped and had "reasonable suspicion" to believe were in the country illegally.[12]

That law, key elements of which the U.S. Supreme Court jettisoned, was one of a slew of harsh and hotly controversial laws in South Carolina, Alabama, Georgia, and other states that restrict access to benefits and jobs and step up law enforcement harassment of immigrant communities in order to deter new arrivals or long stays by foreign visitors. Some new laws have been struck down over the same flaw in Proposition 187: impingement on the federal power to make and enforce immigration law.[13]

Proposition 187 was certainly designed to cause as much misery as possible for undocumented immigrants and their families. The initiative would have made them ineligible for public social services, including child welfare payments or foster care; public health-care services "unless emergency under federal law"; and public education at all levels.[14] It would have required state and local government agencies to report suspected undocumented immigrants to the California attorney general and the federal Immigration and Naturalization Service (INS), today's Immigration and Customs Enforcement (ICE).

In addition, the manufacture, distribution, sale, or use of phony citizenship or residence documents would be a felony. The INS estimated there were roughly 1.6 million undocumented immigrants in California, and the number was rising by 125,000 each year, according to the initiative's ballot summary.[15]

The measure targeted a fast-growing number of undocumented workers who, like today, were filling jobs most Californians generally refused to do—the dirtiest, most poorly paid gigs in agriculture, manufacturing, garment sweatshops, and restaurant kitchens, in addition to staffing the homes and gardens of the wealthy. Proposition 187 asked its recession-scarred voters to use a denial of basic government services—public health care and education—as a chokehold.

To opponents of 187, it seemed peculiarly heartless to target the sick and the young in an attempt to drive families out of the state. It also was obviously counterproductive to the general populace, which would face public health issues from untreated diseases and illnesses and disruption while young people, denied entrance to schools, would potentially lack supervision while their parents were at work.

The shrill language in favor of the initiative was clear in its sweeping populism: "California can strike a blow for the taxpayer that will be heard across America . . . in the same way Proposition 13 was heard across the land," read the pro-187 ballot text signed by state assemblyman Dick Mountjoy, one of its authors, along with campaign leaders Ronald Prince and Barbara Kiley of staunchly conservative Orange County. "Proposition 187 will go down in history as the voice of the people against an arrogant bureaucracy. WE CAN STOP ILLEGAL ALIENS."[16]

William Safire, echoing the sentiments of many conservatives, averred in a postelection *New York Times* column that penny-pinching Ebenezer Scrooge was "his hero." He noted that Scrooge's "neatly theoretical 'economic disincentive' won't disincent—because being miserable here doesn't compare with the misery they ran away from."[17] Lest one mistake him for a softy, he added his own scary scenario: "Do we really want to drive most illegal families deeper underground, many to lives of crime? Would we rather have 300,000 children on the streets, learning costly delinquency—or safely in school, becoming potential citizens and taxpayers?" But also, he noted, "in terms of practicality and of the American spirit, a government policy of making any child's life miserable is still an abomination."[18]

As Safire and others pointed out, much of the initiative was doomed from its drafting to be blocked in the courts, based on prior Supreme Court decisions on the rights of all children to an education regardless of status. Even the state attorney general's official summary of the initiative noted that "the exclusion of suspected illegal immigrant children from public schools would be in direct conflict with the U.S. Supreme Court's ruling in *Plyler v. Doe* that guarantees access to public education for all children in the United States. Consequently, this provision of the initiative would not be effective."[19]

Given that this is exactly how it played out, the yearlong political storm around Proposition 187 could be viewed as nothing more than an expensive tantrum thrown by a segment of the electorate not worried about the legal concept of stare decisis—precedent. Still, the measure passed.

As predicted, three days later, on November 11, 1994, a Los Angeles federal judge, Matthew Byrne Jr., issued a temporary injunction forbidding the state from enforcing key parts of the initiative. In 1997, his colleague Judge Mariana Pfaelzer found most of the law unconstitutional, as it infringed on the federal government's authority over immigration. Governor Wilson appealed, but his successor, Democrat Gray Davis, withdrew the appeal in 1999, and no trial proceeded.

Back in 1994, one only had to look to Texas for guidance on this issue. Only twelve years earlier, the U.S. Supreme Court ruled against a Texas law that denied undocumented schoolchildren a public education. Texans might have voted for a Proposition 187–type measure given the opportunity, but there is no initiative process there. And lawmakers, taking their cue from business leaders, were not inclined to infuriate Mexico, Texas's number one trading partner, by advocating such a law.

In fact, one month after Proposition 187's passage and his own election in Texas, governor-elect George W. Bush went to Mexico to attend the inauguration of incoming president Ernesto Zedillo. In a private meeting with him, later repeated to the media, Bush made clear his opposition to Proposition

187. He was distancing himself from Wilson, with whom Mexican officials, including outgoing president Carlos Salinas de Gortari, had remained furious over his support for the measure. Zedillo made clear his disapproval of California's Proposition 187, saying he was opposed to denying education and health care to undocumented immigrants and that he supported bilingual education.[20]

Three months after it was approved, Jesse Katz wrote in the *Los Angeles Times* that the measure and Governor Wilson "have been widely assailed as symbols of bigotry and xenophobia" in Mexico.[21] Wilson's support of Prop 187 resulted in Mexican officials boycotting a California trade event in Mexico City just prior to the election, Katz reported, and the governor was pronounced persona non grata by the Tijuana City Council.

Wanting to repair any damage in relations with Mexico, Katz wrote that an aide to the governor asked a prominent Texas banker to deliver a note to Mexican president Carlos Salinas de Gortari, but the banker, a Republican, declined.[22] In a comment that would prove prophetic, Governor Manuel Cavazos Lerma of the Mexican state of Tamaulipas said scathingly of Wilson, "You may want to win an election, but you lose your destiny."[23]

There were many moments during the 187 campaign where dignity was absent, but one of the most memorable was Wilson's ominous reelection commercial, still viewable on YouTube today, in which a grim narrator intones, "They keep coming,"[24] over grainy, black-and-white security-cam footage of individuals and families running across Interstate 5 at the border south of San Diego.

> **Announcer:** *Two million illegal immigrants in California. The federal government won't stop them at the border, yet requires us to pay billions to take care of them. Governor Pete Wilson sent the National Guard to help the Border Patrol, but that's not all.*
>
> [Cut to color image of Wilson speaking.]
>
> **Wilson:** *For Californians who work hard, pay taxes, and obey the laws, I'm suing to force the federal government to control the border, and I'm working to deny state services to illegal immigrants. Enough is Enough.*[25]

The scene is familiar to those who today travel on Interstate 5 between San Diego and points north. If cars are whizzing through at a fast clip, one can assume the border patrol is not checking vehicles. But if the traffic slows to a near stop, the checkpoint is operating; vehicles slow to allow border patrol officers to look into each one before being waved through the checkpoint. Sometimes a vehicle is pulled out of the queue and parked, its trunk left gaping open as it sits near the border patrol building while its passengers are being interrogated inside the checkpoint building. As cars slow down before the checkpoint, people being smuggled in can jump out and head for the brush to travel north on foot.

Even Congressman Dana Rohrabacher, an Orange County Republican who was a prominent supporter of Proposition 187, said as recently as 2014 that he would still support 187, though he found the TV ad "polarizing and nasty."[26]

A few Republicans, like Silicon Valley businessman Ron Unz, who unsuccessfully challenged Wilson in the primary election, opposed the initiative, noting that anything that scared away immigrants would be bad for a state economy that depended on their contributions.

"In Los Angeles, the vast majority of hotel and restaurant workers are hard-working Hispanic immigrants, most of them here illegally, and anyone who believes that these unpleasant jobs would otherwise be filled by natives (either black or white) is living in a fantasy world," Unz wrote for *National Review* in its November 1994 issue. "[And] Silicon Valley . . . is absolutely dependent upon immigrant professionals to maintain its technological edge and if they left, America's computer industry would probably go with them."[27]

Former football star, congressman, cabinet secretary, and Republican presidential candidate Jack Kemp made a stir when he defended his position against the initiative during a talk at the Richard Nixon Library in Yorba Linda. He told the angry audience that he could not support a law that would "turn teachers and nurses into agents of the INS [Immigration and Naturalization Service]." He "was so bothered in my conscience that I could not, in good conscience, support it, even though I know it will probably pass." That day, Kemp, along with Reagan's former secretary of education, William J. Bennett, issued a statement saying that they believed Proposition 187 to be unconstitutional and that it would "contribute to a nativist, anti-immigrant climate."[28] When Kemp was secretary of the Housing and Urban Development Department under President George H. W. Bush, he refused to let INS agents inspect federal housing in search of undocumented immigrants.

The contradictions and outright hypocrisy of the state's relation to undocumented immigrants would be cast in high relief throughout the heated 1994 U.S. Senate race between the incumbent, Dianne Feinstein, former mayor of San Francisco, and the Santa Barbara Republican congressman Michael Huffington. Despite their opposing political affiliations, both candidates competed to see who could appear to be tougher on illegal immigration—only to be embarrassed when news of their own employment of undocumented immigrants came to light.

Feinstein, with the media in tow, made trips to the Mexico-California border to highlight her enthusiasm for greater enforcement. She taunted Huffington (who endorsed 187) for failing to vote for beefed-up border security and ran her own tough-on-illegal-immigration version of the Wilson television ad, down to the similar surveillance footage of undocumented immigrants running north across the freeway. A year before Prop 187, Feinstein proposed a one-dollar-per-crossing "transit fee" for those coming into California from Mexico legally, mostly low-income laborers, to help pay for thousands of new border patrol agents and tamperproof work permits.

Feinstein's ad, noting her efforts to secure a tighter border, began airing in July 1994, the same month Wilson's ad was being broadcast. This strategy, bolstered by having fellow Democrat Bill Clinton (whose 1994 budget proposal trimmed ninety-three border patrol agents) in the White House, enabled a preemptive strike on the issue, cracking down at the border itself and perhaps hoping to thereby sate the public's "bloodlust" ahead of Election Day.

Attorney General Janet Reno sent reinforcements, literally, by announcing the October 1 launch of Operation Gatekeeper, designed to beef up security on the San Diego stretch of the border. On October 22, less than three weeks before the election, in what was surely choreographed timing, Clinton and Feinstein balanced their tough border surveillance language by coming out against Proposition 187, declaring it unconstitutional and wrongheaded. "If you turn the teacher and other educators into instruments of a sort of state police force, it's like bringing a Big Brother into the schools," Clinton said at a nationally televised White House press conference.[29]

Feinstein appeared apprehensive in her own comments at a luncheon speech for the Commonwealth Club in San Francisco that day. "I know that this could cost me votes, quite possibly even the election," she said. "But I simply do not believe it will work."[30]

I t is important to understand that the roots of Proposition 187 are deeper than any single politician's ambition. In fact, Wilson did not formally endorse the initiative until late fall 1994, only a few weeks before Feinstein announced her opposition. But whether for or against the measure, politicians on all sides opportunistically fed the anti-immigrant hysteria they claimed was emanating from the citizenry.

As at other times in the state's history, immigrants were scapegoated— for example, in the 1990s by those whose position in the status quo seemed precarious or threatened. By 1994, more than four decades after the height of the post–World War II boom, real wages had been stalled for a quarter century, and the best new jobs in the growing high-tech and health-care fields were not easily accessible to an older generation unused to career-hopping.

Military spending, long the backbone of California's middle class—from the navy town of San Diego to the missile makers of Orange County to the electronics start-ups of Silicon Valley—had briefly but significantly shrunk in the wake of the Cold War's end. Meanwhile, a major real estate bubble that allowed the middle class to borrow heavily against the inflated value of their homes had finally burst. And after decades of relative prosperity, few members of the urban working class, many of whom had once enjoyed solid union wages, were prepared to return to minimum-wage (or below) jobs as fruit pickers, hotel maids, or fast-food cooks.

As with wave after wave before them, those who *would* take those jobs were indigent immigrants willing to live in the most rudimentary conditions, whether to remit cash back to the homeland or scrimp to ensure a better future for their children here. Today, more immigrants come to California from Asia than Latin America, but in the 1990s they flocked from Mexico. Its own flailing economy, under considerable stress from the deregulatory policies of President Salinas and the new North American Free Trade Agreement, spurred the bulk of new residents, many of them simply hopping the fence near San Diego and walking into the state.

Exploiting the fact that then as now many voters are ignorant of economic models that consistently show immigrants, legal or otherwise, are overall an economic boon, 187 backers were effective in singling out the direct health care, law enforcement, and education costs generated by undocumented residents, which came out of the state's general fund. In reality, then as today, undocumented workers also generated taxable profits for companies, paid sales taxes, and were consumers who immediately pumped almost all of their earnings right back into their local economy.

Immigration, both legal and illegal, had been soaring during the boom years of the go-go '80s without garnering much attention. But in a state known for the volatility of its economy (roughly double the national average), when times felt tough, as they did in 1994, perception was more important than individual financial reality, and "native" Californians predictably focused on perceived rivals. As in previous down cycles, immigrants were more likely to be seen as a burden than a boon, and undocumented workers and their families became a target of rising anger.

"Nowhere has this sentiment been more evident than in California,"[31] wrote R. Michael Alvarez and Tara L. Butterfield in an academic paper they produced for the California Institute of Technology. They noted that during the 1990s, California experienced cutbacks in the defense industry and closure of military bases contributing to the loss of nearly a million jobs and the attendant loss of tax revenues. By 1994, the state was suffering through its worst recession since the Great Depression. The authors wrote that the downturn in the economy and the economic insecurity among the populace correlated to the introduction that year of thirty legislative bills and two citizen-initiated ballot initiatives dealing with immigration.[32]

The authors' study used exit polling, economic figures, and other data to show this pattern repeated itself in generating such strong support for 187. It should be noted, however, that the measure's manifestation was in no way inevitable: Contemporary polls of voter priorities actually held immigration to be barely in the top ten or even fifteen issues facing the state. If powerful politicians, especially Wilson, had not thrown their weight behind it, it might have never reached critical mass. What Wilson and other 187 supporters accomplished with their ads and speeches was to explicitly marry the state's budget and economic problems—far and away the number one concern of voters—to the immigration issue. This tactic was used by the 2016 Republican primary candidate Donald Trump with his exhortation against undocumented immigrants: "They're taking our jobs. They're taking our manufacturing jobs. They're taking our money. They're killing us."[33]

Cleverly presented as a commonsense fairness issue, to avoid scaring off voters fearful of being considered discriminatory, Proposition 187's passage was all but assured. Encouraged by a small but vocal subset of legal immigrants expressing anger at how "illegals" were benefiting from cheating (a "fairness" argument that allowed them to deny the proposition was racist) and finding bipartisan support in polls, Republicans were perhaps blind to the political trap into which they were falling headlong. The fact is that while even an old school Democrat like Feinstein could barely muster halfhearted opposition to it, Latinos and other immigrants angry about 187—not only in California but across the country, and especially the younger generation—would hold the Republicans responsible for its creation and sentiment years after the measure marred the California social and political landscape.

It was a watershed disaster for Republicans, who rode a self-righteous, nativist wave right into political irrelevance in the most important state in the country. At the time, however, Democrats gave no indication they understood this; they seemed to feel the wave was crashing on their own heads. Instead of baiting Republicans by aggressively defending immigrants and emphasizing that many Americans had less-than-stellar arrival stories, the blue party's message on 187 was defensive, legalistic, and targeted directly at voters' self-interest rather than their morality or compassion.

As *Los Angeles Times* reporters Patrick J. McDonnell and Dave Lesher wrote, "In explaining their opposition to the proposition, for example, Clinton and Feinstein emphasized two oft-cited potential impacts: an increase in crime by those youngsters denied schooling and left on their own on the streets, and a spread of disease by immigrants who would be unable to obtain immunizations and other health care."[34] Clinton and Feinstein also pounded on the financial costs of 187, particularly the possible loss of $15 billion in federal aid for health, education, and welfare benefits, and emphasized how silly it was to enact a law the Supreme Court would likely dismiss.[35]

"In short, while leading Democrats did not endorse Proposition 187, they fully participated in constructing unauthorized immigration as a political and economic crisis that required uncompromising action, essentially affirming the rationale that fueled Proposition 187," wrote Daniel Martinez HoSang in his book *Racial Propositions: Ballot Initiatives and the Making of Postwar California.*[36]

While most state politicians were either stridently for Prop 187 or weakly against it, organized opposition to the initiative was hampered by a serious internal split between grassroots immigration activists and an establishment group, Taxpayers Against 187, the name chosen for the campaign by two Bay Area Republican consultants hired to run it. "The decision by a Democratic–civil rights–labor coalition to retain a Republican consultancy to derail a deeply radicalized ballot initiative spoke volumes about the limited confidence they had in their own ability to communicate with the electorate about this issue," observed HoSang.[37]

Even the first line of the "No on 187" ballot argument, signed by an interesting alliance—Sherman Block, the Los Angeles County sheriff, and the presidents of the California Teachers Association and the California Medical Association—was an attack on the undocumented: "Something must be done to stop the flow of illegal immigrants coming across the border."[38]

For those who believed most undocumented immigrants were exploited, hardworking people doing essential jobs other Californians were loath to do, this was outrageous. While Taxpayers Against 187, which feared having Latinos as presenters of their arguments, tapped Sheriff Block to be a main spokesperson, the grassroots activists ultimately organized massive student protests that would later be blamed for inciting a greater reactionary response.

With only a few weeks before the election, the split broke into the open on October 16, when an estimated seventy thousand people marched from primarily Spanish-speaking East Los Angeles downtown to City Hall.[39] Media coverage across the state fixated on the colorful images of young Latinos carrying Mexican flags through the streets of California's biggest city like a conquering army. (Years later, refining their message, the predominantly Latino participants in other massive Los Angeles immigration rallies carried American flags.) Over the next three weeks, tens of thousands of students from high schools and colleges across the state would walk out of classes in opposition to 187. For many in that generation of Latinos, it would be their first clear political act, and for some it would be the beginning of a lifetime of civic engagement.

Despite some wildly inaccurate polling that showed a dead heat, Proposition 187 passed easily, with the support of one-quarter of Latino voters. Californians concentrated in glitzy enclaves hugging the state's coastline, in the canyons and hills, or in the luxury high-rises and gated communities could comfortably continue to rely, wittingly or not, on a huge undocumented labor force to clean their houses, weed and manicure their gardens, take care of their children, cook their meals, look after their aging parents, and exercise their horses.

While the word "servant" was not usually in the lexicon of the often-liberal elites, it could not be ignored that the tree-lined blocks of mansions with their lush, landscaped grounds were inhabited mostly by white people and maintained by an impressive force of immigrant labor busing in each morning from some distant barrio. Sometimes they are "live-ins." I recall being at a middle school fund-raiser at a vast two-story private home in the swank Brentwood section of West Los Angeles, where a staff of Latinos attended to the guests. I asked my son's classmate, whose parents owned the home, how many people lived there. His reply: "Ten of us, my family of five and five servants." Needless to say, nobody would be much interested in making such arrangements even more awkward—or expensive—by asking live-in workers for papers.

In the same way, the state as a whole was content to look away from employers who threw a pittance to maltreated farm, sweatshop, and kitchen workers, largely hidden from the public's eye. It was simply easier not to have to question which employers were complying with federal and state labor, employment tax, and health and safety laws.

The Wilson administration, in an exceptional example, did initiate a pre-187, five-year state-federal-local project, Targeted Industries Partnership Program (TIPP), that targeted farm and sweatshop owners for violating labor laws, rather than immigrant workers for being undocumented. The goal was to level the playing field for employers who were obeying labor laws while competitors were shamefully exploiting and abusing undocumented workers, including child laborers, for greater profit. One well-publicized case in 1995 involved freeing seventy-two Thai garment workers held as slaves for six years in a building in the Los Angeles County city of El Monte; they eventually won permanent residency and $4 million in back pay.[40]

For fiscal years 1993–94 to 1997–98, TIPP recovered $14.2 million in wages for workers and $4.6 million in penalty assessments. Garments worth $26.6 million were seized and donated to hospitals, clinics, and charities for women and children.[41] One of the top officials operating the program told me at the time that wealthy garment manufacturers and farm owners whose property had been raided and who had been cited (including for 501 child labor violations) complained to lawmakers in Sacramento. When Wilson left office, the program was discontinued by his successor, Gray Davis.

For politicians during the 187 debate, the issue could be difficult, especially if they sought, as most did, to portray themselves as hard-liners against illegal immigration. Just weeks before the 1994 election, the surging Huffington was flummoxed by revelations that he and his then wife, Arianna Huffington, had employed an undocumented woman as a nanny for five years.

It was a huge embarrassment to his campaign, and he asked his wife back in Santa Barbara to discharge the nanny to mitigate any further damage. (The next time Arianna flew into Washington with their young daughters, they were accompanied by the nanny. Arianna Huffington later told me that the little girls were very attached to their nanny and she did not have the heart to suddenly sever the relationship.)

Michael Huffington countered that Feinstein had also employed an undocumented housekeeper back in the 1980s. The Democrat was legalistic in her response, noting that she hadn't actually broken the law then and that, besides, she had recently come out against the initiative anyway. Huffington narrowly lost the race, by less than 2 percent, despite pouring in some $28 million of his own money. He never ran for public office again.

In retrospect, Wilson and the Republicans in 1994 pursued short-term gain for what became long-term pain. The governor was reelected easily over Kathleen Brown, effectively ending her political career, but in the long run he became permanently associated with "losing" California for the Republicans. Proposition 187 ended up haunting the GOP right through to 2014, when President Obama, whose administration deported more immigrants than all other presidents combined, used an executive order to put into place a controversial partial amnesty, bypassing eternally stalled congressional immigration reforms. Moderate Republicans were frantic that the still-vituperative nativist energy expressed by its party base would doom it to continued failure in presidential elections. That was before Donald Trump upped the ante with his inflammatory rhetoric.

It may seem odd to blame a state proposition for such a long-term national effect, but Prop 187 not only became a debate that even the president entered but was also credited with spawning copycat legislation in other states and even in D.C. For example, Clinton's 1996 welfare reform included the elimination of payments to undocumented families, regardless of need (some of these cuts later were restored).

"It took the idea from Prop 187, this idea that immigrants were a drag to the economy and they were coming for benefits," Joseph Villela, director of policy and advocacy for the Coalition for Humane Immigrant Rights of Los Angeles, told the *Orange County Register.*[42]

In fact, while the common perception, particularly among conservatives, may be that California is teeming with "illegals," more than 70 percent of foreign-born Californians have legal status; 47 percent are naturalized citizens, while 26 percent have green cards or visas. Another 27 percent are counted as undocumented by the Homeland Security Department.

Wilson likely rued the day he made such a poor political bargain, despite success for him personally, with many historians now pointing to Prop 187 as the beginning of a long decline in his party's significance in California that endures today, with ripple effects nationwide. Republican registration has dropped to 27.6 percent in California, where the growing Latino population surpassed non-Hispanic whites in March 2014. (Democrats are at 43.1 percent while 24 percent claim no party preference.)

In recent elections, even in the primaries, California Republicans have not been eager to cozy up to Wilson's legacy, a slight exception being the 2010 gubernatorial race in which former eBay CEO Meg Whitman chose Wilson to be her campaign cochair. It was tantamount to political suicide from a candidate who was trying on the one hand to appear tough on undocumented immigrants and on the other to have ads in Spanish courting Latinos. It didn't help that she fired her housekeeper of nine years, an undocumented immigrant Whitman described as like "a member of the family," two months before the election.[43] The termination was either because Whitman had just learned the housekeeper was undocumented—Whitman's version of the saga—or because the housekeeper asked for help gaining legal status—her version. The woman ended up getting $5,500 in back wages in a settlement with Whitman and her husband.[44] In the end, Jerry Brown got 73 percent of the Latino vote to Whitman's 27 percent.

A 2013 survey on the effects of Proposition 187 on California and the nation by the Seattle-based public opinion research firm Latino Decisions found that 84 percent of Latino voters had "some degree of concern" that Whitman had selected Wilson as her campaign cochair.

In a conclusion two years ago that easily could be taken as a current cautionary note for the Republican Party, a summary of the survey reported: "This should serve as a reminder to the national GOP that the statements and positions taken today could have long-lasting effects on Latino voters if they are seen as negative and severe as the Wilson/187 policies back in 1994."[45]

My former sister-in-law, Sandra Molina (now Madar), is a perfect model to illustrate that point. Prop 187 was one of life's defining moments for her, just as it was for tens of thousands of Latinos, and just as Donald Trump's anti-Latino rants and hurtful words will be defining moments for many others, having a negative impact on the Republican Party nationally for years to come. In Sandra's case, having fled Nicaragua in her early twenties after her brother was killed in the revolution, she was not eager to change citizenship, even after marrying my brother. Nor was she interested in politics. Then came Proposition 187. She was appalled and hurt by the rhetoric of the campaign, which implied, she said, that all Latinos were criminals or gang members or just here to "mooch" off the government.[46]

"The people supporting 187 should have known you can't get any government services if you are undocumented," she said. "We were made to feel discriminated against, like we were not contributing to society. . . . In the kitchens in every restaurant, everywhere in society, we were doing the dirty work the white people did not want to do. And we were not recognized as taxpayers, as hardworking people. It felt horrible. I wanted desperately to become a citizen so that I could vote for the Democrats. I wanted to vote for Bill Clinton."[47] Sandra became part of Clinton's Citizenship USA initiative of 1995–96, which urged more immigrants to become citizens and to line them up as voters.

In June 1996, Sandra gathered with ten thousand fellow aspiring citizens at the Los Angeles Convention Center to take the oath of citizenship, a ceremony that was repeated for another thirty-eight thousand new citizens that month in Texas, Florida, and New York—states with large Electoral College numbers useful in the upcoming November presidential election.[48]

At Sandra's ceremony, which my family and I attended, each immigrant found a voter registration card on his or her chair, and each received a congratulatory letter from President Clinton. We heard a speaker lecture about the vital importance of each new citizen fulfilling his or her responsibility in our democracy by voting, reminding all that they could vote in the upcoming presidential election. When we walked out of the convention center into the bright sunny afternoon, there were about a dozen tables set up with volunteers to register new voters. While the new citizens could choose their party, signage at the tables indicated Republicans staffed only one table, and Democrats staffed all the others. The lines of those registering as Democrats grew as the convention hall emptied.

It all seemed carefully scripted, but to Sandra, who immediately registered as a Democrat, "It felt great, I was so psyched."[49] Sandra subsequently was divorced, remarried, moved to Connecticut, became a preschool teacher, and returned to college to study speech pathology. She became a lifelong Democratic political activist, volunteering for Democratic officeholders, and even involving her two children in campaigns. She was pictured on the cover of a 2012 campaign brochure for Democratic Congresswoman Elizabeth Esty, of Connecticut; she assumed she had been invited to be photographed with the congresswoman in order to attract other Hispanics to the candidate, and she was happy to oblige.

It is probable that Sandra would have registered as a Democrat without having lived through the Proposition 187 campaign, but its stinging rhetoric created an insult whose scars were so deep that it energized a lifetime of loyalty to the party. Sandra's example is borne out in the aforementioned report by Latino Decisions, which found: "the number of Latino voters grew quickly in response to perceived attacks on the Latino community," and that compared to states including New York and Texas that were not experiencing an anti-immigrant climate, "the research clearly demonstrates that Latino voter registration in California increased much faster than anticipated by population growth alone." They found an increase in Latino votes for the California Democratic Party throughout the 2000s. "Not only did more Latinos start voting, they started voting heavily against the Republican Party."[50]

With wisdom from the past, one can better see the future: The disaffection for the Republican Party that has grown among California Latinos for decades may presage the negative ramifications for the Republican Party nationally due to Trump's anti-immigrant remarks. Back in 1994, half of the fifty-two-member California congressional delegation was Republican; by 2015 it was 26 percent. By 2015, thirty of California's fifty-three congressional districts (nearly 57 percent) were at least 30 percent Latino, including nine of the state's fourteen districts represented by Republicans, who could be vulnerable in future elections.

GOP congressman David Valadao recognizes that as much as anyone. The son of Portuguese immigrants, Valadao represents a Central Valley agricultural district that is 70 percent Latino. When he announced at a community meeting in the summer of 2013 that he supported a path to citizenship for undocumented immigrants, he was wildly cheered. At least two other California Republican congressmen from heavily Latino districts made similar statements.[51] They are not alone among Republican officeholders in the state.

Republican politicians in California today must contend with the fact that every year since 1994, the state's electorate has been getting less Anglo and less Republican, providing more Latino votes to Democrats. The lesson from California for the rest of the nation is pretty clear, but although the sirens have been sounding a warning in Washington, congressional Republicans in the nation's capital continue to head their party ship straight for the rocks.[52]

In mid-2014, Texan Ted Cruz and his Tea Party cohorts in Congress crashed a compromise immigration bill and came up with one that would ease deportation of undocumented immigrants brought to the United States as children, which seemed more likely to solidify far right support than become law anytime soon. Neither the Canadian-born Cruz nor members of his Cuban immigrant family ever had to worry about their status in this country; Cruz's mother was an American citizen, and Cubans who left the island and set foot on U.S. soil have had a special status guaranteeing a fast track to U.S. citizenship.

Cruz's anti-immigrant tactics make fellow Texan and heavy-duty Republican Steve Munisteri's hair stand on end, judging from an interview with the

New Yorker's Ryan Lizza in November 2012. Munisteri, who served as Republican Party chairman in Cruz's home state from 2010 to 2015, predicted his party's demise in Texas and nationally if Republicans do not do more to attract Latinos.[53]

Lizza wrote: "Munisteri . . . turned to a chart showing Texas's population by ethnic group over the next few decades. A red line, representing the white population, plunged from almost fifty-five per cent, in 2000, to almost twenty-five per cent, in 2040; a blue line, the Hispanic population, climbed from thirty-two per cent to almost sixty per cent during the same period."[54]

Munisteri wants his party in Texas and nationally to do something to avert what happened with the African American community, whose voting bloc has been solidly for the Democrats for decades. He told Lizza, "You can't do that with a group of citizens that are going to compose a majority of this state by 2020. . . . By 2040, you'd have to get over a hundred percent of the Anglo vote."

While every syllable of Donald Trump's rhetoric was being translated into future votes for Democrats, and the Tea Party was finding its voice as a xenophobic movement, California was moving in the other direction, and some Republican political realists in the state took notice.

"We're finally breaking out of denial," Allan Hoffenblum, a longtime Republican consultant in state politics, told the *New York Times*. "Until we solve our Latino problem, we're not going to be a viable state party, and it's hard to understand how that's possible without fixing immigration."[55]

The polarizing Prop 187 campaign and the outpouring of protest it elicited "changed our lives forever," state assemblyman Luis Alejo told the *Orange County Register*. Alejo, the grandchild of fruit pickers brought to California by the bracero guest worker program, said, "Many of us were driven into political activism because of that draconian, anti-immigration proposition."[56]

Kevin de Leon, the first Latino elected to serve as state senate president pro tem in more than a century, also became an activist during that historic fall, helping organize one of the massive Los Angeles rallies. In 2014, de Leon got in the final word on Proposition 187 when he wrote a measure to repeal the remaining unenforceable provisions of the initiative that were still in the record.

Governor Brown signed the bill given to him by the Democratic-majority legislature, hammering the final nail in the law's coffin.[57]

It was just one of many new laws passed by the Democratic-controlled legislature and signed by Brown that have eased burdens on undocumented immigrants, including enshrining in law the right of undocumented students to receive in-state tuition rates at public colleges and to apply for loans at those institutions, to apply for professional licenses, to be licensed to practice law, and to work in polling places. Most dramatic, perhaps, on January 1, 2015, those with no legal right to be in the state became eligible to apply for a California driver's license; fifty thousand new drivers passed their tests and were licensed to drive by the end of that month.

These laws, accepting the presence of the undocumented immigrants and allowing them access to state resources, were maddening to a large number of conservative Californians, many of them still clustered in rural and suburban counties—the "red" portions of California—especially those who identified with the Tea Party phenomenon. By 2014, however, they seemed resigned to their own minority status in the state's political ecosystem. When Obama's executive order to protect about five million undocumented residents from deportation sparked outrage across the country, protests in California were small and generally ignored.

"Other parts of the country are experiencing the same kind of demographic and cultural shifts that California did some time ago, so now they're struggling through the same policy debates that we've already experienced," said Dan Schnur, a former Wilson spokesman who heads the University of Southern California's Jesse M. Unruh Institute of Politics. "History doesn't repeat itself," he said. "It just moves east."[58]

That California is now a standard-bearer for more moderate, liberal government, its position on immigration may seem like a given, especially in the light of the general—and largely incorrect—reputation the state has as a bastion of leftist "bleeding hearts." And if one reads shorthand journalistic accounts of how California went from hard-line Proposition 187 to the current wave of pragmatic legislation, it can seem quite simplistic: The initiative upset the rising demographic Latino group, resulting in a seismic political shift. The reality, however, was much more gradual and subtle. In fact, not only did Proposition 187 win passage, but it was followed up in the two succeeding elections by other populist, conservative "fairness" initiatives that sharply divided the state. In other words, change happens, if not always overnight.

Neither the anti–affirmative action Proposition 209 on the November 1996 ballot nor the anti–bilingual education Proposition 227 in 1998 directly targeted immigrants, yet they shared many similarities with 187. For example, none of the three was generated directly by political elites in Sacramento but rather were pushed forward by passionate individual ideologues with deep pockets and powerful political connections. They were furious at what they perceived as institutionalized unfairness to the Anglo majority that had dominated the state in all aspects for more than a century and how that disrespected "American" values.

Proposition 209 banned state and local governments from considering race, gender, or ethnicity in public education admission, employment hiring, and contracting agreements. It was drafted by two academics and had several fathers, but it became closely associated with its most aggressive and supportive public proponent, Ward Connerly. Appointed to the University of California Board of Regents by his longtime political benefactor, Pete Wilson, the African American land-use consultant convinced his fellow regents to ban UC's long-controversial affirmative action policy in 1995. He scored a bigger victory on the issue the following year, when the ban was extended to all government agencies.

Prodded by the evolving civil rights movement that had shown that changing laws was not always enough to transform society, President Kennedy thrust the term "affirmative action" into the civic discourse in 1961. He issued an executive order to the federal government to "take affirmative action to ensure that applicants are employed, and that employees are treated during employment, without regard to their race, creed, color, or national origin."[59] Hundreds of years of suffering discrimination, abuse, and enslavement had left such scars, the argument went, that equal opportunity for minorities was not going to happen within an acceptable time frame unless elite institutions took "affirmative" action.

As United States policy, it was reaffirmed by President Johnson four years later with an expanded order to prohibit government contractors from discriminating and extended the policy to protect women two years after that. The concept eventually became the norm for universities, Fortune 500 companies, and other institutions eager to create a mechanism to hasten integration, whether because of public relations or because they believed that diversity would strengthen the institution or organization.

In June 1978, the Supreme Court had ruled on a discrimination lawsuit brought by Allan Bakke, a white male who believed he was unfairly excluded from a University of California medical school because of quotas that reserved 16 percent of incoming classes for minority applicants. Signaling the way they would handle affirmative action cases for the next few decades, the jurists returned a ruling with six separate opinions affirming the constitutionality of affirmative action but rejecting strict quotas, making it much more difficult to accomplish.

The Bakke case became a rallying cry for white conservatives and, later, some Asian Americans who feared that affirmative action quotas would undermine their growing numbers in university admissions. Yet mainstream politicians in California had no desire to aggressively champion a cause that could make them look harsh or even racist. It would take a Pete Wilson crony, who was African American himself, to serve as the triggerman for the execution of affirmative action in California. Step one for Connerly was leading the UC Regents—mostly political appointees who were large donors to winning campaigns—to altogether ban the practice for the state's top-tier university system. With that accomplished in 1995, and the concept of opposing affirmative action normalized, he successfully barnstormed on behalf of Proposition 209.

It was a political tour de force that made the previously anonymous Connerly one of the most cheered and reviled Californians almost overnight. Meanwhile, his political patron, Wilson, who was running for president, decided to use the fight against affirmative action as a central plank in his campaign.

Although Wilson did not gain traction as a candidate, 209 became a legitimate debate topic, with President Clinton opposing it and eventual GOP nominee Bob Dole giving support. Soon, the Republican establishment swung in behind 209; the national party platform for 1996 called for support of the state proposition "to restore to law the original meaning of civil rights."[60] While the reach of Proposition 209 went far beyond the state's illustrious university system, it was the issue of admission to these springboards to the middle class that dominated debate both before and after the measure's passage (54 to 46 percent), keyed by the state's steadily declining yet still politically dominant prosperous white male demographic. According to a *Los Angeles Times* exit poll Jewish voters (58 percent) and females (52 percent) rejected the measure, as did three-quarters of blacks and Latinos. Voters aged eighteen to twenty-nine split 50-50, while the wealthier and more conservative the voters, the more likely they endorsed 209.[61]

The consequences of its passage, for those appalled by the already proportionally tiny enrollment of most minority groups in the state's university system, were shocking. In 1995, the year before 209, the freshman enrollment of self-identified African American students (945), Native Americans (248), and Chicanos/Latinos (3,432) to University of California campuses was at an all-time high; by 1998 all three demographic groups had seen those numbers plummet.[62]

Of course, for those who had fought for Prop 209 on the basis of fairness— the so-called "level playing field"—minority enrollment decline after its passage was a validation, not a problem. Equality of opportunity was the alleged goal of the mainstream, yet for most this meant transparent and fair entrance requirements and some scholarship support; any factor that was difficult to measure—racism, for example—was inconvenient and messy.

It would take a full decade, until 2006, for the number of African Americans to return to 1995 real-number levels—Native Americans never have— and by 2013, the percentage of black UC freshmen enrollment stalled at 4.0 percent, compared with a similar 4.3 percent two decades earlier.

Latino enrollment bounced back more, and more quickly. By 2014, for the first time in the state university system's history, the percentage of incoming UC Latino freshmen (29.6 percent) surpassed that of non-Hispanic white people (27.8 percent). In the state's general population they comprise 39 percent and 38 percent, respectively. Asian Americans (14.1 percent of the state population) were 38.3 percent of freshman admissions. By January 2015, four UC campuses boasted Latino undergraduate enrollments of more than 35 percent.

Because Proposition 187 had been immediately and successfully blocked in the courts, many opponents hoped the same would happen for 209, which they considered equally reactionary. But lawsuits failed to block the initiative's implementation in both the short term and long term; the new state constitution language was upheld by the federal courts in 2000 and has remained in effect ever since.

From 2012 to 2014, the state legislature bandied about a Senate constitutional amendment to essentially repeal 209. But after it passed and appeared headed for the 2016 ballot, the measure ran aground in the Assembly amid massive opposition from Asian Americans, claiming it was an example of "Yellow Peril" racism.[63]

A year after the Proposition 209 election, activist Republicans, pleased with their success in rolling back liberal policies in two successive elections, went after a third one in June 1998 that proved just as divisive as the others. Wealthy businessman and failed 1994 gubernatorial candidate Ron Unz gave financial backing to Proposition 227 to kill bilingual education, which Unz and other conservatives believed was a wrongheaded product of liberal-endorsed multiculturalism. Arguing that rapid assimilation of immigrants was to everybody's benefit, the proposition was quite detailed in mandating specific rules for Limited English Proficiency (LEP) students in the public K–12 schools.

As with 187 and 209, the proposition's backers insisted there was no malice toward any particular ethnic or racial group underlying their "common sense" solutions, yet many in immigrant communities certainly felt targeted.

"I think Latino voters and families are feeling threatened and they're feeling undue attention on them," Guillermo Rodriguez, executive director of the statewide Latino Issues Forum, told a *Contra Costa Times* reporter.[64] "Somehow they are being questioned on how American they are."

Other observers wondered if the details of the educational micromanaging inherent in 227 were flying way over the heads of both the media and the general public. And was "bilingual education" an actual problem or just a hot button issue to symbolically affirm an "English only" defense of Anglo America? While education and linguistic experts could be found on either side of the debate, teachers' unions were appalled on principle: Why should politicians or even voters be managing how education was delivered at the classroom level?[65]

Conservatives answered that bilingual education was itself a cultural artifact of the 1960s national-identity movements rather than a well-founded educational approach, foisted on the country by Chicano activists hoping to protect their culture from assimilation.

Univision billionaire A. Jerrold Perenchio, previously a donor to Wilson, made a last-minute $1.5 million donation to the campaign to oppose 227, and the biggest California teachers' union also kicked in $2 million. Spanish-language Univision also ran frequent editorials against the initiative. But all that would prove to be too little, too late; 227, or the English for the Children Act, would prove even more popular than 209 and 187 before it, winning in a landslide, 61-39 percent.[66]

In hindsight, the shrillness of the English-only crowd seems somewhat absurd in an era when McDonald's now markets a hamburger with both Mexican jalapeño peppers and Thai Sriracha sauce, the children of middle-class suburbanites pay inordinate sums to gentrify urban cores made interesting by the cultural richness of immigrant communities, and the increasing frequency of intermarriage means that many Californians consider themselves to be living embodiments of multiculturalism.

What was clear about Prop 227 is that while mostly white conservatives concerned with rapid demographic change in California had secured another victory at the ballot box, it didn't change the fact that their state was going to continue to become more Latino and Asian every year for the foreseeable future.

I n the end, a funny thing happened on the ride to a conservative, hard-line California run by populist initiative: The steam ran out. With the 2003 recall of the Democratic governor, Gray Davis, and the election of charismatic Republican action hero Arnold Schwarzenegger, Republicans could be forgiven for fantasizing about a return to power. But the very initiative process that they had found so much friendlier than the liberal state legislature, dominated by Democratic heavyweights like Willie Brown and John Burton, proved Schwarzenegger's Waterloo when voters, in a major blow to his political career, rejected his 2005 conservative-supported special election "reform agenda."

There were eight measures on the ballot, four measures for which the governor strenuously campaigned. Those would have slowed the growth of state spending, redrawn congressional and legislative district lines, made public-school teachers work longer to gain tenure, and restricted the spending on political campaigns by public employee unions. The latter two concepts galvanized teachers, nurses, and firefighters, and their unions' expensive ad campaign against the governor was quite damaging to his popularity. Four other measures on the ballot also were rejected; the cost of waging the eight campaigns totaled $417 million. Polls showed that people did not want the expensive election, did not like the governor so much at that point, and were unhappy about the way the state was headed. There was a respectable turnout of 50 percent, but voters wanted to show their anger. Schwarzenegger was chastened.

The lesson with propositions 187, 209, and 227 was that when it came to carefully crafted "fairness" initiatives attacking policies generally unpopular with the mainstream—bilingualism, illegal immigration, affirmative action—Californians were willing to overlook what critics saw as underlying racism or xenophobia. Yet, despite this, the state was gradually becoming more diverse, more Democratic, and more tolerant of cultural difference, not just in the cities but in the increasingly nonwhite suburbs.

The California propositions, whether gummed up in the courts or not, were important symbolically but were not game changers as policy; furthermore, they inflamed and radicalized a generation of young minority leaders who might otherwise have accepted the "postracial" view of America a half century after the height of the civil rights movement. If the goal had been partly to beat back the rise of "identity politics," the backers of propositions 187, 209, and 227 had instead only confirmed to many its importance.

By 2015, California was home to one out of every four foreign-born people in the United States—more than 10 million immigrants, greater in number than any other state, and Latinos had passed non-Latino whites as the biggest ethnic/racial group. Roughly half are naturalized citizens and another quarter have some form of legal status; the rest are undocumented, according to the Public Policy Institute of California. While the state's rate of immigration has slowed since a whopping 2.4 million immigrants arrived in the 1990s, a still-formidable 1.3 million came in the 2000s.[67]

People of color have become California's majority—61 percent of the state's residents—while as of 2015, the new minority of non-Hispanic whites rests at 38.4 percent while Hispanics are 39 percent. Asians compose 13 percent, while blacks and African Americans are 5.7 percent of the state's 39 million residents. These figures are practically the inversion of the population of the total fifty states, which is 37 percent people of color and 63 percent Anglo.

"Demographics is destiny, and, at the core, we're seeing a historic shift of almost a reconquest,"[68] Chapman College political science professor Fred Smoller told the *Orange County Register* for a twenty-year retrospective on the impact of 187. "The state is changing permanently."[69]

Assimilation does happen over time, of course, through intermarriage, co-education, and generational drift, particularly for those who attain middle-class status. But the process is not always fast, consistent, or inevitable, especially if economic, cultural, and geographic isolation are in play. In a state and country where the expansion of the middle class has stagnated and is now receding, islands of self-segregation have persisted, despite the globalization of the

English language and the admission of representatives of every group into the educational and corporate hierarchies.

Whereas the backers of propositions 187, 209, and 227 argued for "color-blind" government, at least partly on the basis that assimilation is a fundamental American value, those hoping to "Americanize" immigrant and minority groups pragmatically might be better off supporting anything that will help them prosper. The more education and employment people have, the more likely they are to integrate into mainstream culture and accept its norms and laws.

Such is the hidden premise behind new laws like Assembly Bill 60, nicknamed Drive California, which are the antithesis of the Proposition 187 ethos. This aforementioned driver's-license measure is symbolic of the state's changing demographics that helped deliver Jerry Brown the governor's office. It also is a perfect example of changing sentiment among voters. Up until 1993, undocumented residents could obtain a driver's license just like any other resident of California. But the immigrant bashing surrounding Proposition 187 prompted the legislature to pass a law requiring license applicants to prove they had legal status. Governor Gray Davis, fighting for his political life and facing a recall election, signed a bill revoking the 1993 law, but it was short-lived. Public sentiment at the time was against providing the privilege of driving to people in the country illegally.

Signing the bill hurt Davis and helped his main opponent, Schwarzenegger, who promised in the recall campaign to rescind the law—which he did. The position against granting licenses to undocumented people, which nearly a dozen other states had taken, was foolish, since drivers without a license—the only alternative for thousands of undocumented people who needed to get to work and drive their children to school—did not have to pass written and driving tests proving their proficiency behind the wheel or to obtain insurance. The personal cost to them also could be great: getting caught driving without a license could result in having their cars impounded and sold at auction and being processed for deportation. But those days, and those fears, have ended.

On the last evening of the 2013 legislative session, in the frenzy that overtakes the capital in the hours before the midnight deadline to get bills passed, a legislator ran into Brown in the capital and mentioned that the driver's license bill had been taken off the calendar, killing it for the session. Brown told him if the legislature passed it, he would sign it. Last-minute scrambling ensued, and the senate resuscitated the bill and sent it to the assembly, where it was approved before midnight, to take effect in January 2015.

Legislators were taken by surprise. Brown had campaigned in 2010 against granting driver's licenses to undocumented drivers, saying at the time it should be part of a comprehensive federal immigration reform package. But after two years with no action from Washington, Brown and the legislature acted. Upon passage of the new law, Brown commented, "Hopefully, it will send a message to Washington that immigration reform is long past due."[70]

On January 2, the first business day of 2015, nearly 9,300 Californians made advance appointments with the Department of Motor Vehicles, while others lined up as early as 4 a.m., in freezing weather in some parts of the state. In the first three months of the law taking effect, nearly five hundred thousand new undocumented drivers were issued their license with a special designation: "Federal Limits Apply." By the end of 2015, that number grew to 605,000. The state expects to issue 1.4 million licenses to undocumented immigrants through 2017. One positive side effect is that all of these drivers will be required to carry liability insurance. "It's going to be a big change," San Leandro construction worker Francisco Galvez told the *San Jose Mercury News* at the Hayward DMV. "I can get to work without fear. I can have a normal life."[71]

California's move was followed in 2015 with federal regulations allowing undocumented immigrants with legal-resident children or spouses to have work permits and protection from deportation. The principle is the same: If you can drive, work, and live without fear, you will be less isolated, more productive, and less of a potential burden on the society as a whole.

Just as Jerry Brown has been helpful to Latino assimilation, that demographic group came through for him in 2010, giving him 64 percent of its vote to Meg Whitman's 31 percent, and again in 2014,[72] when Brown rolled over his Republican opponent, Neel Kashkari, 73 to 27 percent among Latinos closely matching Barack Obama's 71 percent of the Hispanic vote in 2012 to Mitt Romney's 27 percent.

None of this is lost on the Republican Party of California, which itself has become a model in reaching out to long-alienated groups by softening hard-line positions offensive to them. It has responded in a constructive way to the very cultural and demographic shifts in the state and nation that the national party chooses to ignore, at its peril. The California party leadership and membership have done this by taking action to attempt to expand their tent by being more welcoming of groups long alienated from the Republican Party.

In March 2015, for example, the state party voted overwhelmingly (75 to 25 percent) to welcome as a charter member the gay Log Cabin Republicans of California. One delegate noted, "It would have been the complete opposite fifteen years ago. The fringe does not control the party anymore."[73] At least that is true in California. Just six months later, in a better-late-than-never moment, delegates to the party's statewide convention proposed adding "sexual orientation" to the list of groups protected from housing and employment discrimination.[74]

After the reach-out to gays, and with no sign that Donald Trump would cease spewing his anti-immigrant rhetoric, convention delegates took an important if in some ways symbolic step of voting to change the party platform on immigration. Party members voted to delete the words "illegal alien"[75] from the platform language and softened the tone if not the intent of other immigration-related positions. For example, the phrase "new immigrants should be required to learn English, and businesses should be able to require employees to speak the English language while on the job" was substituted with "learning English is a vital part of life in the United States. Therefore, fluency in English must be the goal of California's education programs."[76]

The party's position that all election ballots and government documents should be printed only in English was eliminated, as was a statement that "allowing illegal immigrants to remain in California undermines respect for the law."[77]

The platform changes were drafted by Marcelino Valdez, the Central Valley chair of the state Republican Party, who said the new language was approved by the platform committee with 75 percent of the vote and by about 90 percent of the general assembly, including some Tea Party delegates. Valdez referred to the new platform as "an anti–Proposition 187 plank" and called it "a monumental day in California politics."[78]

That old specter continues to haunt, however. Harmeet Dhillon, the state Republican Party vice chair, was realistic, telling *Los Angeles Times* political reporter Cathleen Decker at the convention: "There are going to be people that if we made the chair of the party and the top of the ticket somebody born of immigrant parents, it would not convince them that we are the right party for them because of the history of 187 and other issues."[79]

One of those "issues" is the party's new spoiler, Donald Trump, who "brings back a lot of rancor of the 1990s, and I think that will hurt us,"[80] said Republican state assemblyman Rocky Chavez, of Oceanside, in San Diego County, a retired Marine Corps colonel. He was both optimistic and realistic: "We're evolving. Anything that doesn't evolve and change dies."[81]

7

Gold Rush, Fracking, and Electric Cars

Whiskey is for drinking, and water is for fighting over.

—WESTERN SAYING (OFTEN FALSELY
ATTRIBUTED TO MARK TWAIN)

The love affair Californians have with the environment is well known and often reviled by big coastal property owners, oil interests, developers, and others who have a financial stake in seeing "green" regulations cast aside to enable their projects. Sometimes years-long courtroom battles have been waged for developments to get the "go" or "give up" signal. One coastal property owner, tech billionaire Vinod Khosla, has been fighting the state for five years in court over his blocking public access to the beach on his $32.5 million property near Half Moon Bay in Northern California. Antifracking activists hound Jerry Brown at public appearances for not being aggressive enough by not banning the practice. But these clashes are hardly new in the Golden State.

California's first big environmental battle was fought within a few years of the gold rush of 1849. In the forested foothills of the Sierra Nevada, gold miners had reinvented an ancient Roman technique for exposing precious metals, blasting out entire hillsides using hydraulic energy. Using more than five thousand miles of flumes, ditches, and canals winding down through the woods to build pressure, the water was then forced through sheet-iron hoses and shot out of eighteen-foot-long forged nozzles with astonishing force.

At the North Bloomfield Gravel Company site near Nevada City, seven of these monsters each fired a million gallons of water an hour, twenty-four hours a day.[1]

Once screened for gold, the vast quantities of mud and gravel knocked loose by these water cannons were then washed down into the rivers, deltas, and bays of central and coastal California, promptly clogging farmers' irrigation systems, wiping out fisheries, causing floods, and even blocking steamboat passage. Over two decades, hundreds of thousands of acres of farmland and orchards were destroyed or damaged. It is estimated that in some areas, land levels were raised as much as seven feet by the aquatic transfer of some twelve billion tons of earth, the equivalent of eight times the earth that was removed to carve the Panama Canal.[2]

While devastating for riparian wildlife and the lifestyles of California's native hunters and gatherers, it was the effect on farmers and town dwellers that brought the situation to a climax in the new state. In 1875, deadly floods caused by hydraulic activity wrecked the towns of Marysville and Yuba City, leading to widespread outrage.

"I have no objection to the miners digging all the gold they can find but I don't want them to send the whole hill down upon my ranch and bury me and all I have," said farmer James Keyes at a postflood meeting in Yuba City, according to the historian Robert Kelley. "And that is just what they have done and are doing. I want to be let alone."[3]

By 1880, the farmers' revolt against this abuse of the commons by a small set of profiting companies had spawned the Anti-Debris Association, an advocacy group complete with a seventy-man-strong uniformed guard. They were locked in mortal political combat with a new industrial-scale mining industry backed by financiers in San Francisco and London (hermit panhandlers were already anachronisms).

While mountain and valley newspaper editorials jousted over who had the right to do what to the land, Judge Lorenzo Sawyer of the Ninth Circuit Court adjudicated the decisive battle in the case of *Woodruff v. the North Bloomfield Gravel Company*. Sawyer, who had himself come west in 1850 as part of the gold rush, and had even spent a few months as a miner before returning to the law, ended decades of giving miners free rein to do pretty much as they pleased when he found for the farmers, ruling that the "injurious nuisance" of hydraulic mining was unacceptable.[4]

The Marysville newspaper reacted as if a great war had ended, although it took some years for the decision to be fully implemented. "Exactly at one o'clock the first message was received, announcing in the most positive terms, a complete victory for the valley. In a few moments the steam whistle at Swain & Hudson's mill began a shrill and prolonged shriek . . . soon the church bells were ringing out the most joyful peals ever heard in Marysville."[5] Farming communities from Chico to Bakersfield threw huge civic parties, with marching bands, fireworks, and bonfires.

This pitched battle over the management of the environment, one of the first in the country, foreshadowed many in California, in that it was centered on the issue of water and the consequences of new technology. It would set the stage for other future state battles to protect the environment, as it pitted powerful economic interests against each other and the state and ultimately led to a lot of political strife and complex litigation. Such battles would come to define California and cement its place as a national leader in the environmental movement. It was also a reminder that for all its epic scale, the state was not immune to the depredations of man.

Along with Colorado, Alaska, Hawaii, and other states, California has always been strongly associated in the public mind with its natural splendor. From Yosemite to San Francisco Bay; from the world's biggest trees to the country's tallest continental peak to the lowest, hottest, driest place in North America; from desert to forest to ocean cliff—the state has long been celebrated internationally by naturalists and explorers, among them John Muir, Jack London, and Ansel Adams.

But despite its stunning scenery, California is in some ways quite a harsh environment. First of all, much of the water was not originally where folks ultimately decided it needed to be. And prone to drought, wildfire, flood, and, of course, earthquakes, the state has surprised successive waves of immigrants who flocked to its promised land with sometimes biblical-proportion assaults. In 1862, for example, California was struck by a so-called "arkstorm."

"It rained for forty-five days straight," Lucy Jones, of the U.S. Geological Survey, recounted more than a century later to National Public Radio's Jon Hamilton. The storm "bankrupted the state, destroyed the ranching industry, drowned 200,000 head of cattle, [and] changed California from a ranching economy to a farming economy."[6] It also forced the state capital to temporarily move from Sacramento to San Francisco because of the flooding.

The 1906 earthquake and fire of San Francisco, which killed four hundred people and decimated the biggest city west of St. Louis, was another epic disaster. Nor are such events only a thing of the distant past. A deadly tsunami destroyed Crescent City in the state's far north in 1964; massive earthquakes struck the San Fernando Valley (Los Angeles County) in 1971, Santa Cruz and the Bay Area in 1989, and Los Angeles in 1994; and an inferno that started as a brushfire blew through a swath of the Oakland and Berkeley hills in October 1991, killing 25 people and injuring 150. It destroyed 3,469 residences and damages exceeded $1.5 billion.

But nature wasn't the only source of the state's disasters. Human activity resulted in debacles that were more subtle but no less destructive. By the 1970s, for example, air quality had reached crisis levels, while the state's bays and waterways—and the soils they water—had become dangerously polluted with toxic chemicals and heavy metals. By the will of the voters, activist environmental groups, and enlightened lawmakers, California, home of the Sierra Club, became the driving heart of the national environmental movement that arose in that decade. Californians had already been conditioned to care about the polluted air they breathed, especially since they often could actually see it in the form of smog.

California has always been on the cutting edge in this area, by necessity. By the 1940s, residents of Los Angeles complained about a haze that made their eyes water, and soon their fast-growing geographic area came to be referred to as the "smog capital of America."

Not forgotten by those who were around in the summer of 1943 was the smog, referred to as a "gas attack," that struck Los Angeles. As reported by the state Air Resources Board's history of air pollution in the state, "Visibility is only three blocks and people suffer from smarting eyes, respiratory discomfort, nausea, and vomiting."[7] Two years later, the city of Los Angeles established a program to control air pollution.

By the 1960s, Southern California politicians began demanding that Detroit produce cleaner cars. And because California was such a major market for automakers—accounting for 12 percent of revenue for new car sales in the United States—Detroit had to listen. California was the first state to establish emission standards for new cars in the 1960s and has set the pace for the nation and even the world ever since.

In 1961, the first automotive-emissions-control technology in the United States was mandated by California to control hydrocarbon crankcase emissions; it went into effect in 1963 on all domestic passenger vehicles sold in California, which eventually meant everywhere, since California was, and remains, the biggest market for all new and used vehicle sales in the country. That was followed by tailpipe-emission standards, which were established in 1966, also the first in the nation.

The Federal Air Quality Act of 1967 included a waiver for California to set and enforce its own more stringent emission standards for new vehicles sold in the state. Four years later, the state Air Resources Board adopted the first nitrogen oxide standards for automobiles in the nation; in 1975, the first two-way catalytic converters came into use in California. The following year, the state limited lead in gasoline, which also spread nationwide, followed over the years by demands for cleaner diesel fuel and tougher emission standards for off-road and marine vehicles.

It was also in 1976 that the South Coast Air Quality Management District (SCAQMD) was established to deal with the infamous Los Angeles smog, and other areas of the state eventually established their own AQMDs.[8]

All California drivers reregistering their vehicles annually must participate in the California Smog Check Program, started in 1984, which requires biennial inspections of vehicles' emission-control systems to make sure they are effective and not in need of repair. A Californian cannot renew his or her vehicle registration when due unless it has passed the "smog test."

In another example of how California is ahead of the nation, the California Clean Air Act (CCAA) was passed into law and signed by Republican governor George Deukmejian in 1988, establishing the framework to direct the state in how to manage air quality in California for the next twenty years. The federal Clean Air Act, signed into law by President George H. W. Bush, "relied largely on elements of the CCAA, and required a number of new programs aimed at curbing urban ozone, rural acid rain, stratospheric ozone, toxic air pollutant emissions and vehicle emissions."[9]

The "big seven" automakers agreed in 1996 to produce zero-emission vehicles, and, two years later, new emissions standards for marine and off-road vehicles were initiated. In 2001, a government mandate to increase the sale of zero-emission vehicles was upheld, with modified requirements. Automakers wishing to sell cars in California—again, all automakers—were required to produce between 4,450 and 15,450 zero-emission cars starting in 2003.[10]

The state Air Resources Board adopted the nation's first "greenhouse gas" rule in 2004, which required automakers to begin selling vehicles with reduced greenhouse gas emissions by model year 2009. The federal Environmental Protection Agency got into the act in 2009, issuing the first greenhouse gas standards demanding lower-emission vehicles throughout the nation in 2010.

In California, this transition already was well under way. In 2008, six of the ten U.S. cities with the highest registration of new hybrid vehicles were in California, and out-of-state visitors often commented on the ubiquity of the Toyota Prius, in particular.[11] Four years later, California approved new rules requiring automakers to reduce tailpipe pollution by 75 percent and ensure that, within thirteen years, one out of seven cars sold can run on electricity.[12] By September 2014, sales of hybrid and plug-in electric vehicles in California totaled 40 percent of the national market for such environmentally friendly cars.[13]

Almost without exception, the rest of the country eventually mandated the innovations that California had already implemented—sometimes after great political and legal conflict. For example, the administration of George H. W. Bush tried to block the national implementation of the stringent exhaust standards mandated by California "phase 2" emissions standards in 1996.

The growing California population and massive number of vehicles on the road inevitably led to deteriorating roadways, a need for more public transportation, and often terribly long daily trips for commuters, some of whom spend an hour or more on the road to get to work every day. In 2006, California's voters passed Proposition 1B, authorizing nearly $20 billion in bonds to be sold to fund improvements to the state's roads and public transportation, with a secondary goal of improving air quality. Yet, despite all these investments, controls, agreements, and incentives, the ever-growing population of California means the state is always fighting an uphill battle. By the end of 2014, the state's 38.8 million people had 25 million licenses and 33.6 million registered vehicles and drove 300 billion miles a year,[14] using 15 billion gallons of gasoline while producing more than 1.2 million tons of nitrogen oxides and hydrocarbons.[15]

As with other aspects of California life, technology is looked to as a savior. Beyond cleaner fuel and more efficient cars, state policy is supporting several competing clean-car technologies, some of them controversial, including ethanol, fuel cell, all-electric cars, and even driverless vehicles. The latter vehicles depend on technology—radar, GPS navigation, laser sensors, and cameras—to be able to see more than a human driver can and sense trouble before it happens. Google started testing such cars in 2009, and after a 2012 state law allowed autonomous vehicles to be test-driven on public roads, seven companies, including Mercedes-Benz and Nissan, received permits to hit the road at speeds not exceeding twenty-five miles per hour.

The iconic Toyota Prius Hybrid became the state's best-selling car in 2012 and repeated the feat in 2013 before being overtaken in 2014 by the Honda Hybrid, validating the government's push to force automakers to produce greener vehicles. But while liberal cities like Berkeley and Santa Monica are overrun with unassuming earth-toned Priuses, much of the state still loves its muscle, sports, and luxury cars, as well as pickup trucks and SUVs, and the state uses larger vehicles in its corporate, industrial, and public transportation fleets. Moreover, hybrids, while fuel-efficient, still burn gasoline (the Prius does have a plug-in model, but most sales are still for the hybrid).

In the exacting, egomaniacal style of Apple's Steve Jobs, PayPal billionaire

Elon Musk is pushing his Tesla Motors to upend the status quo of an entire manufacturing industry and create a new product niche with fast, beautiful, expensive cars. That they are all electric makes them a green gearhead's fantasy. While garnering a fabulous amount of media attention, by the end of 2014, the Palo Alto company's Fremont plant had only produced one model car, the Model S, which starts at around $70,000. Still, according to Green Auto Blog, Tesla, the well-financed start-up founded in 2003, was moving a respectable 2,150 of the Model S each month in 2014 nationally, and it was set to launch the new SUVish Model X by 2016 at a more affordable midrange price.[16]

While hybrids made it into the mainstream and all-electric cars were carving out a niche among short-commute urbanites, the state was pushing an even more revolutionary technology through mandate and incentive policies, encouraging hydrogen fuel-cell technology. Despite concerns about danger related to Fuel Cell Electric Vehicles' (FCEVs) use of explosive hydrogen, the Air Resources Board expected automakers to "introduce FCEVs to the early commercial market in the 2015 to 2017 time frame. By 2020, automakers expect to place tens of thousands of fuel cell electric vehicles in the hands of California consumers."[17]

California at the end of 2014 had less than a dozen publicly available hydrogen fueling stations but approved more than $200 million in funding to build at least a hundred more by 2024. By 2016, there will be an estimated fifty-five hydrogen-fueling stations in California.[18] Automakers have said they're concentrating on sales of fuel-cell vehicles in California and will expand to other states as more hydrogen-fueling stations come available.

Outside the motor vehicle realm, the state legislature and voters have been steadily enacting innovative and aggressive regulations for decades, over not only pollution and toxic elements but also the health of the environment itself—namely, climate change. The passage in 1970 of the landmark California Environmental Quality Act (CEQA), signed by Governor Ronald Reagan, brought the term "environmental impact report" (EIR) into the state's lexicon.[19] The act essentially regulates all development and planning in the state to determine its impact on the environment. These are just the regulations that the former Texas governor Rick Perry and fellow conservatives cite as antibusiness and an assault on "freedom."

Voters enacted Proposition 20 in 1972 to create the California Coastal Commission, initially for a term of four years. The commission was made permanent in the California Coastal Act of 1976, which prioritized public access and marine protection over private ownership and controlled all development and use of land and water along the state coastline. Powerful local and state panels of appointees have protected the public's access to beaches up and down the coastline, sometimes fighting private property owners in court and shutting down private development that threatened such access.

The Safe Drinking Water and Toxic Enforcement Act, passed by voters as Proposition 65 in 1986, requires the state to list publicly all naturally occurring or synthetic chemicals known to cause cancer, birth defects, and other reproductive harm. That list, available on the state's Web site, must be updated annually; it contained about eight hundred toxic chemicals as of January 2015. Most important, the law prohibits toxic discharges into drinking water and requires businesses to disclose what toxic chemicals they use and where. This is done by labeling consumer products, posting signs at workplaces, or distributing notices at rental properties or in newspapers.

This labeling by California has had an influence on other states by virtue of its size as a consumer market. For example, the country's two largest soft-drink producers—the Coca-Cola Company and PepsiCo—agreed to change the caramel-coloring process for their drinks in 2012 to avoid having to place a "known carcinogen" warning label on their Coke and Pepsi drinks in California.

This decision to remove the cancer-causing chemical 4-MEl followed a report by the Center for Science in the Public Interest on its presence in the drinks.[20] Coca-Cola changed its formula throughout North America. Pepsi-Co and Goya Foods, following a *Consumer Reports* study of 4-MEl in soft drinks, were named defendants in a class action lawsuit filed in January 2014 in California accusing them of hiding how much of the chemical is used in their drink products.[21] The case is ongoing.

While some real progress has been made, particularly in air and water quality, it has been blunted by the reality of a prosperous, carbon-consuming population surging past thirty million, most of whom still dream of owning a McMansion and a two-car garage, and by industrial and agricultural sectors at the root of endemic shortages of water, power, and space.

In the fall of 2014, more than 67 percent of voters had approved Proposition 1, which authorized more than $7 billion in bonds for water-infrastructure projects in an effort to better use and protect what is available. The National Resources Defense Council, a major mainstream environmentalist group, hailed it as a good compromise that would promote reduced use, increased recycling, and better protection of limited freshwater supplies. Other green groups opposed it, arguing that it would drive funds toward the creation of new dams and diversion tunnels. Some agreed that it was a lot of money and would not help the state in the short term.

One project opponent, the California Water Impact Network, urges an assessment of water quantity in the state and cautions that, drought or no drought, water rights claims exceed by five and a half times the amount of available developed water. The network encourages more conservation, development of local supplies, more equitable distribution, and desalination projects like the one in San Diego County that is pumping 50 million gallons a day of Pacific Ocean water for use by residents and businesses, meeting 7 to 10 percent of the region's water needs, or for about 300,000 users.

The $1 billion project was built by an Israeli-owned company, IDE Technologies, which has built similar plants in China, Israel, Australia, and India. More than a dozen more desalination facilities are being planned along coastal California. The plant is not free of environmental issues; salt concentrations in the brine that is a product of the desalination process can harm plants and wildlife, and the water intake process kills larvae, eggs, and invertebrates. The Carlsbad project involved restoring fifty-five acres of wetlands to help mitigate such damage.

Desalination could go a long way toward helping California's water shortage, but even then droughts pose a serious threat to the state.

That became clear when the state's ski resorts closed for much of the winter of 2014–15. The drought—an issue that previously had been mostly relevant to farmers and water managers—began to blossom into public conscious-ness. At the end of 2014, the state was facing the fourth year of increasingly severe drought, forcing severe reductions in water usage that were imposed throughout California, pitting north against south, city dwellers against farmers and ranchers, and neighbor against neighbor, especially if one was seen watering his lawn more than the allowable two times a week. Expansive green lawns at private golf courses and estates generated fierce opprobrium, while brown foliage in its death throes became a symbol of good citizenship. Those who suffered the most were Californians who were left with no running water at all, some for more than a year, after their wells ran dry. By July 2015, the strict conservation policies ordered by Brown paid off when Californians had lowered their water usage by 27 percent. Freak summer thunderstorms and hailstorms briefly cheered Californians, looking for a sign of the arrival of El Niño, the rains that would relieve the parched land-scape, though not necessarily end the drought.

After more than a century of radical human engineering on a truly massive scale—resulting in a seven-hundred-mile aqueduct, world-famous freeways, and some of the most impressive bridges on earth, California's environment seems to be reasserting herself and imposing new limits on the state's aspirations. A lack of water has the state's various alliances gearing up for new battles in California's long-running water wars, famously depicted in the classic film *Chinatown*. The news that it takes one gallon of water to grow one almond captivated the news media and appalled the populace, who couldn't seem to stop talking about it.

As discussed in the "Tale of Two States" chapter, how to balance develop-ment with the wise use of natural resources is a debate long split along po-litical and regional lines. In the minds of Rick Perry and other staunch conservatives, the environment is a basket of resources to be used by humans until the free market can unlock or develop new ones. This attitude was well illustrated in 2008, when vice presidential candidate Sarah Palin debating Joe Biden famously repeated the chant "Drill, baby, drill!"

Perry and others sued the government to turn back key federal Environ-mental Protection Agency rulings: that greenhouse gases were subject to regulation under the Clean Air Act and that the EPA has the authority to regulate air pollution that wafts across state borders. The U.S. Supreme Court ruled in favor of the EPA in both cases in 2014. To the extent that environmental problems are admitted at all in Texas, they are seen as quantitative technical challenges to be adapted to rather than qualitative moral dilemmas that must be faced.

In California, on the other hand, after decades of taking a backseat to economic and criminal justice issues, the environment again became the hot topic, with Governor Brown, having long been something of a cheerleader for the notion of limits, well situated to lead during the period of devastating drought. In 2012, facing certain reelection to his record fourth term as governor, he was touting another in a long line of water-bond initiatives, fighting a rearguard action against antifracking activists who stalked his public appearances, and continuing to push hard to advance climate-change policies initiated by his Republican predecessor, Arnold Schwarzenegger.

Brown rightfully has always been described as an environmentalist by the media and his supporters. The slogan of his 1980 presidential campaign was "Protect the Earth, serve the people, and explore the universe." In his first two terms as governor, urged on by the rise of the new national environmental movement, he was active and frequently successful in promoting solar power, energy-efficient building design, getting lead out of gasoline, antismog regulation, a moratorium on the construction of nuclear power plants, federal protection for state rivers, and blocking offshore oil drilling.

"He has never really gotten the kind of credit he deserves,"[23] Max Neiman, a professor at the Institute of Governmental Studies at the University of California, Berkeley, told the *New York Times* in 2010, arguing that Brown was one of the first nationally prominent politicians to see that fossil-fuel reliance was a dead end. Pragmatically, he found that he could deflect opposition by forcing all the interest groups fighting over a particular environmental issue into negotiations by creating powerful oversight or coordinating boards or offices. "Jerry Brown kind of invented environmental conflict resolution at the state level," Richard Charter, a veteran coastal activist in California and senior policy adviser at Defenders of Wildlife, said in the same *Times* story:

> Brown's trick, Charter said, was the creation of the Office of Planning and Research . . . which was charged with coordinating activities among coastal counties, city councils, mayors, the attorney general, fishing interests, and conservation groups. This local pressure bubbled up to Congress, where nearly every member of the California delegation, regardless of party affiliation, voted to block new leases in 1981 and 1982. . . .
>
> The California coast would look much different today. You would probably have offshore drilling off Big Sur and Mendocino had it not been for the anticipatory strategy employed by the Brown administration.[24]

After his nearly two-decade hiatus from statewide political office ended with his election to California attorney general in 2006, Brown once again used his office to pursue environmental causes through the courts. For example, he employed the California Environmental Quality Act credited for inspiring a state law and the Obama administration's policy push along the same lines.

"Far too many environmental efforts are long on promises and short on delivery," Dan Kammen, chief technology specialist at the World Bank and an expert on California energy policy, told the *New York Times*. "Not so of Jerry. He can spot a good idea and will be relentless in digging to the bottom of it."[25]

Yet he can be unpredictable, especially when it comes to signing or vetoing green legislation. In 2013, the Sierra Club criticized him in its annual legislative report card for paddling so hard on the right side of his theoretical canoe that he was leading the state in circles. Specifically, the granddaddy of environmental groups gave him a 43 percent score and accused him of being too cozy with industries, particularly oil and timber, with which he had tangled so aggressively in the past.

The group cited the two bills he signed regarding harvesting of trees that were supported by timber industry "giants, including Sierra Pacific Industries, the largest private timber lands owner in the state, best known for its aggressive clear-cutting practices."[26]

When the issue of hydrofracture drilling, or "fracking," heated up in Brown's third term as governor, attention was drawn to contributions he had received over the years from oil companies. A detailed examination by Robert Gammon of the *East Bay Express* noted that from Brown's race for attorney general through 2013, his campaigns received more than $2 million in donations from oil and natural gas interests ($500,000 alone from Occidental Petroleum), with just less than a third of that going to Brown's Oakland charter schools and the remainder going to his campaigns for attorney general, governor, and the tax-increase measure Proposition 30.[27] These donations garnered attention when Brown was too noncommittal to please his environmental constituency on the white-hot controversy over fracking.

Hydrofracture drilling is hugely controversial around the nation, dividing environmental groups, oil and natural gas interests, and economists, so it can be useful to look at how California has dealt with the issue. Pioneered in Oklahoma and Texas, fracking involves shooting chemical-laced water and sand with great force vertically and horizontally approximately eight thousand feet into the ground to break up rock formations and release huge amounts of oil and natural gas that would otherwise be trapped and inaccessible.

At the start of the new millennium, a boom in fracking wells transformed the economies (positively) and environments (negatively) of North Dakota and Pennsylvania in particular, as well as other states. Fracking has been credited with revitalizing, in the short term, America's energy profile and boosting exports. One government study projected at the time that a predicted fracking-triggered boom would bring as many as 2.8 million new jobs to California and boost tax revenue by $24.6 billion annually, benefits not lost on a governor who inherited a multibillion-dollar deficit and a high unemployment rate.[28] Economics trump almost all other issues for most, if not all, politicians.

The hazards for groundwater wells and the aquifer as a whole, however, are myriad, especially from chemicals leaking on the way down and oil or gas leaking on the way back up. Images of flammable tap water in the documentary film *Gasland* put fracking firmly into the national consciousness, and the

Hollywood film *Promised Land* used Matt Damon's trusted visage to cement it there, seeing the star in the role of a naive tool of the oil industry, hoodwinking a rural community into signing up for its own destruction.

By 2013, the use of this technique to gain access to reserves of gas and oil that were previously too difficult to get out of the ground had reached California, and politicians were under pressure from environmentalists to regulate or ban the practice. A bill made its way through the legislature to place a moratorium on fracking while the state conducted an extensive environmental analysis on the process. Some green groups wanted a full ban while others accepted it as better than nothing. As expected, oil and gas interests fought it. But so did Brown's own Department of Finance analysts, contending that even a temporary moratorium could cost the state jobs and revenue.

The bill's author amended it, giving up on a moratorium in favor of regulations requiring oil and gas companies to obtain permits, notify nearby property owners of fracking activity, conduct groundwater testing, and reveal the chemicals being used. Four major environmental groups withdrew support for the bill, which passed and was signed by Brown on September 20, 2013, with implementation set for 2015.[29] However imperfect, the regulations were considered the strictest in the nation governing fracking. Characteristically, they were followed by similar federal regulations announced by President Obama in March 2015, and Republicans began their fight to overturn them.[30]

Brown's stance was disconcerting and confusing to environmentalists who had consistently been in his corner due to his stewardship of the environment. But his past reputation was not enough to protect him from the fury of greens on this issue. Protesters began dogging his public appearances. "It's a growing grassroots movement across the state," Rose Braz, of the Center for Biological Diversity, told the *Sacramento Bee* at one of these events. "It's not going to go away. It really is not until the governor acts to halt fracking."[31]

Brown's position was taken as a betrayal. When he signed an agreement a month later with the governors of Washington and Oregon and the premier of British Columbia to reduce pollution that contributes to climate change, about fifty antifracking protesters picketed outside. In a news conference after the signing, *San Jose Mercury News* reporter Paul Rogers commented on the protesters and asked how the governor could "square your support of the fracking process in California with your statement that climate change is an existential threat to the world."[32]

Brown made reference to the legislation he signed, saying it will offer "the most comprehensive analysis of fracking to date." Then, uttering a rare incoherent sentence, perhaps a product of the underlying awkwardness, he added: "In terms of the larger fracking question—natural gas—because of that, and the lowered price, the carbon footprint of America has been reduced because of the substitution of natural gas for coal. So this is a complicated equation."[33]

This was perhaps a bit disingenuous, since the state's Monterey shale deposits, which the U.S. Energy Department initially said could yield fifteen billion barrels of oil (later revised downward significantly), contain not only oil, rather than much cleaner natural gas found in deposits being fracked elsewhere, but dirty oil, and the geology is also more challenging to exploit.

Of course, Brown was well aware that the "Texas miracle" ballyhooed by the media after the recession was largely driven by new oil and gas revenue. Could the Golden State cash in as well? His statement in the news conference made clear there are trade-offs: "You can be sure California is doing everything it can to reduce greenhouse gases and support a sustainable economy."[34]

But it may not be enough for the public; 68 percent of California voters in May 2014 supported a state senate bill calling for a moratorium on fracking until more environmental studies could be done.[35] The oil industry, however, has more clout than the voters, and it poured $1.5 million into lobbying efforts in the three months before the vote.[36] The measure failed.

Bad news for fracking enthusiasts was delivered six months after the state law's implementation when state regulators, forced by an Environmental Protection Agency demand to investigate fracking sites, halted operations at eleven injection wells that were dumping water filled with toxins and carcinogens into natural aquifers. The California State Water Resources Board confirmed to the EPA that three billion gallons of contaminated wastewater had been illegally released and that water samples taken from nearby supplies found excessive levels of arsenic and thallium, among other dangerous pollutants.

"Arsenic and thallium are extremely dangerous chemicals," said Timothy Krantz, a professor of environmental studies at the University of Redlands. "The fact that high concentrations are showing up in multiple water wells close to wastewater injection sites raises major concerns about the health and safety of nearby residents."[37]

In February 2015, Julie Cart of the *Los Angeles Times* reported that data from tests submitted by oil companies to the state in 2014 revealed the human carcinogen benzene in hundreds of wells at levels thousands of times greater than allowed by federal safety standards. On average, benzene levels in fracking wastewater, which is often injected into groundwater, were seven hundred times higher than what is considered safe, the data showed. The *Times* story made note of another critical problem: state oil and gas regulators, who have overseen the fracking industry for years, unintentionally allowed fracking companies to inject the wastewater, called "fracking flowback," into more than 170 wells bored into aquifers that contain safe drinking water, and "an additional 279 disposal wells were allowed to discharge into aquifers containing water suitable for drinking if treated."[38]

The story also faulted many operators for not complying with reporting requirements, so the threat may be even more extensive. And at least 150 other operators reported some results but either failed to test for benzene "or provided no data for benzene and a host of other dangerous contaminants."[39]

The EPA called the state's actions "shocking," while an attorney for the Center for Biological Diversity, which monitors the water-injection program, called the entire situation "a disaster." Krantz called the test readings, which he at first thought were a mistake, "just phenomenal."[40]

Californians' anxiety over harm to humans and the environment was not assuaged when the long-awaited report on fracking by the California Council on Science and Technology and Lawrence Berkeley National Laboratory was released in July 2015. In very nonscientific language, the conclusion was essentially: What we don't know can hurt us. It acknowledged that fracking requires the use of highly toxic chemicals that could be contaminating drinking water and endangering crops and wildlife, but, because of gaps in data gathered and inadequate testing by the state, the extent of any threat is not known.

The *Los Angeles Times* reported that "the risks and hazards associated with about two-thirds of the additives used in fracking are not clear, and the toxicity of more than half . . . remains 'uninvestigated, unmeasured and unknown.'"[41]

It noted that an estimated 1.7 million Angelenos live or work within one mile of an active oil or gas well, and pollutants near those sites "can present risks to human health."[42] The scientists suggested that the state should not only conduct more extensive studies of oil company activities and the chemicals being used in the fracking process but also conduct epidemiological studies of people who live or work near the sites.

Every time a well is fracked, it can take up to 150,000 gallons of fresh water out of circulation, according to the Center for Biological Diversity, not a welcome stat in a state suffering from devastating drought. And while fracking in the East generates a lot of natural gas, in California it is dirty oil, which takes more refining and produces more pollutants.[43]

However, while some estimates initially calculated California's frackable oil reserves as the biggest in the nation, extracting it would be particularly problematic because land is so expensive, and valuable crops transfer waterborne toxins to increasingly selective consumers. Moreover, fracking has been blamed for triggering earthquakes—a shaky subject in California.[44] *Bloomberg Business* reported that "the Oklahoma Geologic Survey in 2014 located 5,415 earthquakes in that state, while many more small earthquakes were left unlocated because of the sheer number of earthquakes and limited resources."[45]

In any case, the science on California's frackable reserves may render the issue moot, which would allow Brown and the Democratic-dominated legislature to sidestep the issue. In May 2014, federal energy experts revised down their estimates of how much of California's shale oil was recoverable with existing technology by a whopping 96 percent, to a modest 600 million barrels.[46] Needless to say, this also punched a giant hole in fantasies that millions of new oil-related jobs would be produced and that the United States might reduce its oil dependency.

The problem, it turns out, is geologic: Where the shale layers in other states are layered like a cake, continental plate friction and seismic activity have torqued the West Coast's shale formations into a tortuous mishmash, making it much more difficult for drillers to navigate—explaining why there has been no black-gold rush in the Central Valley, whose landowners sit on top of two-thirds of U.S. shale oil reserves.

Despite being bruised in the fracking fight, Brown remains a high-profile environmental innovator. He aggressively pursued and then touted his highly publicized visits tied to environmental cooperation agreements with other states, provinces, and countries, positioning himself and the state as global leaders in the climate change crisis.

"I believe that from the bottom up, we can make real impact and we need to join together . . . ," said Governor Brown at a speech delivered to the United Nations Climate Summit in New York on September 23, 2014. "We're signing [memorandums of understanding] with Quebec and British Columbia, with Mexico, with states in China and wherever we can find partners, because we know we have to do it all."[47] Optimistic pledges were also made with the states of Oregon and Washington to mutually back high-speed rail, zero-emission vehicles, and pricing carbon emissions. All of these deals, of course, depend on legislators and officials in each locale following through.

Yet California is such a huge market, it doesn't have to wait for others to jump in the pool; it can make big waves on its own. In September 2014, Brown and his party doubled down on the car-crazy state's pioneering history of mandating that automakers decrease pollution spewed from the cars they sell, pushing through legislation seeking to place more than 1.5 million zero-emission cars on state roads by 2025.

"He has taken this very much to heart," Brian Wynne, the president of the Electric Drive Transportation Association, a Washington-based industry group, told *Bloomberg News.* "He's doing what he sees as the right thing for his constituents and also being a leader nationwide."[48]

This was one of nineteen bills related to climate change that Brown signed into law in a single day, using both carrots and sticks to increase solar-panel installation, use of car pool lanes, and investigation of ways to decrease the release of methane, among other things.[49]

"It's real, it's here" has become a mantra for Brown, who blames climate change for an increase of disastrous drought and wildfires in the state.

The governor was able to bring this message to the world stage on July 21, 2015, when he was a keynote speaker at the Vatican's symposium on climate change. The former young Jesuit seminarian was comfortable in that venue, joining forces with a pope who shared his vision for mobilizing legions of soldiers in a worldwide battle against climate change. Pope Francis's June encyclical on the dire crisis facing the world inspired Brown, who took the occasion of the symposium to attack those who deny the science behind climate change and who oppose efforts to combat it:

> [The] opposition is well-financed, hundreds of millions of dollars going into propaganda, into falsifying the scientific record, bamboozling people of every country. Television stations, political parties, think tanks, PhDs, university personnel, they form a group of people that is attempting to put a cloud of doubt and uncertainty over the clear science.[50]

He then informed the audience of international mayors and other officials of California's efforts:

> California is now deriving 25 percent of its electricity from renewable sources and in that source we don't count nuclear or hydro. Secondly, we have the most efficient buildings, because of our building regulations, in the entire country. As a result, California citizens have saved tens of billions of dollars in energy bills. The same is true for our appliance standards, the most efficient in the country. As far as automobile pollution, we have very strict tailpipe emissions standards. And as a result and because of some changes in Washington, those standards are now adopted as the national standard of

America. And that source of pollution is going down, not fast enough but steadily. We also have 40 percent of the electric cars in the United States.

But we're not stopping there. . . . My commitment is to increase the renewable portfolio to 50 percent of the electricity consumed . . . [and] reduce petroleum in cars and trucks by 50 percent in the next fifteen years. That's quite a challenge, but it can be done. The California economy has steadily reduced its greenhouse gas emissions, particularly on a per capita basis, but its economy is growing over the last decade faster than the economy of the United States as a whole. . . . We have to get on the side of nature and not abuse it or go against it.[51]

New York mayor Bill de Blasio followed Brown to the microphone and thanked the governor for being "the leading voice in the nation" on climate change. De Blasio then said he would follow the efforts of California, the most ambitious in the nation, to cut greenhouse gas emissions 40 percent by 2030.[52]

In his 2015 inaugural address, Brown identified additional goals, including doubling the efficiency of buildings, making cleaning fuels cleaner, and reducing "the relentless release of methane, black carbon, and other potent pollutants across industries. And we must manage farm and rangelands, forests and wetlands so they can store carbon."[53]

Beyond being a global economic leader, the onus is doubly on California to show leadership in this area. With its innovative and forward-thinking legislation and its reputation as the home of "tree-huggers" and "recycling Nazis," the state's liberal political leaders, prodded by activists, keep churning out cutting-edge regulatory laws and policies, though never without critics, whose motives often are profit-driven.

For example, in 2014 Brown signed into law a statewide ban on one-time-use plastic bags for all grocery stores, pharmacies, convenience stores, and liquor stores. Proponents cheered the move as a way to mitigate the environmental hazard caused when the bags, which take years to break down, ended up in waterways and landfills. But the law was put on hold when opponents, primarily from the plastics industry and bag manufacturers, gathered enough signatures to place a referendum on the November 2016 ballot.

While the ban on plastic bags was an example of what conservatives bemoan as meddling, the slew of green laws also made liberal use of incentives designed to encourage the development of green practices on the micro level. One law, for example, sought to increase the pace of homeowners installing rooftop solar by limiting fees cities and counties could charge for construction permits. Another encouraged the use of biomethane—burnable methane gas produced by microbes digesting organic matter—while the extension of the Self-Generation Incentive Program authorized $415 million over five years for rebates to behind-the-meter production of energy through fuel cells, wind, and other alternatives to fossil fuels.

The state's pioneering emissions-trading program, or cap and trade, has been in slow but steady development since it was signed into law by Arnold Schwarzenegger in 2006 and is potentially one of the most important programs in California history. It is not without criticism, however, and it is being hammered by several environmental groups—and Pope Francis—for not being tough enough and allowing polluters to pay in order to continue polluting.

The law, if it works and becomes a model for other states and nations, is groundbreaking. It ambitiously seeks to help the state drastically reduce greenhouse gas emissions to 40 percent below 1990 levels by 2030, mandated by executive order—the most ambitious goal in North America—and 80 percent below 1990 levels by 2050.

The program, the first comprehensive cap-and-trade system in the country, is complicated but essentially puts a price on emissions that contribute to climate change. Rolling out to various sectors of the economy each year since 2012, the law protects the environment and the population's health by forcing sources that create emissions to obtain emission allowances, or permits, through distribution by the state or through an auction system, up to the emission cap that has been set.

A source that pollutes more than the cap would have to buy permits from another source that has maintained emissions below the cap, thus establishing a financial incentive to pursue efficiency and emission reductions. The details are complex, and the state Air Resources Board is in constant negotiation with the major businesses affected—such as refineries, utilities, manufacturers, food processors, and gasoline wholesalers—which collectively emit more than twenty-five thousand tons of carbon dioxide a year.

On New Year's Day 2014, the Canadian province of Quebec became part of the auction process, and in 2015 the program added California's fuel-distribution and transportation sector. California's cap-and-trade program is second in size only to that of the entire European Union, according to state officials.

"California and Quebec have raised more than $1.5 billion recently in carbon market auctions," reported Mike De Souza for *InsideClimate News* on June 12, 2014. All but $56 million of this is in California. "Analysis by [University of Ottawa think tank] Sustainable Prosperity says California could raise about $7.7 billion by 2020 through the auction."[54]

None of this impresses Pope Francis, who is unsparing in his criticism of cap and trade: "The strategy of buying and selling 'carbon credits' can lead to a new form of speculation which would not help reduce the emission of polluting gases worldwide. This system seems to provide a quick and easy solution under the guise of a certain commitment to the environment. But in no way does it allow for the radical change which present circumstances require. Rather, it may simply become a ploy which permits maintaining the excessive consumption of some countries and sectors."[55]

Others are also displeased with cap and trade. A 2014 California Chamber of Commerce analysis argued the auction process "amounts to a multibillion dollar tax on carbon that would push jobs into other jurisdictions without real reductions in greenhouse gases."[56] Yet, as with the gold miners exploiting land they controlled to the misery of those downstream, cap and trade is based on the idea that the common good requires that destructive activities be penalized rather than on the pretense that the only true rights are those of free trade and private property.

California, with its pursuit of hydrogen-fueled and electric cars, international cap-and-trade markets, and strict air pollution regulation, is set apart from the nation. It may not be doing enough—it assuredly is not—yet it clearly is doing more and trying more new approaches than any other state.

In Texas, Kansas, and many other states in the thrall of neoliberal or libertarian cant, "regulation" is seen as an extremely dirty word. Just consider the organized Republican officials' opposition to the federal Clean Power Plan announced by President Obama in August 2015. Yet for those hoping to leave a planet to our children that is not completely ravaged, smart carrot-and-stick laws that can incentivize green behavior and discourage environmental damage is likely the best way forward.

California has continued to move in that direction, passing legislation to protect groundwater supplies from toxins and addressing previously ignored pollutants such as plastic microbeads (used in cosmetics) and black carbon (linked to regional climate change). The Sierra Club, so critical of Brown the year before, gave him an A plus at the end of 2014.

"Political scientists say that elected officials who are in their last term of office are more likely to vote their conscience, and that typically means they vote more with the public interest than industry interest . . . ," the club's report stated. "In January, he will be entering the last four years of one of the most interesting political careers in California history, if not U.S. history. We think he deserves the benefit of the doubt given his latest score. We hope for more hundred-percent scores in the next four years, including on bills that challenge carbon-producing industries."[57]

For his years of leadership on the issues of global warming and climate change and for making the state a role model for a healthier future for the nation, Brown deserves all the accolades he receives. He has earned the right to call out the "troglodytes," as he has referred to climate-change deniers such as the Republican senator Ted Cruz, of Texas. This man contends that government researchers are falsifying data and "cooking the books . . . actually adjusting the numbers. . . . I'm saying that data and facts don't support [climate change]."[58]

Cruz chooses to stick not to science but to a simpleton's view that there is no global warming because "I just came back from New Hampshire and there is snow and ice everywhere."[59] As pointed out by *Time* reporter Philip Elliott: "Science . . . does not back up Cruz's position. Geochemist James Lawrence Powell, an adviser to Ronald Reagan and George H. W. Bush, reviewed peer-reviewed science journals and found that only two articles rejected climate change during 2013. His sample size: 10,885 articles."[60]

Jerry Brown doesn't suffer fools, and he did not hold back when he heard Cruz make a similar comment on the eve of Cruz's announcement for the 2016 Republican presidential race: "That man betokens such a level of ignorance and a direct falsification of the existing scientific data," Brown said on *Meet the Press.* "It's shocking and I think that man has rendered himself absolutely unfit to be running for office."[61] It is worth noting here that with the singular exception of Senator Lindsey Graham, the sixteen Republicans in the field of the early 2016 primary campaign didn't believe the warnings of 97 percent of climate scientists on the issue, flat out deny it is taking place, or oppose efforts to combat it.

A *Los Angeles Times* story about President Obama introducing the EPA's Clean Power Plan captured the reality of California's leadership on the subject of climate change in its opening paragraph: "President Obama's plan to cut pollution from power plants over the next 15 years will force states to address climate change by pushing them to act more like California."[62]

The federal plan is not as strict or ambitious as the Golden State's, and opposition comes from across the spectrum—some environmental groups, conservative Republican governors, and states that rely most heavily on coal-fired plants to generate electricity. Nationwide, 39 percent of electricity generated in 2014 came from coal; in contrast, in California in 2013, the latest year this information was available, 8 percent of electricity was generated by coal-fired plants and 19 percent came from renewable sources.[63]

In making his announcement, Obama harkened back to his days as a student at Occidental College in Los Angeles from 1979 to 1981, when people were advised to stay indoors during smog alerts. The Twitter crowd questioned whether it was true. It is. In 1979, the year Obama moved to Los Angeles, the *Los Angeles Times* published a story that began: "Eye-searing, throat-burning smog smothered the Los Angeles area in a bourbon-colored blanket . . . sending scores of persons to hospitals with respiratory trouble and forcing school children to stay indoors, out of the noxious air."[64] The city was in the midst of a stage 2 smog alert.

I was a California kid, growing up in the coastal city of San Diego before moving north to attend UCLA, and that's when I first noticed that I could see the air. (It's where I first heard this joke: "Knock, knock." "Who's there?" "UCLA." "UCLA who?" "UCLA when the smog goes away.") The area is often referred to as the "Los Angeles basin" because of its valleys and mountains, and it is that geography that traps the pollution. It wasn't bad in the beach city where I lived, where the ocean breezes kept the smog inland and the air clean and fresh, but as I drove inland into downtown, where I worked at the *Los Angeles Times*, I was struck by the brown haze I could see ahead of me. To escape the daily two-hour, traffic-jammed commute, I moved in 1978 to a downtown high-rise.

It was extremely disconcerting that looking out from my unit on the twenty-eighth floor, I could see a thick brown blanket of yuck hovering over the city, the tops of the tallest buildings puncturing the thick smog. Over the years, enforcement of strict emission controls and other pollution-control laws have had an effect. I look out the same window today and, on many days, can see for miles across a landscape that in the heart of winter reveals snow-capped mountains in the distance; in the 1970s, there were many days when the mountains were not visible at all. Today that still happens, but with less frequency.

Los Angeles last had a stage 1 smog alert—advising everyone to avoid strenuous outdoor activities—in 2003, the first since 1998.[65] It has had no stage 2 alerts—advising everyone to remain indoors—since 1988. The worst case, a stage 3 alert, when a general holiday is declared (schools and commercial and industrial establishments must close, and drivers would have to exit the highways) last occurred in 1974.[66]

There is no respite, however; vehicles produce 50 percent of air pollution in California, according to the Air Resources Board, and, although cars have been getting cleaner, commute times and traffic have been getting worse. The American Lung Association ranks pollution in the Los Angeles region among the worst in the United States for ozone and particle pollution, while six other California cities, all in the Central Valley, also routinely appear in the top ten worst American regions for air quality.[67] Continued diligence is required, and the battles against pollution and climate change—while there may be some disagreement on tactics—are ones Californians support.

That is one reason Brown was so angry when a key part of his climate change agenda collapsed at the end of the 2015 legislative session. It was a highly unusual and painful defeat for Brown at the hands of oil companies. The industry lobbying group Western States Petroleum Association heavily lobbied Republicans and moderate Democrats to force an amendment deleting a goal to cut petroleum in gasoline 50 percent by 2030 in Brown's climate change bill. The group spent hundreds of thousands of dollars alone on television ads against the measure.[68]

After the stinging defeat, Brown was motivated to ratchet up his criticism of the energy industry to uncharacteristic volume: "Oil has won the skirmish," he said of the defeat. "But they've lost the bigger battle, because I'm more determined than ever to make our regulatory regime work for the people of California—cleaning up the air, reducing the petroleum and creating the green jobs that are going to put hundreds of thousands of people to work." His anger was tinged with a characteristic rhetorical flourish when he added that his "zeal has been intensified to a maximum degree."[69]

A month later, Brown proceeded to sign into law what remained in the bill, new standards requiring the state to generate half its electricity from renewable sources such as wind and solar by 2030 and double efficiency in factories, offices, and homes.

I n the end, some environmentalists believe that California can make the governor's goal of 50 percent less fuel consumption. His efforts will be helped in the years ahead both by federal standards for fuel economy[70] and by state mandates for carbon reduction that require oil companies to blend their fuels with biofuels (dating from the administrations of Gray Davis and Arnold Schwarzenegger).[71]

Propelled by Brown's intensified zeal, this could get California to the 50 percent goal he desired.

8

Crime and Punishment

As with issues such as the environment and immigration, Californians in recent decades have reconsidered the overall direction of the state regarding its policies on criminal justice. For several years, Californians went through a costly "tough on crime" phase that led to the biggest and most costly prison buildup the world has ever seen.[1] This resulted not only in a skewed disposition of justice and federal sanctions for prison overcrowding but also, over time, in a deeper examination by voters of what these laws they once supported had wrought. As a result, in two recent elections, they rejected overstrict laws they earlier had passed, partly for humanitarian reasons and partly because the crimes did not merit the mandatory punishment meted out.

The 1994 "three strikes" law, for example, enacted in response to the murder of twelve-year-old Polly Klaas in Northern California by a career criminal, required a mandatory prison term of twenty-five years to life for anyone convicted of a third felony. This made more sense when the third felony was violent. But in one case a man was sentenced to twenty-five years to life because his third strike was stealing a slice of pizza from some kids on the Redondo Beach Pier in Los Angeles County.[2] Another was sentenced to fifty years in prison for shoplifting a couple of videotapes, a charge that was elevated from a misdemeanor to a felony because he had two previous felony burglary convictions. Even some prosecutors and judges voiced opposition to the mandatory sentences in which judges had no discretion.

Voters in 2012 passed Proposition 36, which modified the 1994 law so that life sentences could be imposed only if the third-strike felony was "serious or violent." It also allowed for resentencing of inmates then serving life sentences if their third felony had not been serious or violent and if a judge determined they were not a threat to society. This permitted roughly three thousand felons serving life sentences to petition for a reduced sentence, which would result in an estimated savings to the state of $150 million to $200 million annually.[3]

The following year, Brown, under pressure from a federal court order to diminish the inhumanely crowded prison population, signed a bill into law that mandated "realignment" of how prisoners in the state were housed, pushing those with less horrific rap sheets down from the costly higher-security state prisons to less expensive jails in their county of origin, along with state funds to cover the county's costs.

Then, in 2014, with the overwhelming (59 percent) passage of a citizens' initiative, Proposition 47, the prosaically titled Reduced Penalties for Some Crimes Initiative, voters took it upon themselves to continue to liberalize treatment of criminals and decrease prison overcrowding by turning certain felonies into misdemeanors. Brown, who has consistently had a tough-on-crime stance, had earlier vetoed a similar measure saying reform should be part of a comprehensive justice-system overhaul.

Brown had said in our interview in February 2013 that he wanted to focus on the "justice" issue in his final term, and he is doing that.[4] In his January 5, 2015, inauguration speech he showed signs of softening his hard position. He gave a detailed history of the growth of the prison system and reaffirmed this emphasis on reform, noting that the voters passed multiple criminal justice reforms through the initiative process.

"All these changes attempt to find less expensive, more compassionate and more effective ways to deal with crime. This is work that is as profoundly important as it is difficult, yet we must never cease in our efforts to assure liberty and justice for all," Brown said. "The task is complicated by our diversity and our divisions and, yes, by shocking disparities."[5]

Nine months later, he vetoed eleven crime-related bills, writing a message to accompany nine of the bills he rejected, noting "each of these bills creates a new crime—usually by finding a novel way to characterize and criminalize conduct that is already proscribed. The multiplication and particularization of criminal behavior creates increasing complexity without commensurate benefit."[6]

He reminded people of the past penchant for excessive penalties: "Over the last several decades, California's criminal code has grown to more than 5,000 separate provisions, covering almost every conceivable form of human misbehavior. During the same period, our jail and prison populations have exploded. Before we keep going down this road, I think we should pause and reflect on how our system of criminal justice could be made more human, more just, and more cost effective."[7]

That's exactly what the voters had in mind when they enacted Proposition 47. Within a few months, the changes were evident: hundreds of prisoners had been released, while those who remained were serving out more of their sentences, no longer released early for the state to comply with court-mandated overcrowding rules. "For decades, Los Angeles County jail inmates divided their sentences by five, ten or twenty to calculate the time they would actually spend behind bars," reported the *Los Angeles Times*. "Because of overcrowding, they left after completing as little as 5 percent of their sentences. Now, as Proposition 47 begins to reshape the California criminal justice system, they are serving much more of their time."[8]

For Brown and his generation of Californians, the state seemed to be coming full circle. As Allen Hopper, criminal justice and drug policy director for the American Civil Liberties Union of California (ACLU), told the *Sacramento Bee,* "There's a shift in the national consciousness. I think that 'smart on crime' sort of captures the mood of the nation now."[9]

Once upon a time, and for much of the last century, California's punishment system was based on indeterminate sentencing, a concept that was born out of optimism that prison could be a place of rehabilitation. But it became a weapon used against those groups society already oppressed. When a convicted Californian had been given a sentence of ten to twenty years, it gave the system an opportunity to reward transformation and good behavior while doing time. Some sentences were even much broader, such as "five years to life," which gave parole boards enormous discretion to determine the consequences for a particular crime.

Such open-ended sentences were born from early-twentieth-century progressive beliefs in the capability of scientific-based bureaucratic structures to solve societal ills. Those ills proved resilient, however, and old human foibles such as racism found ways to exert control over the levers of supposedly blind justice. Specifically, it was noticed by civil rights advocates that judges and parole boards, whose members tended to be Anglo, wealthy, and well connected, reflected the dominant group's biases against minorities, immigrants, and poor people, and there were not enough checks and balances against their power. This is not unique to California, of course.

It is a tragic irony, however, that this push for clearer boundaries around sentencing to protect convicts from overimprisonment would, when conflated with the war on drugs, actually contribute to a massive escalation in the percentage of poor and minority (mostly African American) men and women locked up. Frightened suburbanites whipped into a frenzy of fear by news and entertainment media coverage of drug use, as well as rising gang violence and other urban crime in the 1970s, gave opportunistic California politicians a way to kill the proverbial two birds with one stone: enact mandatory sentencing laws to make the system seem both fairer and tougher at the same time.

In 1976, in an effort to decrease disparities in sentencing, Brown in his first term signed a watershed determinate-sentencing law that proscribed fixed terms for most crimes, giving judges no discretion in sentencing. Two years later, he signed another one that mandated paroled prisoners must be supervised for three years after prison, two years longer than before. Soon, the state began changing policies so that it became increasingly difficult for parolees to stay out of trouble, with even minor infractions of behavior leading to a return to prison to complete the maximum sentence. By the end of the century, nearly 70 percent of parolees were sent back for further imprisonment for violations.

Deindustrialization and the loss of good working-class jobs, the crack cocaine and methamphetamine epidemics, many new laws recriminalizing most drugs, and—perhaps most important—the passage of a series of bond measures to build new prisons across the Central Valley resulted in the skyrocketing of the state's convict population over the next three decades: 500 percent from 1982 to 2000. From 1984 to 2005, the state completed twenty-four new prisons at a cost of $280 million to $350 million each, while the state budget for corrections grew to nearly 8 percent of general fund expenditures, roughly the same as what the state spent on public higher education.[10]

One strange aspect of this unprecedented expansion of the state's prison system, detailed by City University of New York professor Ruth Wilson Gilmore in her investigation of the subject, *Golden Gulag: Prisons, Surplus, Crisis, and Opposition in Globalizing California* was that the major surge in both the number of convicts sentenced to prison terms and the building of a new gulag "archipelago of concrete and steel cages"[11] to house them happened *after* crime rates began to decline. Per capita murder and forcible rape numbers, for example, both peaked in 1980, beginning an erratic decline that continues to this day. Illegal drug use, too, began to decrease even earlier, in the mid-1970s.

Of determinate sentencing, Brown at the time boasted, "It is the most far-reaching criminal-justice reform in the last fifty years."[12] He later admitted, however, that in hindsight it was a disaster. In 2003, according to the *Los Angeles Times*, Brown, then mayor of Oakland, called it an "abysmal failure" and described California's prisons as "postgraduate schools of crime."[13]

Not only had the determinate sentences mandated by the new laws proved longer than their indeterminate predecessors, but structural discrimination actually appeared to have grown worse. Beyond the now infamous discrepancy between sentencing for possession or sale of powder cocaine (favored by the wealthy) versus rock cocaine (the cheap high of the urban poor), many of the new tougher laws tended to lead to convictions based as much on who "the criminal" was and where he or she lived as on what harm was done.

In her academic examination of the root causes of the resulting prison boom, Gilmore sleuthed out a number of reasons why the prison population kept growing even as the crime rate was falling. She uses economic data and political history to show that building prisons was structurally convenient rather than historically inevitable and had very little to do with punishment or crime prevention.

Gilmore is careful to note that she sees no signs of a conspiracy, simply a systemic reaction to certain complex and difficult realities. After the energy crisis and recessions of the early '70s and a decline in defense spending, many jobs permanently evaporated, and there was a surplus of low-skilled workers. A political shift rightward, illustrated by Prop 13 and the vilification of "welfare queens" (perceived to be women of color, though the majority of people on welfare were white children), meant the state was no longer authorized to build capacity for a social safety net. Depressed land values in the rural and agricultural regions of the state, where farm mechanization was simultaneously drastically reducing job opportunities, made those communities and their political representatives desperate for government investment, and financiers saw a huge opportunity to profit off California bond measures.

Panicked by the chaotic social upheavals of the '60s and '70s, voters approved a series of massive bond measures to turn the California Department of Corrections (CDC) from a bureaucratic backwater to one of the most powerful institutions in the state, and its prison guards' union into one of the most influential.

Gilmore writes that depressed towns throughout the middle of the state were receiving visits from the CDC with promises that new prisons would bring prosperity in jobs and increased housing equity. Some locals did benefit, particularly the largest agribusiness interests that were able to leverage their political clout to sell their worst farmland to the CDC at vastly inflated prices.

Clear losers, however, were the urban communities—mostly African American—that were sending many offenders to this far-flung collection of particularly restrictive gated communities. Where the philosophical basis for the state's prison system had once been rehabilitation and punishment, it was now admitted to be a giant experimentation in incapacitation; the hope was that if all the "bad guys" were locked up, even those who are not violent or sociopaths, the streets would be safer. As we can see now, looking at the cold data, this is a tragic case of false logic: the urban communities steadily lost thousands of their young men to prison and became more violent, depressed, and dysfunctional.

I n an era when California had decided to end the affirmative action policy governing admission to public universities, the disproportionate imprisonment of impoverished minorities from hopeless neighborhoods eventually became awkward for a state that still likes to think of itself as optimistic and progressive. Critics described it as the "prison industrial complex," an echo of the military-industrial complex against which President Dwight Eisenhower warned the American people in his farewell speech.

Prison also became the boardroom for the state's criminal empires, run by transnational gangs inside and outside the gates. Also empowered were the guards, whose union became over time one of the most powerful political forces in the state, able to negotiate, with the complicity of political leaders, lucrative salaries and an overly generous pension plan that threatens the fiscal stability of the state down the road.

In interviews with former political leaders of the state, Governor Gray Davis's 34 percent raise for prison guards, granted when he became governor in 1999, and the sweet pension deal they received from him and the Democratic-majority legislature were brought up as contributing factors to out-of-control pension costs. Over the years, the California Correctional Peace Officers Association has donated millions of dollars to legislators and governors. Davis received more than $3 million from the union for his campaigns, including $250,000 within weeks of the pay increase's negotiation, according to *Bloomberg*.[14] Prison guards can retire after thirty years of service and receive a pension equal to 90 percent of their last year's salary.

The former assembly speaker Willie Brown recalled in an interview how devastating that turned out to be: "None of us [in the legislature], not till 2000, did we start paying attention to the pension funds. And then Gray Davis, in the late nineties when he was governor, really enhanced with the legislative approval, the pension benefits, not understanding how incredibly horrible financially that could ultimately be."[15]

Meanwhile, no matter how fast the prisons were built, they were still overcrowded and dangerous—even crumbling, nineteenth-century anachronisms like Folsom and San Quentin had perennially dodged planned closures—sparking a string of successful constitutional lawsuits against the state for cruel and unusual punishment.

Finally, a drumbeat of scandals involving the treatment of prisoners, including accusations that guards staged fights so they could shoot inmates and that female prisoners were manipulated into being sterilized, made Californians queasy. In 2011, and again in 2013, massive hunger strikes by prisoners demanding an end to widespread and open-ended use of solitary confinement—one inmate was sentenced to solitary in a small cement cell for forty-three years—called more unwelcome attention to what Amnesty International described as "an affront to human rights."[16]

The 2013 protest, with approximately thirty thousand inmates statewide participating in the early stages, was the largest hunger strike in state history.[17] While most began eating food after a week or two, forty continued on for nearly two months. Given a promise that the state legislature would hold hearings on the use of solitary confinement, the strike ended, but not before it brought worldwide attention to the inmates' cause.

One high-profile observer who took notice was President Obama, who, in a July 2015 speech to the NAACP, called for an overhaul of the criminal justice system and ordered the Justice Department to review the practice of solitary confinement, noting: "Do we really think it makes sense to lock so many people alone in tiny cells for twenty-three hours a day, sometimes for months or even years at a time? That is not going to make us safer. That's not going to make us stronger. And if those individuals are ultimately released, how are they ever going to adapt? It's not smart."[18]

The following month, a California inmate's lawsuit, *Ashker v. Brown*, filed in 2012 and approved for class-action status two years later, was settled in a landmark action by the state Department of Corrections and Rehabilitation and the Center for Constitutional Rights. It ended confinement of inmates in solitary for more than ten years except for individuals who cannot be moved, to protect their safety. It also ended indeterminate sentences in solitary and the practice of putting inmates into solitary just because of their alleged gang affiliation. About two thousand inmates were released into the general prison population as a result. The settlement was a national media story, and officials in more than a dozen states are rethinking solitary confinement in their prison systems.[19]

In California, a spotlight was focused on the state justice system when Democrats in 2012 returned to supermajority power in Sacramento and faced a considerable and complex criminal-justice crisis. With the recession-bred education budget shortfalls highlighting how much taxpayers were spending to keep so many locked up, as well as federal judges hounding the state over overcrowding, a re-examination of priorities seemed in order. However, the combined internal and external lobbying power of the state Department of Corrections and the prison guards' union was a strong incentive to stay the course.

Brown sought to challenge the competing narratives with a disruption he opined was the "boldest move in criminal justice in decades."[20] Diverting thousands of convicts from state prisons into county jails and probation departments, termed "realignment," would be an "encouraging and stimulating" challenge for sheriffs who would then find "creative alternatives" to overcrowding and recidivism by "evolving" the use of day-treatment centers, counseling, education, and job training as alternatives to jail.

At first, the effects were dramatic. The number of prisoners in state-run facilities dropped by nearly thirty thousand, or close to 20 percent. The state's bean counters calculated that this shift would reduce prison spending by $1.4 billion and that about two-thirds of that would be passed on to counties.

"The prison emergency is over in California," Brown crowed in January 2013,[21] asking a three-judge panel from the Ninth Circuit Court of Appeals to lift its standing 2009 mandate to decrease the state inmate population, then 162,000, to 110,000 (137.5 percent of capacity) because he claimed its demands would be met by that June. The order, affirmed by the U.S. Supreme Court in 2011 after an unsuccessful appeal by Brown, was imposed because the state was not able to provide adequate medical and mental health treatment for inmates.

Fifteen months after the rollout of realignment, the situation—still early, to be sure—was not as rosy as was hoped. "The numbers tell a different story," reported the *Los Angeles Times* in a review of the effects of the new policy: "Today, California is spending nearly $2 billion a year more on incarceration than when Brown introduced his strategy in 2011. The prisons are still overcrowded, and the state has been forced to release inmates early to satisfy federal judges overseeing the system."[22]

Jails—primarily designed to hold people awaiting trial or convicted of minor crimes meriting a sentence of no more than a year—are being expanded to confine and rehabilitate inmates serving decades-long sentences. Brown's response to critiques was to take the long view. "Sometimes we get a problem," he said, and "the solution makes things better than what we had before."[23] It was Brown at his Zeniest.

Finally, the respected Public Policy Institute of California in September 2015 pronounced the realignment program "largely successful"[24] thanks to several factors. Along with the passage of Proposition 47 and the release of nonviolent inmates into the community, the prison population finally met the federal government's target number of inmates, although there was still a big price tag—$10.1 billion for the 2015–16 fiscal year, compared with $9.65 billion spent in 2010–11; the study attributed the higher spending to increased costs for inmates' medical and mental health care, the lack of which was the impetus for the court order. Another $1 billion or so, partly generated from the Proposition 30 tax increase initiative, is paid by the state to local governments to reimburse them for their additional incarcerated populations.

The counties' increase in incarcerations was a net gain for those who believe California has drastically overincarcerated offenders who committed minor crimes, since overwhelmed jails were forced to release thousands of nonviolent inmates early. Twice as many inmates as those earning early-release in the past were freed before doing half their time, according to the

Los Angeles Times investigation, and some counties were even refusing to accept parole violators back into their jails.[25]

"On any given day, Los Angeles County has 4,300 offenders walking the streets who would be in jail if there were room,"[26] Terri McDonald, the assistant sheriff overseeing the jail system, told the *Los Angeles Times* ominously. Unnoted was that in previous eras, before harsher determinate sentencing, most of these men and women would have been out on parole in the first place.

In a way, Brown was proving he had learned a painful lesson back at the advent of the Proposition 13 era: If you make it too easy for citizens not to feel the downsides of their political decisions, they would have no impetus to correct them. Whether or not it will work, realignment has forced localities to wrestle with the sheer volume of prisoners their own police and prosecutors have culled mostly from their most damaged communities.

To keep the prisons from filling back up, however, will take changes outside their walls, whether legal, social, or economic. The timely and overwhelming passage of Proposition 47 in November 2014 may have been one such step. The initiative, backed by such odd bedfellows as the ACLU, Jay Z, and Newt Gingrich, made nearly five thousand convicts eligible for immediate release by changing a number of nonviolent drug and property-crime felonies to misdemeanors. It also specified that certain crimes that had been "wobblers," potentially charged as either felonies or misdemeanors, could now only be charged as the lesser.

In so doing, exactly two decades after passing what would stand as the second (Washington State was first by a few months) and most draconian three-strikes law in the country, setting off a national wave of copycat statutes, California was again a pioneer, this time embracing a new leniency.

"It's the first time that criminal justice reform of this nature has been endorsed by public referendum," Will Matthews of the ACLU told *Al Jazeera America*. Voters, he said, were realizing that "simply locking up as many people as we can is not the smartest or most fiscally prudent way of approaching crime and punishment."[27]

Gingrich noted in a *Los Angeles Times* op-ed shortly before the election that California spends $62,396 per prisoner annually and only $9,200 per K–12 student, while the average salary for a new teacher is just under $42,000.[28] He also noted that in thirty-three years, the state built twenty-two prisons and only one additional public university.

While the full consequences of the more moderate approach to charging as misdemeanors such crimes as shoplifting, minor drug possession, and writing bad checks are not yet known, the nonpartisan Legislative Analyst's Office estimated that Proposition 47 could save the state "potentially in the high hundreds of millions of dollars annually" that could be spent by a new Safe Neighborhoods and Schools Fund, "on school truancy and dropout prevention (25 percent), mental health and substance abuse treatment (65 percent), and victim services (10 percent)."[29]

Proposition 47 was not a hot news story, like many of California's controversial initiatives have been, and it appeared in an election year notable for widespread disinterest. Nor were the changes it has made to the state's criminal code extreme; it is telling that the powerful prison guards' union did not help fund 47's outspent opposition. Yet those who have been denouncing the drug war for decades hope the initiative heralds a sea change in attitudes toward crime prevention.

Brown is one of those whose attitude changed. In 2016, he worked to qualify for the November ballot a measure that would make it easier for nonviolent prisoners to obtain parole. Speaking to an audience of crime victims, he criticized himself for signing the 1976 determinate sentencing law, noting, "You create a problem, you figure out how to solve it."[29]

For states and the District of Columbia in the 2014 election cycle legalized or decriminalized marijuana use, while in 2015, Oregon established a 25 percent sales tax on cannabis sales, Texas legalized cannabis oil, and California enacted four medical marijuana-related measures. One targets growers who damage the environment by dumping chemicals and wastewater, removing trees, or killing wild animals, and three establish licensing and operating rules for growers, retail medical marijuana outlets, and manufacturers of cannabis-related products.

While many in California believe the plant, a profitable crop that is the backbone of the economy in many California rural counties, is already quasi-legal, it is not. Although if you are middle or upper class, or white, you could be forgiven for this misunderstanding, since the law is so inequitably enforced.

According to the state attorney general, in 2013 there were nearly 14,000 felony marijuana arrests, more than half of which involved African American (18 percent) or Hispanic (39 percent) suspects. Another more than 6,500 misdemeanor marijuana arrests were made. For comparison, African Americans were arrested for marijuana crimes at nearly three times their percentage of representation in the state (6.6 percent), a pattern that echoes national statistics that show while African Americans compose only 14 percent of regular drug users, they are 37 percent of those arrested for drug offenses. On the other hand, felony marijuana arrests have come way down since 1973, when there were more than 100,000 arrests, according to California NORML, a marijuana advocacy group.

A citizen-drafted initiative to legalize marijuana for adults is headed for the 2016 ballot in California. It would tax and regulate cannabis like alcohol. Kamala Harris, the state attorney general running for Barbara Boxer's seat in the U.S. Senate in the 2016 election, said in an interview with *BuzzFeed News* that she is "not opposed" to California's legalizing marijuana. "I think there's a certain inevitability about it.[30] A Public Policy Institute of California survey in March 2014 revealed that 53 percent of likely voters favor legalization.[31]

Lieutenant Governor Gavin Newsom was more aggressive, offering to campaign for a legalization initiative for the 2016 ballot if it was the "right initiative," addressing age limits, advertising, and other issues.[32] While neither Harris nor Brown seem eager to take even that cautious step, it is hard to imagine who will fight hard to defeat such a measure in the current political climate other than illegal growers and dealers themselves, many of them with connections to transnational gangs run from prison. These folks risk losing profits if they face legal and open competition.

As the left-leaning economics magazine *Dollars and Sense* described it in 2012, the economic stakes are sizable:

The trade journal *Medical Marijuana Business Daily* currently estimates that a fully legalized cannabis market [nationally] could be as large as $46 billion per year, while more conservative observers peg it at anywhere between $10 billion and $40 billion.

There are about 7.6 million frequent marijuana smokers in the United States, according to the 2012 National Survey on Drug Use and Health. Nearly 23.9 million Americans use the drug semi-regularly. . . .

Washington placed a 25 percent excise tax on marijuana with its new law, and Colorado voters [approved] a 15 percent excise tax and a 10 percent sales tax on recreational marijuana. These measures are expected to raise hundreds of millions of dollars in revenue for each state, including a projected $500 million for Washington alone by 2015.[33]

California's marijuana production dwarfs that of all other states, as well as other state cash crops, so the potential revenue stream is that much greater. Growers in the state produce an annual crop of top-grade marijuana estimated by scholars and government agencies to be worth anywhere from $5 billion to $15 billion at the retail level, despite decades of federal raids on grow operations (and partly because of them, since they drive up production costs and scarcity inflation). "Emerald triangle" counties Humboldt, Mendocino, and Trinity in Northern California are so dominated by the marijuana industry that law enforcement officials provide de facto authorization for many growers in an attempt to semiregulate the business.

Of course, widespread legalization could shift production to other states or countries, to the overall detriment of California's economy. Yet it seems unlikely that the combination of experience, growing conditions, and investment capital concentrated in Northern California already wouldn't allow adaptation to full legalization. This would be comparable to Silicon Valley's continued dominance of the tech sector. That could mean more money for the ever insatiable public education system, once the envy of the nation until funding plummeted along with tax revenues.

To Teach His Own

A ny discussion of California as a model for the nation inevitably raises the question: What about education; what happened to California schools? It's a fair question. Let's begin with the notion that there is nothing more important to most Californians, or to people in any state, for that matter, than the education of their children. We care about the quality of their teachers, class size, educational materials, and safety on and off campus. But higher education has a special pull. Parents wealthy enough to not have to worry about tuition costs want their children to get into the "best" universities—ones with big names or that are recognized in national rankings (academically or in sports), those that grant a degree assuring graduates a place in a prestigious professional home. For other parents, especially low-income immigrants and others who themselves do not have a college degree, their children attaining one is a ticket to a better life, a more comfortable future, realizing the American dream.

In the Golden State, in my own youth, one could earn a degree at a top-ranked public institution of higher education, be taught by renowned professors, including a number of Nobel laureates, and not have to ask his or her parents for a penny because it was tuition-free—whether a two-year community college, a state university, or a campus of the prestigious University of California. But then that world turned upside down.

To get a good perspective on where the higher education system in

California stands today, a look back at the foundation upon which it was built can be illuminating. Every state in the country has a public university system, but there is only one Berkeley. Wisconsin's gets respect, as does the 190-year-old University of Virginia, founded by Thomas Jefferson; New Jersey co-opted venerable Rutgers from a private men's college to public coed school to boost its cred, and Ann Arbor hosts the impressive University of Michigan. Yet none of them can boast the most Nobel laureates or the birthplace of the atomic age or be spoken of in hushed tones by aspirational grandmothers in rural China. Founded more than 800 years after Oxford and 232 years after Harvard, the University of California became a world-class university and the top public school in the United States in less than a hundred years, a stunning achievement. That it is simply the flagship for a massive three-tier university and college system makes credible the state's claim to being a model for public education for much of the last century. Consider that six of the top eleven public colleges and universities, as ranked by *U.S. News & World Report* in 2015, are in the UC system, with Berkeley at number 1 for the seventeenth consecutive year, UCLA (tied for number 2 with the University of Virginia), followed by UC San Diego (8), UC Davis (9), UC Santa Barbara (10), and UC Irvine (11). Throw in top private universities Stanford (number 4) and the California Institute of Technology (10) in Pasadena (Los Angeles County), and the state clearly stacks up well against New England and blows away every other region.[1]

Another very different but important index, the *New York Times*'s 2015 College Access Index, lists the "Top Colleges Doing the Most for Low-Income Students." It measures the efforts top private and public colleges make on economic diversity. The University of California campuses led the nation, with six of the top seven campuses: Irvine, Davis, Santa Barbara, San Diego, and Los Angeles; Berkeley was in seventh place after the University of Florida.[2]

The California public university model was born in the progressive movement at the beginning of the twentieth century—progressive politicians believing, perhaps naively, that an educated populace would stand up to the corporate trusts (particularly Southern Pacific) that then dominated the politics of the day. The goal was to create a clear path for young people to move up into a then small middle class. By 1920, state support for UC Berkeley was a lordly $3 million, a second campus (UCLA) had been added, and real momentum had been created.

Eventually, California's system of having a far-flung network of top-tier universities (eleven so far), more modest four-year "state" schools (twenty-three), and open-enrollment two-year community colleges (112), would be copied far and wide as a model for higher education in a modern democracy. The Democratic-majority legislature, in a bill signed by Brown in 2014, extended the system by giving a green light to fifteen community colleges to offer four-year bachelor's degrees in vocational fields, as an experiment. Brown continues to push for online courses to help alleviate the overcrowding and high costs in the state's colleges and universities.

"The campus is no longer on the hill with the aristocracy but in the valley with the people," UC Berkeley's first chancellor and later president Clark Kerr once boasted.[3]

Kerr's reign seemingly cemented UC's populist success when he oversaw the implementation of the revered California Master Plan for Higher Education in 1960 as the system faced the entry of a huge surge of baby boomers. Much of the plan involved organizing or endorsing previously established policies, yet it proved internationally influential as a clear, compelling vision. *Time* magazine put Kerr on its cover, labeling him a "master planner."[4]

The plan codified a mandate that said the University of California must offer a spot to the top 12.5 percent of the state's graduating high school seniors tuition-free, and the top third were guaranteed access to a California State University (CSU) campus, also tuition-free. Moreover, it promised that any student who succeeded at a two-year community college would be allowed to transfer directly to a state or UC campus. Best of all, for students and their families, the colleges were inexpensive. The branches of the higher education system charged fees, but tuition was banned for California residents under the Master Plan. It was firmly believed that an educated populace would benefit the state and society and that the state had an obligation to avoid imposing a financial burden on students to get that education. For tens of thousands of families, this was the promise fulfilled. When my brother was a student at a community college in San Diego in 1978, he paid $25 a semester for various fees; his charges at San Diego State University came to around $200 for the year, while the University of California fees totaled $320 when I graduated from UCLA in 1970.

As late as 1985, UC tuition and student fees combined were about $1,200 a school year. By 2015, however, that had increased to $13,456 per year, while state college tuition was $5,472, prohibitive for many families. If the tax-increase Proposition 30 had not passed, tuition and fees would have been higher.

A chart of university fees for the past century looks like the Loch Ness monster: a series of undulating dips and rises before the neck and head come rearing up in the past decade and a half. Community colleges, meanwhile, which had been almost entirely free, saw tuition and fees go up 80 percent in 2007 and 2012. One reason was clear—competition for funding—with the state prison system, discussed in detail in chapter 8, a big villain in this drama.

As journalist Andy Kroll reported in 2012: "Thirty years ago, the state accounted for nearly 70 percent of public higher education funding; today, it's 25 percent. . . . The prison system saw its state funding in dollars leap 436 percent between 1980 and 2011. Back then, spending on prisons was a mere 3 percent of California's budget; it's now 10 percent."[5]

The university system replaced much of its funding decline with increased reliance on corporate and military contracts, leverage of patents, and increased enrollment of full-freight-paying out-of-state students, and foreign students, who pay a much higher tuition. Yet, increasingly, the California students and their families are bearing the costs. With fees and tuition increasing, middle-class students—many of whom don't qualify for significant financial aid—have been especially hurt. They have had to scuttle college plans or enter community colleges instead of the four-year institutions or take out huge loans to pay for their education.

Unable to keep opening new campuses at the pace of population growth, and suffering from severe budget decreases, the university systems capped enrollment and cut costs by reducing faculty and classes offered. Not only were fewer students being admitted but often those who were admitted took longer to graduate because they could not get the classes they needed to earn their degrees. By 2013, community college enrollment dropped to a twenty-year low.

The problem facing California State University Long Beach in the fall of 2012 described by its president to *Los Angeles Times* writer Carla Rivera, perfectly illustrates what was a common scenario: [Cal State], "which typically admits 9,500 new students each fall, will admit about 6,800 for the fall of 2012. The school received about 78,000 applications, up 10% from the previous year. It will be forced to cut about 1,800 classes and will ration course loads to a maximum of 13 credit units."[6] Thus, students who were admitted would take longer to graduate and incur additional costs before they could graduate and enter the job market. And as the recession forced massive state budget cuts, Cal grant money dried up.

One young member of my family with a bachelor's degree in business decided to go into the medical field and went back to college in 2014 to complete four science classes she needed for a nursing degree. Enrollment in each class at Los Angeles Community College, all of which were oversubscribed, was selected by lottery. Fortunately she got into the classes she needed, while a colleague's daughter with the same plan for nursing school failed to get into any of the same classes, had to sit out the semester, and hope she could win a seat in the next semester's lottery.

Making it more difficult to graduate is not in the state's long-term interest. While the UCs have among the highest graduation rates of any public system in the country and CSUs and the community colleges crank out seventy-five thousand graduates with bachelor's degrees and a hundred thousand graduates with associate of arts degrees each year,[7] the state is failing to meet its economy's voracious need for educated workers. A 2015 Public Policy Institute of California survey cited a pending shortage of 1.1 million college-educated workers by 2030.[8]

The question is: What happened? Proposition 13 had much to do with it, although the first heavyweight attack came twelve years earlier, when Ronald Reagan rode into the governorship partly by attacking UC students as spoiled rabble-rousers who needed to be taught a lesson. In an ominous precursor to the tax revolt a decade later, Governor Reagan fought for, and won, cuts to what he said was a bloated public university system. He engineered the firing of President Kerr and got the university's governing Board of Regents to start charging tuition, euphemistically referred to as "fees," lest they be accused of violating the Master Plan for Education. That ballyhooed Master Plan, the country's model for a public school system, began slowly tipping, like a hull-breached ocean liner beginning to sink. Especially hard hit by an increasingly competitive and limited-access higher education system were low-income and minority students.

It would take several decades for the slow slide to turn into what felt to many like a near collapse after the Great Recession of 2008. Finally, as tax revenues plummeted and the budget crisis peaked, the precarious state of the higher education system got the state's full attention. Helping to grab the lapels and shake the body politic were the students themselves, who in 2011 began a concerted protest campaign—joined by teachers, administrators, and sympathetic Occupy activists—against the rising cost of getting an education in California. Walkouts, building occupations, and even the shutdown of a UC Regents meeting raised a clear challenge that politicians were loath to ignore, considering that these students' mostly middle-class parents were watching and that they tended to vote.

Faced with the shock of the mortgage crisis and soaring unemployment, it would not have been surprising if Californians had become more stingy, not less. Yet, even as the worst effects of the crash were working their way through the system, there were signs that Californians were tiring of all the bad news about what many still remembered as a strength. In March 2010, 60 percent of respondents told the Field Poll they thought education was among the most important issues in deciding whom to pick for governor (second highest issue, the budget deficit, selected by 68 percent).[9] And the following April, the Public Policy Institute of California reported that a "strong majority" of surveyed residents would back increased taxes on the wealthy to maintain K–12 spending.

It was against this challenging backdrop, with more cuts ahead for schools, and tentative signs of a shift in public thinking, that Brown asked Republican legislators' help to enable a basic exercise in a democracy: Join Democrats in asking voters to renew some fees that were about to expire to avert the impending funding cuts to education, K–12, and the university systems. Only three Republican votes were needed to attain the two-thirds vote for the legislature to put a fee-extension measure on the ballot. Not one Republican would break rank. So he went to the voters with a citizen initiative that became Proposition 30, on the November 2012 ballot. His proposal to bridge the huge budget crevasse, for a term of seven years, went against the grain of nearly a half century of bombastic antitax rhetoric.

Proposition 30 revenue was desperately needed not just for the higher education system but for K–12 public schools, which had suffered massive cuts over the decades since Proposition 13. Once considered one of the top education systems in the country, California's K–12 schools plummeted after Prop 13 into some of the lowest indexes for determining educational excellence in the nation. This has been humiliating for the state but especially hard on parents and their young children.

It is often easier to be compassionate in theory than in practice; humans, capable of altruism, have a powerful selfish drive. For Californians, like other Americans, this conflict is perhaps most glaring in how we collectively care for our young—especially, as education scholar Lisa Delpit once referred to them, "other people's children."[10]

Let a parent, grandparent, or even neighbor loose on his or her local school and you may see a whirlwind of selfless giving—time, money, and love. They will bake; build Halloween haunts; volunteer in classrooms; donate supplies, carpentry, gardening work, and cold, hard cash when asked, perhaps after a glass or two of wine at the annual fund-raiser. It adds up: In 2014, Berkeley High School, a diverse public school of 3,200 students, boasted more than two hundred active parent volunteers who donated hours every month, as well as an affiliated parent-founded nonprofit that raised hundreds of thousands of dollars between 2004 and 2014.

Thanks to several special city taxes and bond measures supported by one of the most liberal communities in the country—one, Measure A, was projected to generate $25 million in 2014–15 alone—the once dilapidated school now boasts multiple new classroom buildings, a new gym complex, new fields, and even a new cafeteria serving healthy meals influenced by the famous chef Alice Waters and her Edible Schoolyard project, embraced by First Lady Michelle Obama. In addition to the army of adult volunteers, the school—six years removed from the Great Recession—was blessed with a brace of support staff, including two librarians, nine counselors, and a full score of security guards ably patrolling the site's myriad exits, hallways, and courtyards.

Berkeley High School's parents and teachers admit the school is not perfect. But despite the usual drug issues and the occasional brawl, one would be hard-pressed to look at the large school and see the sort of "crisis" in American education weary citizens have been hearing about periodically since the 1970s—talk that escalated in deficit-plagued California in the wake of massive budget cuts across the state between 2010 and 2013. Berkeley's mostly middle- or upper-middle-class parents generally have positive things to say about the city's public schools (taking into account nearly half of the city's children attend private school), and even the students are surprisingly positive.

Yet, like the Indian fable of the blind men and the elephant, any analysis of the state of education depends on what part of the animal is being examined. If we move ten miles south and two years earlier to the neighboring city's biggest public high school, we find a very different picture. There, Skyline High—built in 1960 to cater to wealthy Oakland hills residents, who fled to private schools after busing and open enrollment brought the children of the poor onto campus—faced a growing set of resource limitations.

Even when factoring in the smaller student body, the contrast to Berkeley High was stark: Skyline no longer employed a librarian or *any* counselors—all were laid off after successive years of $1 million budget cuts. With most students living in low-income households, there were no significant parent donations, no functioning nonprofit, a small number of strained parent volunteers, and only five security guards for a sprawling forty-five-acre campus. No new buildings, other than an armada of aging portables, had been built in half a century, and fierce windstorms felled many of the pine trees planted at the school's founding.

There were many reasons for these contrasting situations. Some, like the predominance of working single mothers with little time to contribute to the Parent Teacher Student Association (PTSA) at Skyline, were commonplace. A parcel tax to provide more funding for the district's schools had failed after the teachers' union opposed it, one reason being that some of the money would have gone to controversial charter schools accused of "cherry-picking" the best students and drumming out the underperforming.

In 2003 the state had taken control of the district after it fell into bankruptcy, stripping authority from the locally elected school board but later returning it to local control still tens of millions of dollars in debt. Rapid gentrification, which brought in younger, wealthier residents with no or fewer children, pushed out the larger, less affluent families after the dot-com boom of the late '90s. That and the creation of new charter schools had cut the district's noncharter enrollment significantly; it would ultimately plummet by nearly nine thousand students (16 percent) between 2000 and 2008 before stabilizing.[11]

Nevertheless, local differences, no matter how inevitable, were not supposed to make providing a good education so much more difficult from one district to the next. The Supreme Court of California had said so, in a series of rulings in the 1970s known as the *Serrano* decisions, which were based on a challenge brought through the California courts alleging a school-funding system that was de facto separate but not equal.

Separate but not equal was the case for every student. When John Serrano of Los Angeles filed suit in 1968 against the state on behalf of his child, public elementary school districts in the state were spending from $407 to $2,586 per student, an amount based simply on the location of a school, since they were dependent on local funding. Factoring in private donations to these public schools, the numbers were even more skewed toward the wealthier ones, with the disparity becoming greater over time. A UCLA study in 2010 found that "low-poverty" schools collected an average of $167,797 in private funding annually, compared with $21,319 for "high-poverty" schools. In other words, private funding was eight times greater for schools that were already better off.[12]

Consider the moral issue: How are children to have equal opportunity in a democratic society if the quality of their education is tied to where their parents can afford to live? This is a question Jerry Brown would address more than forty years later.

When the *Serrano* case was filed, the underlying issue was that roughly two-thirds of school funding came from property taxes, and the more affluent a neighborhood with high residential and commercial building values, the greater amount of money was generated for local schools. Not-so-affluent towns were forced to raise taxes on their less wealthy residents.

This was noted by the California supreme court in a 1976 follow-up *Serrano* opinion: "Affluent districts can have their cake and eat it too; they can provide a high quality education for their children while paying lower taxes. Poor districts, by contrast, have no cake at all."[13]

While the patent unfairness of this system should have been corrected by the legislature, it was ultimately left to jurists: California, with its stark district-to-district disparities, they said, had failed "to meet the requirements of the equal protection clause of the Fourteenth Amendment" of the U.S. and California constitutions. Those with less money, many of them long-suffering minority groups, "are required to pay a higher tax rate than [taxpayers] in many other school districts in order to obtain for their children the same or lesser educational opportunities afforded children in those other districts." The court ordered lawmakers to decrease the disparities between school districts to no more than $100 per pupil, establishing in 1977 a six-year timetable for compliance.

But just one year later, the funding of California's public education was upended with the voters' passage of the landmark Proposition 13 of 1978, which forced a radical retooling of the state's school-funding systems, making them reliant on the state rather than local taxes. Over the years, trying to achieve equal funding was not so much about uplifting poorer schools as it was about giving wealthier schools less support. Former state Board of Education executive director John Mockler argued that the way California responded to *Serrano* was a death knell to the state's claims of educational exceptionalism: "This was like having a crippled arm and a good arm and making things equitable by crippling both arms. We defined mediocrity and then insisted on it. That was the beginning of the end for public schools."[14]

The once much-vaunted K–12 public education system in the Golden State, which had been perennially ranked in the top two or three state systems in the country in key indexes—class size, per-pupil spending, and test scores—tumbled to the bottom quartile, brushing shoulders with rural, poverty-stricken states in the rankings.

The decline had a lot to do with money. As discussed in chapter 2, the handout to local governments for education, which exceeded $1 billion, delayed Proposition 13's devastating impact on education funding. Yet the effect since then has been akin to a slow-moving landslide, infamously shifting the financial foundation of public education.

Further confusing the issue, voters in 1984 approved creation of a state lottery operation, ostensibly to generate education funds—more than $1 billion a year, today. Yet this was a bit of a snow job, since an amount equal to the revenues taken in for schools by the lottery could be redirected from the state's general funds to any other programs—for example, the rapid expansion of the state's sprawling prison system and its infrastructure, including prison-guard salaries and pensions, which realized huge increases while education suffered large cuts.

The upshot of all this push-pull activity was what *Sacramento Bee* columnist Peter Schrag in 2000 dubbed "Mississippification"[15] of California schools—the dramatic decline in the per-pupil funding for K–12 students, which resulted in the education system's precipitous fall to the level of a poor southern state, including low test scores and the hiring of teachers who were not fully certified. For example, the U.S. Census report on public education finances for 2013 showed per-pupil spending to be $9,220 in California, compared with the District of Columbia ($17,953) and New York State ($19,818). California ranks sixteenth of the fifty states and D.C. Spending in California was even lower before the passage of Proposition 30.[16]

As Jerry Brown has pointed out, urban teachers, and to some extent their rural peers, face a more challenging daily task than those in the 'burbs, including more behavior problems; less parental support; higher rates of child abuse, PTSD, and undiagnosed special needs; and fewer volunteers and support staff. All of these challenges contribute to perhaps the biggest problem of all: high teacher and administrator turnover, leading to inexperienced, demoralized faculty members or even to classes taught by a series of short-term substitutes. Teacher turnover in American public schools runs about 15 percent annually (teaching is a tough job in any school) but rises to 20 percent or more in urban schools; in a school in free fall, the number can be much higher.

When one of my sons began teaching in Oakland, he was offered a job at a public charter school that was returning zero out of twelve full-time staff members—the only teacher or administrator coming back from the previous year was the part-time music teacher. My son immediately was offered a job at the beginning of the interview; he chose another offer, at the aforementioned Skyline High School.

While some additional help, particularly federal Title I funds, are available to such schools with more "at risk" youth, this often feels to principals like a trickle falling into a bucket full of holes. At Skyline High, the school-site council was forced to decide whether to use its Title I money to retain either a remedial reading program or the school's translators for parents who don't speak English—the program they did not fund would disappear.

The disparity between the education offered students in urban schools that serve a low-income population and students in wealthier schools became particularly clear to Jerry Brown between his two stints as governor, when he was the mayor of Oakland. It was in that position that he got an up-close-and-personal look at the conditions and challenges faced by California's urban public schools. He announced in his 2013 state of the state speech that he wanted to level the K–12 playing field by giving more state money to schools with lower income parents than to schools in wealthier districts, signaling a historic shift in school funding mechanisms. He elaborated on this in one of our interviews.

"*Serrano* was saying that you have to have equal spending for children, whether they're living in Beverly Hills or Compton. This is saying that you have to have unequal spending, because people are in unequal circumstances. . . . You can't treat unequals equally and arrive at a just result."[17]

He stated the obvious, which also explains the challenges that exist in the state: In California, "there's about 23 percent kids in poverty . . . three million kids who are speaking in a foreign language at home . . . And there's widespread immigration that has seen millions of people who were not in anything called a middle-class culture moving into California to work in the fields, work in construction, and work in restaurants and warehouses and other low-skilled occupations, and their children are certainly going to have more difficulty than people who come from a more literate or more affluent background. . . . There are places, the Central Valley and places throughout the state, where you have a stratification that is extreme."

He had criticism for public sector business executives who use their financial largesse to influence the public and school administrators to push certain and often-untested education reforms: "The social stratification, the language, the income—all of that weighs on the equation. So the latest effort principally by hedge fund and other individuals at the top of the income scale to apply business practices, performance metrics, to the school, is an untested set of propositions, there's not empirical data that justifies them."

Diane Ravitch, professor, historian, and former assistant secretary of education, reinforced the evidence that children's learning is affected by their economic status. "Poverty clearly affects children's readiness to learn and their success on standardized tests," she said in an interview for *Educator,* a publication of the California Teachers Association.[18] "The achievement gap exists before children enter school. Some children have consistent access to good nutrition, good medical care, educated parents, safe and healthy neighborhoods—and some don't. All of this affects children's readiness to learn. We know that economic conditions affect test scores, because every testing program shows differential success in relation to family income: Children from affluent families have the highest scores, and children whose families have the least income have the lowest scores."[19]

O ver the last decade or so, parents and public school students grew used to drastic cuts to education programs; having a music or art class, a librarian, nurse, or counselor became considered a luxury. When the science teacher at Skyline lost funding midyear and was not able to purchase items for experiments for the rest of the school year, she posted her needs on the nonprofit Web site DonorsChoose.org and was funded by donors sympathetic to students' educational needs.

By the 2011–12 school year, all but core-studies classes were threatened or eliminated, the Center for Investigative Reporting noted in a report,[20] pointing out that only one in four public schools was staffed with a credentialed librarian. California had the highest student-librarian ratio in the country, according to the American Association of School Librarians, with one librarian for every 5,124 students; the national ratio was one to 916.[21]

These cuts were taking a toll on Californians throughout the state, humiliated nationally by the slide in the status of their public school system and concerned that their children were not getting the quality education that they themselves had enjoyed and from which they had benefited. Corporate and business leaders were also concerned with the declining state of education, as they were largely dependent on these graduates for their workforce.

Some of the most shocking revelations came to light in the class action *Williams* case in the year 2000, when a group of students, parents, and education advocates decided to shine a light on some appalling physical conditions— particularly in low-income schools—just as *Serrano* exposed disparities in funding between wealthy and low-income districts. In the lawsuit brought in San Francisco Superior Court on behalf of children from eighteen urban school districts, the American Civil Liberties Union argued that low-income students were forced to study in rundown, sometimes rat-infested classrooms that were often extremely cold or hot and frequently lacking enough textbooks.

The case was named for San Francisco middle-school student Eliezer Williams, in whose school five social studies classes had to share the same set of textbooks; a dead rodent lay decomposing in the gym; the school had no librarian, no computers, and no art classes; and two of three bathrooms were locked at all times. The third was locked during lunch and at other times of the day.

Governor Gray Davis bypassed the state attorney general, Bill Lockyer, to defend the case, arguing the state was not the responsible party, and hired O'Melveny and Myers of Los Angeles, one of the state's most elite, politically connected corporate law firms. It cost taxpayers $2.5 million the first year alone, and attorneys put the eight- to seventeen-year-old witnesses through grueling depositions. Two brothers, age eight and eleven, asked to have their aunt testify in their place because their mother had been killed just weeks before in a drive-by shooting; their father had died in an auto accident the prior year. The state's attorney said no, and the younger boy dropped out. The older child testified that he had fainted in his ninety-degree classroom one day.

Ten months after Arnold Schwarzenegger became governor, the state settled the case and provided $1 billion for textbooks and supplies, maintenance, physical improvements, and accountability procedures that require each school to file an annual report on school conditions to ensure their compliance with *Williams*.[22]

A William and Flora Hewlett Foundation report conducted the same year as the *Williams* case settlement attempted to determine whether the condition of schools affects academic performance; the answer could have been assumed, but the details were unsettling. Based on interviews with more than a thousand teachers across the state, the report concluded, "conditions in the schools attended by high-risk children are so seriously inadequate that they do not provide an equal opportunity for a quality education."[23] It was an all-too-familiar refrain.

Governor Brown, while focusing in his funding strategy on students at the lower end of the economic spectrum, noted the accomplishments of those who have more advantages: "If you take the higher end of the students, you'll find that California does very well both nationally and internationally," he said in our interview.[24] "The attendance of four-year colleges, two-year colleges, are all very high; there is a very skilled workforce; this is a very sophisticated economy, one of the most sophisticated in the entire world. And so I think statements about how bad things are [are] distortions."

Or maybe not. According to the RAND Corporation, there wasn't good data to compare academic performance among the states before 1990, but other indicators put California well above the national average back in 1970 in spending per pupil.[25] The 1980s saw a growth in student-teacher ratios, followed by a decline in spending for facilities. The Silicon Valley Education Foundation placed California forty-second in its overall 2015 state rankings, standing at fortieth in school financing (a step up in this rank due in large part to funding from Proposition 30 revenues), and thirty-third for K–12 achievement.[26]

Funding, of course, is not the only issue when it comes to education, and California, while often in the vanguard nationally, is hardly isolated from the trends and forces operating across the nation. In public education, a war has been raging for several decades that roughly posits two overly simplistic models for "fixing" education, not just in the Golden State but everywhere.

On the one hand, there are the high-powered "reformers," a shifting, sometimes uneasy alliance of politicians from both parties, education nonprofits and corporations, billionaire philanthropist/activists, parent groups, and charter school advocates whose central philosophy rests on the concept of "accountability"—for students, teachers, schools, and districts. In practice, this primarily has meant increasing the frequency and importance of state testing, as well as working to weaken teacher job security and opening the door to publicly financed though mostly independent charter schools.

On the other hand there are teachers' unions, student activists, and old-school, pre-"triangulation" liberals, portrayed by these reformers as stodgily defending an outmoded status quo, who believe the fundamental problem facing troubled schools centers on inadequate school funding, unequal resource distribution, and the problems that plague the larger society—poverty, racism, child abuse—that spill over into the classroom. In California, this viewpoint was bolstered by the fact that, in 2011, the state would have had to increase its K–12 spending by $8.8 billion—roughly what it spends on prisons—just to meet the national per-pupil average, and $61.6 billion to match the generous New York State per-pupil average.

Brown, whose own education philosophy was honed in part when he was mayor of Oakland, has strong opinions about these educational reforms. As he wrote to former Secretary of Education Arne Duncan regarding his draft proposal for President Obama's Race to the Top education plan (which Brown rejected in favor of the alternative Common Core State Standards Initiative): "You assume we know how to 'turn around all the struggling low performing schools,' when the real answers may lie outside of school. As Oakland mayor, I directly confronted conditions that hindered education, and that were deeply rooted in the social and economic conditions of the community or were embedded in the particular attitudes and situations of the parents. There is insufficient recognition in the draft regulations that inside and outside of school strategies must be interactive and merged."[27] He suggested Duncan develop "a little humility" in assuming what makes for "educational success."[28]

Brown put his philosophy to work more than a half dozen years before his letter to Duncan, when he founded two charter schools in Oakland as mayor: Oakland Military Institute, which accepted its first students in 2001, and Oakland School for the Arts, which opened in 2002. The governor, who has shown irreverence to many institutions and their prescriptions for success his entire life, is dismissive of what he considered a slavish devotion to untested or recycled reforms. Much of what he says can be overlaid on the blueprints of educational experiments implemented across the country. As he told me in our interview:

> The notion that some of these so-called education reformers have developed in the last decade—and developed, I might say, in a history of almost [decades of] education reform [are] notions that come in and come [out] and pass with regularity—these notions of performance pay, extreme and extensive data collection, frequent testing on multiple-choice questions, and then holding teachers to account on all of this.
>
> These are all ideas. There's not a scintilla of evidence that this is going to transform the stratified society in terms of its educational outcome.
>
> There will always be isolated cases in a charter school or a particular school with a very charismatic leader that will be transformative. You always can find that. But in terms of general performance on the part of hundreds

of thousands of schools, the social stratification, the language, and the income—all of that weighs on the equation. So the latest effort principally by hedge fund and other individuals at the top of the income scale to apply business practices, performance metrics, to the school, is an untested set of propositions. There's not empirical data that justifies them.

And I've seen [California over] the last forty years through the creation, the implementation of dozens, dozens, and dozens of programs, there's a lot of fashion in education; things are tried, and then they're discarded and something new is tried. And because politicians come and go, and there's a short-term memory, people even forget that they're doing the same thing, something like it, just with different words.[29]

He also spoke strongly against the stereotype of California's K–12 system as being in free fall, instead emphasizing that averages and generalizations hide the huge and widening disparities between the successful schools and their students and those struggling. While noting that math and language scores overall have been on the rise for the past ten years, he explained certain results, such as one exam given to high school seniors, in which the state performs poorly—as being the product of a sort of reverse bell curve; those mainly immigrant and minority students, generally at the bottom in terms of skills, are so far behind they are dragging the state's average down dramatically:

The school gets children for a very small fraction of the week. And the rest of the time, young boys and girls, or young high school students, are with their parents or in the neighborhood, or wherever they happen to be living; some of them are in foster care, some are even under more adverse circumstances. And it is completely evident, although a lot of people like to turn their head away from it, that those with the lowest income, as a rule, do considerably worse than those with higher incomes. And just look at any school, look at the demographics, and look at the state test scores, and there they are.[30]

These facts aside, Brown didn't arrive in office with a mandate to launch a new war on poverty (though many liberals wish he would do more). And, having experienced a modicum of failure along with success in his exceptionally long and varied political career, he knows better than most that you can't bully the California electorate. A tax increase was needed to support education, but how best to get public support for that? Regretting the hits to education as the Prop 13 saga unfolded and as revenues for education plummeted after the 2008 meltdown, he was aware that a proper scare might do more to arouse voters than any number of well-intentioned sermons from the bully pulpit.

In January 2012, Brown played that ace, revealing his latest state budget with the warning that public education could suffer $4.8 billion in cuts if voters didn't approve his plan for temporary increases in sales tax and taxes on the wealthiest Californians. The school cuts would be draconian, possibly forcing the school year to end five weeks early, Los Angeles's school superintendent, John Deasy, warned.[31]

"We won't have enough days for seniors to graduate. The year will end before APs [Advanced Placement exams], before graduation. . . . And things will get progressively worse each year from now on," Deasy told audiences in the months before the election.[32]

The campaign for Proposition 30, sometimes left for dead by outside observers, would be a stunning success. In rescinding the most extreme of the cuts, Brown received credit for staying the sword of Damocles hanging over all levels of public education, while also limiting the rippling economic damage of the budget crisis. It was, said as stodgy a source as the Standard & Poor's bond-ratings agency, "the linchpin to the governor's broader, multiyear strategy for reversing the state's negative budget position."[33]

But Brown was not content to leave it at that. As important as Prop 30 was for the state and Brown, for the education system it was only a rearguard action to limit the recession's ravages, not a challenge to the prevailing status quo. To really shake things up, Brown, with the help of the Democratic legislature, quickly moved over the next year to develop the first major overhaul of state funding for K–12 schools in years, a collection of reforms emphasizing decentralization and resource redistribution. Unlike the court orders of *Serrano*, Brown's proposals sought not just to equalize funding but rather to imbalance it further, in favor of the most needy students and schools.

"Growing up in Compton or Richmond is not like it is to grow up in Los Gatos or Beverly Hills or Piedmont," Brown told lawmakers, comparing two cities that are majority black and Latino with three wealthy white cities. "It is controversial, but it is right, and it's fair."[34]

To do this, he and the legislature revamped the absurdly complex funding formulas to shift money toward schools and districts with higher percentages of students who are poor, English learners, or living in foster care.

"Gov. Jerry Brown is cutting through years of legislative torpor with his proposal to simplify the unwieldy and often unfair formula that determines how schools get funded and to provide extra funds to those students who need it most," the *Los Angeles Times* editorial board wrote of Brown's plan. "For four decades, California has used a school funding formula that could justifiably be called lunatic."[35]

Brown's years of listening, ruminating, and opining about poor kids and special needs; forces outside the classroom that never were factored into data gathering; bureaucratizing teaching and learning; and throwing money hither and yon to no useful purpose all seemed to have jelled into this plan. Brown's formula was locally focused, designed to give all school districts an equal per-student base grant. Some would receive an additional 35 percent for each "high need" student: poor enough to qualify for federally subsidized school lunches, not fluent in English, or in the foster care program. Districts where more than half the students are disadvantaged would receive an additional "concentration" grant. Districts would be required to use the extra money primarily for the benefit of the disadvantaged students.[36]

Not everybody was thrilled. Wealthier districts that would see less of the total pie over time as the new plan rolled out over four years successfully fought for changes softening the numbers before passage from the legislature to Brown's desk for signature. The law in 2014 sent an estimated $2.1 billion more to the most needy districts that were also being given more control over how to spend this money. In 2015, that increased to $3.5 billion.

Local control "is aimed at the idea that . . . the problems can be handled best by people who are engaging in them," Brown explained in our February 2013 interview.[37] He bemoaned the many layers of bureaucracy—federal, state budget, superintendents, school boards, state education code, court orders—issuing many rules and mandates that can be confusing and have "many things going at cross purposes. Given all that, I think more freedom at the local level and the vitality of democratic participation should guide things, as opposed to these kind of ideological prescriptions that many of the reformers are claiming will transform schools, even though as far as I know there's no evidence to support their claims."

On the same day Brown signed the K–12 measure into law in hopes of decreasing the expanding gap between the haves and have-nots, he signed another education bill passed by legislators designed to shore up the state's middle class by providing up to $305 million annually in reduced university tuition on a sliding scale for students whose families earn less than $150,000 a year. In September 2014, the first wave of 73,000 recipients received scholarships. This number is expected to double or triple over the coming years.

By 2015, Brown's $115.4 billion budget allotted K–12 education a 45 percent increase ($6 billion) over four years earlier and $3.5 billion to implement Common Core standards. State colleges got $97 million, a 4 percent increase promised for two years, while the University of California received $25 million, a 4 percent increase promised each year for the next four years with a freeze on tuition increases for two years.

Challenges for education in the state remain: economic and language gaps, high teacher turnover, rising student debt, and on and on. And although California spends more than any other state on education, the spending per pupil is still low compared to most states. But finally, after the dark days of 2008 to 2012, things are looking up for education advocates in California. A number of factors—Brown's insistence on prioritizing student learning rather than testing, the postrecession bounce in the economy leading to increased revenues, the $6 billion a year generated by Proposition 30, and the progressive redistribution and decentralization of the local funding formula—have all helped generate some breathing room.

The state of education, financial stability of California, and the legacy of Jerry Brown would have been strikingly different if Brown had not gotten his initiative on the ballot in 2012 and if Californians had not voted to tax themselves. Up until the end, it was not a foregone conclusion.

10

Jerry Brown 2.0

t was a pleasantly mild November evening in Los Angeles, three days before the 2012 statewide election that would seal the legacy of Governor Jerry Brown. In a little more than seventy-two hours, he would be recognized as one of California's great and most effective governors, or his prestige would be delivered a body blow of sufficient force to hinder his ability to carry out his agenda throughout the remainder of his term.

Just two years earlier, voters had great expectations for Brown when they gave him a third opportunity to govern the state, but the task was more fraught this time around. On Inauguration Day in January 2011, California was reeling under a $26.6 billion deficit, and everything now was riding on Brown's Proposition 30, which he had skillfully maneuvered onto the ballot. Voters would decide whether to tax themselves more to save the state's education system and relieve the deficit.

If Brown was suffering any anxiety over the weight of the election's uncertainty that November night or over the fact that the measure in which he had so heavily invested his political and personal capital had been declining in recent polls, falling to 49 percent that very weekend, it did not show.

Rather than huddle that evening with campaign staff at his Oakland Hills home to discuss last-minute strategy, he appeared relaxed as he meandered alone, through the crowd of partygoers who had come to celebrate the seventieth birthday of Larry Flynt, the man whose business empire includes X-rated magazines, strip clubs, a casino, and a global on-demand porn business worth more than $30 million.

Guests arriving at the Flynt home in the West Hollywood hills on this clear night were greeted by a spectacular view, a seemingly endless sea of lights sparkling across the vast expanse of Los Angeles. They relinquished custody of their cars to a line of cheerful uniformed valets. Names were checked off the guest list to allow entry past a discreet security presence, not for the governor but for Flynt, a subtle and ever present reminder of the crazed man who had tried to assassinate Flynt years ago, shooting him and leaving him paralyzed and wheelchair-bound. Close friends, work colleagues, and acquaintances were gathering in the lush yet modest backyard, its swimming pool covered by a faux-grass-topped wood deck to accommodate tables and chairs.

It would be safe to generalize and say that most politicians would not enter the orbit of the famed pornographer, particularly with journalists in the vicinity, but then California is not in the Bible belt, and Brown has never seemed to care a whit what people think of his personal life. But he is practical, and one might assume grateful for the $25,000 Flynt gave to Brown's Proposition 30 campaign in mid-September and another $75,000 in early October. On September 5, a couple of weeks before the first contribution, when the measure was becalmed before the stormy days that precede a particularly close election, Brown called Flynt. The governor unknowingly had interrupted a late breakfast the publisher was having with *New York Times* reporter Brooks Barnes at the posh Four Seasons Hotel in Beverly Hills, where Flynt dines daily.

It seems Barnes was exploring Flynt's views on politics for an article that would come to be titled "Pornography and Politics" when one of Flynt's bodyguards walked up with a cell phone and whispered that the governor of California was on the line.[1] The reporter's heart must have skipped a few beats; perfect moments like this just don't come along in every interview. Flynt apologized to the journalist for taking the call and explained that it was probably a plea for money.[2]

Flynt and Brown were not strangers. And while the publisher has derided many politicians as hypocrites after the impeachment of Bill Clinton—

famously offering $1 million in 1998 and again in 2007 for verifiable information of an illicit affair involving a member of Congress or other high government official—he believes so strongly that Brown has been good for California in every state and local office he has held over the years[3] that he contributed $54,000 in 2013[4] to help return Brown to the governor's office before Brown announced he would seek a fourth term.

While most people only think of Flynt as a pornography peddler, journalists, lawyers, and free speech advocates also know him for his landmark First Amendment victory before the U.S. Supreme Court in 1988, memorialized in the hit film *The People vs. Larry Flynt*. In that case, centered on a cartoon in Flynt's *Hustler* magazine depicting the conservative firebrand Jerry Falwell having sex with his mother in an outhouse, the justices unanimously held that parody of public figures is not libel. This was good for Flynt, whose hobby seems to be parodying public officials, but he is also a seasoned political junkie who contributes to many campaigns and follows their progress. At the time of Brown's call that September morning, Flynt surely knew the tax measure was in trouble, given the media's saturation coverage of polls.

Now, shortly after Flynt dropped those thousand C-notes into the Proposition 30 coffers, here was Brown at Flynt's backyard birthday soiree. In between acknowledging greetings of guests with handshakes, Brown periodically glanced at his cell phone, as if alerted by a breaking news app or a message from a staffer hard at work; the polls would open in less than sixty hours.

Just that morning, a story in the *New York Times* reported that voter support for Proposition 30 was going south in three polls, with just about half of likely voters in favor, following similar reports in the previous weeks in media across the state. A 50 percent "in favor" poll on a tax measure, which needs more than 50 percent to win, is seen as very weak heading into election day.

One obstacle to passage was Proposition 38, a competing ballot measure that would also have raised taxes for education. It was being heavily funded by the personal fortune of its author, Los Angeles Democrat and civil rights attorney Molly Munger. In Los Angeles, the Munger name is synonymous with enormous wealth. Ms. Munger would end up spending $47.7 million of her own money for Proposition 38, while her brother, Republican Charles Munger Jr., a Stanford PhD in physics, donated more than $36 million to the Small Business Action Committee, which aimed to defeat Brown's Proposition 30. Some of his money also went to pass an antilabor measure, Proposition 32, which would have prohibited unions from using automatic payroll deductions to raise money for political campaigns.

The sire of the siblings is Charles Munger Sr., vice chair of fellow billionaire Warren Buffet's Berkshire Hathaway, founder of the prestigious Los Angeles law firm of Munger, Tolles & Olson, and a major-league philanthropist.

Unlike Brown's measure, Munger's Proposition 38 would have raised taxes not just on the wealthiest but also on all Californians except the very poorest. And it would have bypassed the state legislature and distributed the funds directly to schools, a distinction Munger's anti-30 attack ads hammered, appealing to voters' distrust of state government.

The Democratic Party establishment and organized labor groups formed a campaign committee to work against Munger and line up for Brown, asserting that her measure had less chance of passage and would draw needed votes from Brown's plan. The *Sacramento Bee* reported "emails and conversations within the education community suggested the possibility of 'murder-suicide,' a scenario in which Munger's [attack] ads lead both multibillion-dollar tax initiatives to defeat," ultimately hurting schoolchildren.[5]

Munger pulled the ads in mid-October. But damage was done, with support for Proposition 30 falling several points in polls. Proposition 38's poll numbers indicated it had no chance of passage.

Proposition 30 had its genesis in California's near failed-state status, at the time of Brown's election in 2010. Its out-of-control deficit and spiraling unemployment had made national headlines. Voters had soundly rejected his Republican opponent, former eBay CEO Meg Whitman, who had spent $144 million of her own money on her $178.5 million campaign to Brown's $36.7 million from contributors.

Less than a month after Brown took the oath of office, he implored the legislature to pass an emergency measure to ask voters to extend temporary fees they had been paying since 2009 to avert $12 billion in cuts to education and public safety. He had campaigned on a promise never to raise taxes without voter approval, and tax revenue was desperately needed to take a bite out of the multibillion-dollar deficit and help prevent millions of dollars in further cuts to school funding. A statewide poll released in the previous December had 53 percent of voters saying they would support such a tax increase measure. By then the media had been saturated with stories of California's precarious financial position: government workers had been forced to take unpaid furlough days off,[6] schools were laying off teachers and eliminating classes,[7] and state parks were closed,[8] to name just a few ramifications of the recession.

But in a blow to democracy and out of blind partisan loyalty, legislative Republicans refused to give Brown the votes he needed for a two-thirds majority to call a special election and let the voters decide if they would accept extending the expiring fees. Some of the lawmakers told Brown privately they would vote for it, but publicly they could not break with the "no tax" policy of the party.[9] Brown said getting Republican legislators to vote for a tax was as likely as "inviting Hezbollah into the Knesset and asking them their ideas on how to manage Jerusalem."[10]

Nine months after he took office, in an interview with *Calbuzz,* Brown said some Republicans told him "it's basically a death sentence" to do anything to enable a tax increase, even though it would have been the voters, not the legislators, deciding the measure.[11] Brown's only alternative, then, was to go straight to the voters, gathering signatures to put a citizens' initiative on the November 2012 ballot. But now, instead of asking voters to extend expiring fees, the measure, Proposition 30, asked voters if they would increase sales tax one-quarter cent for four years and income tax on those with an income over $250,000 for seven years.

While the sales tax is primarily a regressive tax, the fact that the state would also go after the wealthy, about 3 percent of the population, with the progressive increase on the income tax was a reversal of decades of American and Californian reluctance to pursue any policies that could be labeled "class warfare."

In a country and state where many of the poor believe they will someday be wealthy or famous, or both—all statistics to the contrary, which show the United States actually has a quite low rate of class mobility—it is rare to have leaders support straight tax-the-rich policies. Credit the recession, the almost absurd wealth of the tech nouveau riche, and the Occupy protests for paving the way for a renewed Democratic populism.

But most important, Prop 30, if passed, would require a renewed commitment on behalf of Californians to public schools, from pre-K through twelfth grade—and to putting their money where their hearts were. Since Prop 13 had passed more than thirty years earlier, liberals had been complaining about its affects on education; yet, even with a clear majority both in the legislature and among registered voters, they had done little to rectify the situation.

Prop 30's tax increases initially would generate funds that were earmarked not for any increase in funding but to support myriad programs on the chopping block and rescind $6 billion in automated education cuts the legislature had already approved, which would have in turn triggered massive teacher layoffs, class-size increases, and even shortened school days and the school year for K–12 students by as much as four weeks in some districts and five in Los Angeles, the nation's second-largest school district.

Its passage meant twenty thousand more students would gain access to the state's community colleges, while the California State University and the University of California systems each would avoid projected $250 million midyear budget cuts that would have led to massive and instant tuition increases, as much as 20 percent, and layoffs. The state Department of Finance estimated that the new revenues would total approximately $8.5 billion in the initiative's first two fiscal years, $6 billion through fiscal year ending in 2017, and smaller amounts after that.

While the details can be mind numbing for all but the most eager bean counter, it was hard to overstate the ramifications for California if Prop 30 and its rival, less popular proposition, Prop 38, both failed. The ballot text for

Proposition 30 noted that, since 2008, "California has had to cut more than
$56 billion from education, police and fire protection, health care, and other
critical state and local services. These funding cuts have forced teacher layoffs, increased school class sizes, increased college fees, reduced police protection, increased fire response times, exacerbated dangerous overcrowding in
prisons, and substantially reduced oversight of parolees."[12]

The competition was fierce between Brown's Proposition 30 and Molly
Munger's Proposition 38. By the end of October, the pro-30 camp was
worried—except, it seemed, the governor himself. He was immune to the
contagious panic of many of the measure's supporters in the campaign's waning days. After keeping a low profile throughout the campaign, for which he
was criticized by some supporters, he spent the last few weeks hustling votes
on college campuses around the state. He seemed to enjoy himself as he rallied support from students.

College campuses were a comfortable milieu for him, and these were relatively easy votes to capture. Tuition had been increasing as state revenues
dropped and stood at nearly $13,000 by 2015—a tenfold increase from two
decades earlier. It was destined to climb precipitously again if Prop 30 did not
win the assent of voters. No one knew this better than Brown's campus audiences, who were enthusiastic and attentive.

D espite the flurry of Proposition 30 death-knell stories the weekend before
the election, Brown was upbeat the night of Larry Flynt's birthday party.
Seeing the governor standing alone, I seized the moment and crossed the
lawn to greet him. I had known Brown professionally for many years, most
closely when I was the *Los Angeles Times* bureau chief in Sacramento during
his second term. My journalist's curiosity was piqued when I saw him glanc-
ing periodically at his cell phone, and I wanted to know what was grabbing
his attention. He was friendly when I approached and asked what he was
doing. Checking last-minute poll numbers? Breaking news?

"No, no, we're okay! We're gonna win!" he said, surprising me with his great confidence that was backed up, he said, by "our polls." It was as if the outcome of the election were no longer an issue. "It's the Supreme Court! They're meeting tonight, right now!" Brown has a way of animating a conversation when he wants to make a point. I knew instantly why they were meeting.

"The Arizona case!" I responded. That *was* news. Here it was, late on a Saturday night, and the state supreme court justices were meeting in an extraordinary session to debate an issue that could impact the election. Okay, so maybe you have to be a government and politics junkie to appreciate it, but this was significant. As often happens in politics, there had been a mysterious last-minute infusion of money, in this case $11 million, that was donated just three weeks before this evening to the aforementioned Small Business Action Committee, whose donations clearly were from conservatives who wanted to bury Prop 30 and see the antilabor measure win. But who were they? Shouldn't the public know who was trying to sway an election? That's what the justices were discussing.

The fact that the identity of the true source of the individual contributions was kept hidden infuriated Brown, who long had detested the influence of big money in politics. He slammed the $11 million donation in a press conference as "money laundering."[13]

Just six months earlier, a provision in campaign funding law was implemented to require donors who give money to nonprofits to be identified if they know the funds are destined for a specific campaign in California. The state's election regulators, the Fair Political Practices Commission (FPPC), stepped into the case and asked the high court to enforce that provision in this case.

Given the imminent election, the court had to act swiftly. So now, with just hours to consider and deliberate the issue before polls opened, the governor anxiously waited at this Saturday-night party for the justices to act.

Amid the well-dressed professionals and seductively clad wait staff, the governor politely greeted guests who approached to shake his hand. At times he was standing alone, creating the impression that he knew few people present. Shortly thereafter, the buffet tables along the perimeter were fully staffed and loaded with steaming entrées, and a long line immediately formed.

After filling his plate and negotiating through tables to find a place to sit, Brown joined the table where my journalist husband, Robert Scheer, and I were dining with the *San Francisco Chronicle*'s former editor, Phil Bronstein, and former managing editor, Robert "Rosey" Rosenthal, both former colleagues at the newspaper, where I was deputy editor; both were now at the Center for Investigative Reporting, and the four of us might have been among the few guests present, other than the host, who personally knew the governor.

When it was time for dessert to be served from the buffet tables, a lineup of statuesque dancers began to perform in pairs atop a camouflaged plywood dance floor that had been placed over the swimming pool. Not far from our table, they shimmied in duos to the beat of loud rhythmic music, stripping off items of colorful costumes until there was little left.

The governor, his back to the dancers, was engrossed in a conversation with Rosenthal, who exercised remarkable visual discipline in avoiding the entertainment to engage the governor in discussion about what book he happened to be reading at that time.

Brown has a reputation for being well read with a wide range of literary interest, and this question was almost always guaranteed to elicit a fascinating response. It seems he was reading a quite compelling autobiography by a nun who was born in the 1300s. He was discussing this woman and turned to ask me: "Have you read it? It is really an amazing story! You should read it!" It was quintessential Jerry Brown: the dancers were invisible to him, the loud music an obstacle to surmount in order to hear and be heard—and a historic nun held center stage.

The next afternoon, Sunday, the California Supreme Court justices came to a decision after conferring by phone: by a vote of 7-0, they ordered the Arizona nonprofit that made the $11 million contribution to turn over its records on that donation in one hour, at 4 p.m.

Attorneys for the Arizona group, Americans for Responsible Leadership, scrambled, asking for an extension, saying they could not meet the deadline. The justices denied the request, and the lawyers filed a letter vowing to appeal the decision to the U.S. Supreme Court.

In stepped "the best looking attorney general in the country,"[14] as President

Obama famously praised California's attorney general, Kamala Harris. She accused the nonprofit's attorneys of trying to "obstruct the process and run out the clock" until after the election.[15] But early the next morning, the group caved, reaching a settlement with the commission, admitting to money laundering and agreeing to turn over the names of the groups involved without naming the individual donors or submitting any transaction records, which is legal under federal law.[16] But that would not be the end of the matter for the state, Americans for Responsible Leadership, or the group's donors.

After all that eleventh-hour drama, the state supreme court ruling ended up not mattering much in terms of saving or losing the election. It came very late, and Brown turned out to be right when he had said emphatically two nights before that voters would approve the tax increase.

For those who wondered if millionaires would be willing to tax themselves more, the answer was a clear yes. Proposition 30 was approved statewide 55.4 percent to 44.6 percent, with especially strong support in the state's three wealthiest counties, whose taxpayers would pay the most: Santa Clara, home to Silicon Valley's tech billionaires (62.5 percent yes vote); Marin, a Golden Gate Bridge ride from San Francisco (67.9 percent); and San Mateo, adjacent to San Francisco (63 percent). Conservative counties were considerably less enthused, though not a significant factor in the outcome.

The tax vote made national headlines, and Brown was widely praised and credited with the Prop 30 win.

"Of all the state election results across the nation, few can top the shocking good sense of California voters approving temporary tax increases to raise $6 billion a year to shore up the state's tattered public schools and university system," a *New York Times* editorial stated on the morning after the election. "That's right: There were voters in these hard times agreeing to be taxed despite the 'no new taxes' mantra of simplistic conservative politicians."[17]

California media was equally effusive.

"The measure's passage was a huge win for the governor,"[18] said the *San Francisco Chronicle* in its postelection coverage, noting that Brown had been blasted the year before for thinking the state's voters would support such largesse. "The governor has been dogged in his determination to hold such a public vote and started a signature-gathering effort to place the measure on the ballot. He has spent the past few weeks barnstorming the state on the issue, sometimes visiting multiple cities a day, and was assisted by a strong union push."[19]

As it turned out, California's new online voter registration statute, which Brown signed into law, brought in nearly one million new voters, most of them young.[20] The large number of young voters raised Proposition 30's yes vote by about 4 percentage points. An exit poll conducted by the Associated Press and various television networks revealed that 28 percent of people voting for Proposition 30 were age eighteen to twenty-nine and that two-thirds of that age group supported the proposition. There also was an explanation of why the polls were off: the Associated Press reported there "was a higher percentage of young voters than the preelection polls used to show the measure faltering among likely voters."[21]

The election was over, but the state's investigation into the $11 million donation shrouded in secrecy was just beginning. It would have major ramifications. If the biggest state in the country was becoming more liberal, it was going to keep attracting conservative money from outside the state, as it did from Utah in drawing support for the anti–gay marriage initiative, Proposition 8, in 2008. Making sure donors of these outsourced monies adhered to state rules was increasingly a priority for Brown and the state's Democrats.

Under federal law, political organizations outside California that funnel money to political action committees in the state are not required to reveal the names of individual donors; that is precisely why some donors take this route and why campaign finance reform advocates want more transparency. In California, if a group donates money for a specific purpose—in this case, to kill the tax-increase initiative and support the antilabor measure, Proposition 32—it must disclose donors who contributed to the sum.

Federal law also allows nonprofit groups to withhold the identity of individual donors. This practice dramatically increased after the U.S. Supreme Court's January 2010 ruling in the *Citizens United* case, allowing corporations,

labor unions, and "social welfare" nonprofits—501c(4)s in Internal Revenue
Service parlance—to spend unlimited amounts of money to support political
campaigns. Since that decision, millions of dollars in nonsourced donations
from these groups have come to dominate the political arena. The Center for
Responsive Politics reported "spending by organizations that do not disclose
their donors has increased from less than $5.2 million in 2006 to well over
$300 million in the 2012 presidential cycle and more than $174 million in the
2014 midterms."[22]

Following the money to determine the individual donors of the $11 million
was a challenge met by the tenacious Fair Political Practices Commission,
chaired by Ann Ravel, working with Attorney General Harris. The investigation connected the organizations involved to the conservative Koch brothers
and detailed the lengths to which donors go to avoid being identified.

In this case, money was paid to an organization based in Virginia—the
innocuous-sounding Americans for Job Security—later identified by the Fair
Political Practices Commission as "the key nonprofit in the Koch brothers
dark money network of nonprofit corporations."[23] The funds then were fun-
neled through an entity in Arizona, the Center to Protect Patient Rights, and
then to their final destination, the two political committees in California
working in favor of the antilabor measure and against Proposition 30.

The inquiry revealed other surprises. Among the donors whose names
initially had been kept secret were the prominent Fisher family of San Francisco (who gave more than $9 million), owners of the Gap retail chain, for
which the governor's wife, Anne Gust Brown, had worked as chief adminis-
trative officer; San Francisco billionaire investor Charles Schwab ($6.2 mil-
lion); and Los Angeles billionaire philanthropist Eli Broad ($1 million).[24]
That was particularly surprising given that Broad, at an event in Los Angeles
with Brown months before the election, had said he would help the governor
get the measure approved and that "I do support it. Those of us who are
wealthy should pay more."[25]

The investigation concluded nearly a year after the election, on October
24, 2013, when the Fair Political Practices Commission and state attorney

general's office announced a record $1 million settlement to be paid into the state's general fund by the Americans for Job Security and the Center to Protect Patient Rights.

The $11 million donation was "the largest contribution ever disclosed as campaign money laundering in California history,"[26] the Fair Political Practices Commission's press release announced in detailing the deceit. California law required the total $15 million in unreported donations—the $11 million plus an additional $4.08 million that was uncovered—to be turned over to the state by the two California committees that received the money, since it is against state law to receive laundered funds.

Announcing the settlement in the case was the last official act as FPPC chair for Ann Ravel; she later resigned to accept an appointment by President Obama to be one of six members of the Federal Election Commission.

While the penalties were substantial, the end result was less satisfactory. In February 2014, following the fallout from the negative publicity and penalties imposed, the Center to Protect Patient Rights ceased to exist under that name, apparently morphing into American Encore, with the same Sean Noble who headed CPPR at the helm of the new group. The state did collect the $1 million fine from the CPPR and the Americans for Responsible Leadership, but none of the $4.08 million was paid by the California Future Fund, which apparently has since disbanded. In 2014, the FPPC announced that the Small Business Action Committee had paid $300,000 toward what it owed to the state: $11 million.

California already has some of the toughest campaign finance policies in the country, but, inspired by the money-laundering case, state legislators, the governor, and campaign finance reform advocates moved to make the state's campaign finance laws even stricter. They have the support of the people of California, who, as noted in chapter 3, overwhelmingly passed the Political Reform Act in 1974 and, like the rest of the nation—84 percent of them in a June 2015 *New York Times*/CBS News poll—believe money has too much influence in political campaigns. Two-thirds believe only the wealthy have a good chance of influencing the election process and want more disclosure;[27]

that includes three-quarters of Republicans, whose leaders in Congress resist legislation for campaign finance reform that requires identifying sources of money to nonprofit political groups.

California is not waiting for Congress. Establishing a model for the nation, Brown signed new legislation in 2014 that did what has been blocked in Washington—require nonprofit organizations that make political contributions in the state to disclose more information about the sources of their money. This law aims to prevent the money-laundering case from 2012 from being duplicated.[28]

"Governor Brown's signature [on the bill] marks a turning point in the fight to reveal secret funders of political campaigns. It starts to shed light on dark money in California and serves as an example for the entire nation," said Trent Lange, president of the California Clean Money Campaign.[29]

Campaign finance advocates Robert Stern, who wrote the original 1974 Political Reform Act, and the FPPC's former top investigator, Gary Winuk, with the support of Silicon Valley entrepreneur Jim Heerwagen, went even further. They submitted an initiative for the November 2016 statewide election intended to upend *Citizens United* in California and "establish California as the national model for campaign finance disclosure."[30] Their Voters' Right to Know Act calls for full transparency regarding donors to campaigns; anything short of that threatens democracy, according to the initiative's Web site.[31]

The measure would enshrine in the state constitution the right to know the true source of political spending. It would further emphasize transparency by making clear the true identity of those groups and committees that, for example, sponsor initiatives and pay for television ads using deceptive names. An example is an initiative that qualified for the 2012 ballot under the name "2012 Auto Insurance Discount Act"; it was sponsored by an auto insurance industry group. An even better example is the anti-union initiative, one of the two ballot measures that received the laundered money contributions in 2012. It was deceptively called the Stop Special Interests Money Now Act, and it was subsidized by, yes, special interest money.

Proponents are hoping that the Voters' Right to Know Act, if passed, will encourage other states and a recalcitrant Congress to acknowledge the damage from *Citizens United* and mandate more transparency. Already, Maine, Washington, and South Dakota are trying to toughen campaign finance law in those states.[32]

In the case of California's Prop 30 campaign in 2012, huge and secretive political forces had set out to subvert the democratic process. But Californians had the last word. The *New York Times* editorial board wondered if the passage of Proposition 30 signaled a larger shift in the state and national politics: "As is so often the case in California, where the 1978 property tax revolt led by Howard Jarvis became the stuff of political folklore, a new and unpredictable chapter may be opening."[34]

Another way to put it was voiced by California state senator Loni Hancock, a Berkeley Democrat: "The tax revolt began in California in 1978, and it ended in California in 2012."[35]

11

The Pendulum Swings Left

O n Election Day, November 4, 2014, California showed it was moving in a different direction than much of the rest of the country. The Republican Party swept to huge victories in the South, Midwest, and the Plains states, taking control of the Senate for the first time since 2006. Californians again elected Democrats to all eight statewide offices. And whereas Kansas—once the fiscal model for conservatives—racked with massive budget shortfalls caused by large tax cuts for the rich, had doubled down on its support for a new era of small government austerity, the Golden State electorate continued the expansive, liberal mode it has been embracing counterintuitively since the recession.

Along with sending Jerry Brown back to Sacramento for a record fourth term as governor, voters also supported the two ballot initiatives he spent more time and money touting than his own candidacy. Both were at least partially about creating reservoirs of precious resources: one for water, the other for money. Proposition 1, a major-infrastructure bond measure, authorized the generation of billions of dollars to spend on the state's public water infrastructure in order to limit the effect of future droughts. Next, Proposition 2, supported by Republicans, ordered the creation of a rainy-day fund for future budget shortfalls and meant eventually holding a full 10 percent of the state's budget needs in reserve.

The latter was an exemplar of late-stage Brown frugality. Whereas earlier in his career he was famous—or infamous, depending on one's point of view—for creating political wars over modest government expenditures, such as new office furniture (he rejected it), and state-issued briefcases and cell phones (retrieved from staff), he has based this go-around on much more ambitious attempts to build fiscal sanity into the state's operating DNA. As unsexy as a state initiative can get, the Rainy Day Budget Stabilization Fund Act is nevertheless potentially groundbreaking for a state whose "broken" image has largely been triggered by periodic budget deficits.

As discussed earlier, California is prone to wild fluctuations in annual tax revenue because of the unusual dynamism of its economy: the highs are higher, and the lows are lower. Fluctuations can be brought on by a surge or crash in the stock market; by huge increases in personal wealth (e.g., overnight dot-com billionaires); or by the partial freezing of property taxes by Proposition 13, which leads to an overreliance on windfall taxes. In boom years, the state, running a debt it can't pay down, must spend this money, leaving coffers high and dry when the tide goes out during the seemingly inevitable downturn. State controller John Chiang's issuing of IOUs to state employees in 2009—the trough of the recession—cemented the "failed state" meme in the public consciousness.

The Republican approach to balancing budgets, exemplified by Kansas under Governor Sam Brownback, has been to cut income taxes so less money can be spent, period. (Just as we looked earlier at Texas as an alternative governing model to that of California, so too can we scrutinize Kansas as a case study of another state moving in the opposite direction.) Of course, this tactic doesn't address the underlying issue of smoothing revenue year to year in order to prevent the deleterious effects of unpredictable funding; it simply makes shortfalls inevitable.

To soften the blow, defenders of austerity usually argue that cutting taxes will not lead to less revenue because of the Laffer curve, the graphic depiction (drawn on a napkin in a 1974 restaurant meeting of economist Arthur Laffer, Donald Rumsfeld, and Dick Cheney) of an idea developed by Laffer that says cutting taxes leads to a stronger economy, which in turn produces more tax revenue. Consider how Governor Brownback brought Laffer into

Kansas to advise on the Kansas tax cut experiment that has been a disaster, leading to huge cuts in education and other funding. Unfortunately, as even conservative *Forbes* magazine was forced to point out, the Laffer curve is, at this point, a laugher.

"We've tried this experiment time and again. And tax cut proponents such as economist Art Laffer continue to insist they can turn fiscal dross to gold," wrote tax expert Howard Gleckman in *Forbes* in July 2014. "Cut taxes deeply enough and the resultant boom in economic activity will boost revenues. Magic. Painless. Everything a politician would ever want. Except this is fiscal snake oil."[1] The Brownback plan in 2012, when the top tax rate was 6.45 percent, began with getting the legislature to cut individual tax rates by 25 percent, repeal the tax on sole proprietorships and other "pass-through" businesses, and increase the standard deduction. The following year, taxes were cut again with a measure to gradually lower rates even more over the next five years. The plan was to lower the top rate by 2018 to 3.9 percent and to partially restore some of the tax credits it eliminated in 2012. It looked good to those who benefited, but turned out to be a disaster. Revenues collapsed, plunging by 11 percent. From June 2013 to June 2014 individual income taxes fell by $700 million, to $2.2 billion, and all income tax collections fell more than 20 percent, from $3.3 billion to $2.6 billion.[2]

Kansas, long run by moderate Republicans, had of late handed the controls to the same extreme small-government zealots who were once known as Birchers, the self-styled Tea Party, which many have argued is an Astroturf version of grassroots activism driven from behind the scenes by Fox News and the conservative billionaire Koch brothers, who hail from Wichita, Kansas. The result was a self-made budget crisis. Struggling to emerge from a post-recession malaise, the state had essentially committed fiscal harakiri. Perhaps not knowing what they had signed on for, much of conservative Kansas began questioning its leadership, forcing Brownback and other state GOP leaders into unexpectedly tough reelection campaigns.

"Two years ago, Kansas governor Sam Brownback laid out an aggressive program of tax cuts to turn this slow-growing state into a Texas-like economic powerhouse—and serve as a model for Republican leaders in other states," began a June 2014 *Wall Street Journal* article. "So far, the results are serving as more of a warning than a beacon."[3]

In this bizarro land, it was politicians running an ideological experiment, not the economy, that led to school closures, mass layoffs, and savage cuts to basic government services. Thomas Frank, author of the influential book *What's the Matter with Kansas?*, which sought to explain why low-income, Christian white Americans often vote against their own economic interests, unpacked the phenomenon in a *Salon* article in 2014, when Brownback was in a brutal fight for his political survival. Frank noted the "shock-and-awe" quality about the Brownback years," particularly:

> The panorama of disaster [his tax cuts] have inflicted on education in the state Fewer teachers working with more students, cuts to sports and art programs, and even school closings here and there. . . . And now Sam Brownback's reelection campaign is begging voters to persuade themselves that everything they've read . . . is a falsehood; that things are really and truly OK. . . . "The sun is shining in Kansas and don't let anybody tell you any different."[4]

In fact, heartlanders almost did dramatically toss out Brownback and infamously absentee senator Pat Roberts, but on the same day Brown was trouncing his Republican foe in the Golden State, both Kansans won squeakers, riding a Republican midterm wave. Although Brownback only won with 49.82 percent of the vote and was blamed, even by sympathetic members of the media and his own party, for driving Kansas down the road to fiscal disaster, he saw the vote as a mandate rather than a red flag warning; Kansas seemed to be on track to continue pursuing the so-called Texas model without the state's booming energy industry to prop it up. Iowa, Colorado, North Carolina, and six other states sent freshmen Republican senators to D.C., while a slew of rural/suburban electorates chose conservative governors.

In California, on the other hand, Republicans who had held the governor's seat less than a decade ago were now left to celebrate the dubious victory of having narrowly prevented a repeat of the Democratic two-thirds "supermajority" in the state legislature. A survey released a week before the election showed 42 percent of likely California voters didn't even know Brown was up for reelection, the lack of a viable opponent no doubt contributing to the lowest voter turnout in California history for a general election (also 42 percent, coincidentally).

Republicans, who compose 27.6 percent of the state electorate, pulled a few upsets in state legislative races, yet when it came to the big picture, the state continued its leftward drift, postrecession. By the end of 2015, Republican registration in the state's most conservative bastion, Orange County, dropped to 40 percent for the first time in its history; San Diego turned blue in 2008.

It is California's dominance in so many rising sectors, from weed and movies to high tech and health care, combined with its wealthy consumer base, that makes the "failed state" meme seem so ludicrous. Regardless of criticisms that the state has mishandled budgeting, of the messy "direct democracy" of initiatives, of crime and incarceration, of the endless influx of poorly educated immigrants, and of unemployment that until 2015, when the gap closed, persistently hovered 2 percent above the national rate, the state's private economy will continue to be huge and dynamic.

With the notable exception of Texas, which is close behind in terms of Fortune 500 and Fortune 1000 corporate headquarters, other states can only dream of providing the base of operations for the staggering list of California-based twenty-first-century titans, including, among others, Activision Blizzard, Adobe Systems, Airbnb, American Honda, Apple, Charles Schwab, Chevron, Cisco Systems, Craigslist, Del Monte, Disney, DirecTV, Electronic Arts, Facebook, Farmers Insurance, Gap, Google, Health Net, Hilton Hotels, Hewlett-Packard, Intel, Mattel, Oracle, PG&E, Pixar, Sony Pictures Entertainment, Salesforce, Trader Joe's, Twitter, Universal Studios, Virgin America, Visa, Wells Fargo, and Yahoo!.

Even though many of these companies employ up to thousands of workers in cheaper labor markets, national and abroad, and their executives and shareholders often park their money in tax shelters elsewhere, the simply phenomenal revenue streams and stock prices of these and smaller, growing firms have still managed to lead to spectacular climbs in housing and retail rental and purchase prices in the desirable Bay Area, Los Angeles, Orange County, and San Diego markets. Gentrification of urban areas in this latest corporate tech boom has accelerated after the recession, as the foreclosure boom paved the way for a generation of well-paid young workers in the tech and entertainment industries to buy steeply discounted homes.

Gritty urban areas like the flats of Oakland, previously mocked by elites for crime and "diversity"—a code word that can be positive or negative depending on how it is used and interpreted—have rapidly become playgrounds for winners in the state's, and nation's, postindustrial economy, where the inequity gap continues to widen between the haves and the have-nots. The irony of downtown Oakland—host in October 2011 to one of the most radical and persistent Occupy Wall Street occupations—rapidly being taken over by twentysomething entry-level software coders making two or three times the salary of a local teacher or bus driver and five to six times that of a food-services worker, has been painful to many who believe the city is losing its soul.

With rent-control laws implemented in the 1960s and 1970s mostly lifted or eroded by court rulings and lobbying, soaring rents meant neighborhoods and whole cities were aggressively gentrified at a pace difficult to fathom by locals. West Oakland, for decades an impoverished ghetto of African Americans geographically isolated by freeways and the bay, was now becoming a bastion of young professionals, mostly white and Asian. Locals feel out of place, while the newbies can't figure out why cleaning up streets, opening hipster cafés, or setting up neighborhood-watch committees could possibly be controversial.

In San Francisco, locals bemoaned what they considered an uncouth invasion of "brogrammers," mostly white and Asian young men with more money than they know what to do with yet lacking in style or cultural panache. In 2013, locals even began protesting the "Google buses," plush, chartered vehicles that used city bus stops to pick up tech workers from the city and transport them down the peninsula to their jobs in Menlo Park, Santa Clara, and other Silicon Valley destinations they had deemed too boring to call home.

Some of their techie counterparts seek the warmer clime of Southern California's Silicon Beach, aptly named for its location in Los Angeles's Westside—Santa Monica, Venice, Playa del Rey, Playa Vista, and neighboring cities. The beach locale is also attractive to giants in the tech world who have established a base there, including Google, Microsoft, AOL, Snapchat, Yahoo!, *BuzzFeed,* and YouTube, to name a few.

When the NASDAQ collapsed at the millennium, taking a slew of overcapitalized, underconceived dot-coms with it, many locals were happy to see the tide of techie nouveau riche recede somewhat. Yet eventually Silicon Valley, pushed forward by the explosion of mobile phone technology and the so-called Web 2.0 built on social networks like Facebook and Twitter, has revived completely, and what might have seemed like a crazy fad in 1998 looks very much to San Franciscans like the foreseeable future.

The previously rough, poor, and ethnic Mission District, a supertrendy neighborhood, is now overflowing with hipster establishments catering to the young and rich. Yet it is undeniable that a major shift is happening when rents double and triple within a few years, or even months in some cases.

On March 2, 2014, the *New York Times* reported that in the entire seven-mile-by-seven-mile city of San Francisco, not a *single* home was on the market that an average public school teacher could afford to buy on a salary of $59,700 a year. The article highlighted a three-bedroom fixer-upper in the Glen Park neighborhood that hit the market at $895,000 and sold two weeks later for $1.425 million—a mere $530,000 over the asking price.[5]

Forget buying a home—renting is next to impossible for many in the Bay Area or Southern California. Eight of the ten highest-priced rental markets in the country in 2015 were in California; New York City ranks ninth. The most expensive city in the country to rent a home is not San Francisco (number 2), as many would assume, but rather its neighbor to the south San Jose, home to Silicon Valley millionaires and billionaires. But it is in Los Angeles (number 6) where renters fork over to landlords the greatest percentage of their income—48.9 percent—to have a place called home.[6] In the once-seedy downtown area of Los Angeles, whose moniker today is DTLA, hipsters paying $2,700 for a two-bedroom apartment or more than $1 million for a condo share pedestrian space with drug addicts and chronic alcoholics on rapidly gentrifying city blocks.

Sky-high prices for housing, whether owned or rented, remain the central bane for middle- and lower-class Californians and are pushing many families into poverty. The California Poverty Measure, developed by the Public Policy Institute of California and the Stanford Center on Poverty and Inequality, found 21.8 percent of Californians were living in poverty (about $24,000 for a family of four) in 2013, the latest figures available, and was highest among children (24.9 percent). Three of the five counties with the highest poverty rate are booming Los Angeles (26.1 percent) and San Francisco (24.4 percent), along with the wealthy resort town of Santa Barbara (23.8 percent).[7]

The federal Census Bureau's Supplemental Poverty Measure (SPM) showed California with 50 percent more people in poverty per capita than the national average for 2011–13, again the most recent figures available.[8] This was despite the fact that the median income for California is 15 percent higher than the national median income. The report noted that more than 78 percent of poor Californians lived in families with at least one working adult, most of them full-time.[9]

While the rest of the world sometimes pigeonholes California as a collection of celebrities, hipsters, and hippies, it can be a cruel place, where the powerful—from the cliffs of Malibu and bayside homes in Orange County to the forests of Marin to the walled housing estates in San Diego and Redding suburbs—can successfully isolate themselves socially, geographically, and politically.

Even as Apple was building a $5 billion office complex in Cupertino shaped like a spaceship to house its fast-growing staff (average annual pay: $125K)[10] in a region where unemployment hovers at about 4 percent, down south in the Mojave Desert's Imperial County, the jobless rate was more than five times as high.[11] In fact, the endemic poverty in the eight counties of the agricultural San Joaquin Valley has been equated with that of Appalachia and is "one of the most economically depressed regions of the United States," according to the Congressional Research Service.[12]

And, really, we don't have to drive that far from the Pacific to find such suffering; the booming cities of the Bay Area and Southern California appear frequently in lists of income inequality, as measured by various statistical tools. For example, San Francisco was second in both 2012 and 2013 when measured by the income ratios of the ninety-fifth and twentieth percentiles, according to the Brookings Institution,[13] while Los Angeles and Santa Barbara both land in the top ten nationwide when measured by the Gini coefficient, a metric for determining economic class differences.[14] By mid-2015, the homeless population in Los Angeles was growing at a pace of thirteen thousand a month,[15] with ubiquitous multicolored tents and tarps housing their tenants beyond Skid Row, lining overpasses and underpasses and sidewalks of downtown Los Angeles, a minicity within a city.

In famously gritty Oakland, recent college graduates could excitedly eye well-paying jobs created by the rapid expansion of the ride service Uber, which announced plans in September 2015 to redevelop a historic (and abandoned) department store site into an airy office for several thousand workers in the hip, booming Uptown District—even as the city's murder rate continued to be among the highest in the nation (number 2 in 2015 for cities over two hundred thousand), with the victims being almost entirely impoverished nonwhite men.[16]

For those who get Bay Area or Southern California tech jobs, the old adage applies: It's good work if you can get it, since it pays well and often comes with perks such as in-house chefs and free luxury bus service. Yet while news stories daily trumpet (or mock) the luxury lifestyle of Silicon Valley and Silicon Beach techies, the number of people directly employed by the industry is relatively modest, especially considering the sector's book value. Facebook, valued at nearly $250 billion halfway through 2015, employed fewer than ten thousand people; Google, worth some $850 billion after a corporate shakeup in September 2015, employed fifty-three thousand. And "sharing economy" poster children Uber and Airbnb, valued at roughly $50 billion and $25 billion, respectively, employ several thousand apiece, as well as many more "contractors," who rent their property and service at the expense of cabbies and hotel employees.

Of course, these companies are growing, yet others in the industry, like Hewlett-Packard, have been shrinking, and hardware companies like HP and Apple tend to make all their products overseas, greatly limiting the number of jobs for less-educated adults. According to CompTIA, a nonprofit trade association for the IT industry, only about 8 percent of Californians are employed by "tech and innovation" firms, earning an average $139,500[17] (147 percent more than the average private sector wage), although the sector accounts for over one tenth of the state's economy. The big job growth remains in service, education, and health care, where entry and midcareer workers are finding they can't afford to live within a reasonable commute to their workplaces.

A typical scenario might be a unionized teacher, janitor, or nurse who finds his or her rent or mortgage eating up an unsustainable percent of an allegedly middle-class paycheck. For them, the pursuit of the California dream is spending two to four hours a day commuting from inland regions to the populous urban areas for jobs that will allow them to send their children to college.

As the rapid gentrification of urban cores by moneyed professionals is happening in cities across the state, and while most mayors revel in the flood of retail and construction money being thrown around town, liberal and progressive leaders have responded with campaigns for living-wage initiatives in an effort to help those who work in these inflationary communities continue to live there. ("Living wage" is a term preferred by activists to emphasize that a minimum wage should be set in order to provide enough to support a humane lifestyle.) In 2015, the Los Angeles City Council approved a minimum wage of fifteen dollars an hour, and the county of Los Angeles soon followed suit. Los Angeles mayor Eric Garcetti had called increasing the wage scale the "largest anti-poverty program in the city's history" when he first proposed it a year earlier.[18]

Between 2012 and 2014, San Jose, San Francisco, and Oakland all passed increases to raise minimum wages for affected employees to levels three to five dollars an hour higher than the state's minimum wage, which is $10 as of January 2016. In April 2016, the legislature passed and Brown signed a law raising the minimum wage to $15 an hour by 2022. In Oakland, in 2014, a living-wage proposal was passed by 81 percent of the voters, with the eventual winner of the mayoral race, Libby Schaaf, endorsing the $12.25 minimum.

Some business interests and conservatives have opposed these city ordinances, claiming they will hurt small businesses that can least afford it. Others, including Silicon Valley multimillionaire and former Republican gubernatorial candidate Ron Unz, TV personality Bill O'Reilly, and two-thirds of the members of the national Small Business Majority, a nonprofit advocacy group, favor raising the minimum wage, believing it will spur the economy. Opponents see the cities' efforts as representing the kind of government meddling the Texas-Kansas model of governance so abhors, while advocates believe it will stanch the widening income gaps in urban areas and be valuable culturally and in terms of concrete labor and tax revenue.

Yet even if a few businesses shut or flee based on regulations such as living-wage rules or the much-maligned environmental regulations California pursues aggressively, other interventions and investments by the state have clearly continued to ensure its future as an economic powerhouse.

One example of this progressive thinking involved a complex ethical issue that exploded onto the national scene a decade earlier—the use of stem cell tissue in the medical field. It was an outsize political controversy, especially once President George W. Bush eliminated federal funding for research at the behest of antiabortion conservatives, but Californians boldly stepped into the breach with Proposition 71 in 2004.

Passing easily with the support of 59 percent of voters, Prop 71, the California Stem Cell Research and Cures Act, amended both the state constitution, making conducting stem cell research a constitutional right, and the health and safety code. Stem cell research, the exploration and experimentation with the use of human building blocks to solve a variety of ailments and disabilities, is ethically controversial because it sometimes uses, or even clones, human embryo tissue, although advanced techniques are increasingly able to generate them from nonembryo cells.

California was not the first state to buck Bush's heavy-handed stem cell ban, enforced later with a veto of compromise legislation passed by Congress with the support of moderate Republicans. New Jersey's leadership beat California to the punch by a few months, authorizing $9.5 million in June 2004, while several states would soon follow with pledges of tax monies to support research with such vast medical and economic possibilities. However, where these states were setting aside millions of dollars, Prop 71 authorized the sale of a much more significant $3 billion over a ten-year period to support stem cell research by California's already cutting-edge university and biotech empire (embryonic stem cells were first isolated in mice at UC San Francisco in 1981).

Overseeing this investment, normally the purview of federal agencies, was the new California Institute for Regenerative Medicine (CIRM), created by the initiative. In September 2005, before it had even given away any money, voters were validated with their faith in the promise of such research when California scientists announced they had helped partially paralyzed mice walk again by injecting them with human neural stem cells.

In February 2007, CIRM released its first $45 million for research; the following month, it gave an additional $75.7 million in funding to scientists at twelve different nonprofit and academic institutions. In May of that year, Governor Schwarzenegger announced the formation of an International Cancer Stem Cell Consortium, a merger between UC Berkeley and Canada's International Regulome Consortium, boosted by a $30 million donation from the Ontario Institute for Cancer Research.

By 2014, CIRM had funded eleven projects in human clinical trials. In March 2016, the institute reported having awarded $1.9 billion to researchers, companies, and institutions, with $1.4 billion of that having been dispersed, with researchers working to find cures for forty-five currently incurable diseases. The institute claims to have generated 38,000 job-years and having lured more than 130 senior-level scientists and their labs to California.[19]

"What Silicon Valley has done for technology, CIRM is doing for stem cell research in California,"[20] said Dr. Dhruv Sareen from Cedars-Sinai Hospital in Los Angeles at the agency's tenth anniversary celebration.[21] Biotech executives were similarly positive. "In 2008, it was extremely hard for a small biotech company to get funding for the kind of work we were doing," said Eugene

Brandon, of ViaCyte, a San Diego company using stem-cell-derived cells to treat diabetes. "Without that support, without that funding from CIRM, I don't know where the work would be today."[22]

There have been critics, however. In 2012, the National Academy of Sciences dinged CIRM for what it said were conflicts of interest on its board and flaws in its grant approval process. Others were frustrated by the slow development of cures, claiming they were mislead by Prop 71 supporters boasting of miracles soon to come.

"Progress on stem cell research has been significant—but it's been the progress of the tortoise rather than the hare," complained a *San Francisco Chronicle* editorial in May 2014.[23] "It was irresponsible for the backers of Prop 71 to convince the California public that cures were just around the corner, and it is unfortunate that so many Californians are disappointed with the institute because they believed this." Initial funding for CIRM will expire in 2017, and it is unclear what will happen after that, though it is already clear that the state's claim to leadership in this promising area has been firmly established.

In looking at the California electoral map, the votes for Proposition 71 echoed that of almost every election: The liberal viewpoint dominates in a great blue arc stretching from Arcata in the "emerald triangle"; down through the booming Bay Area; through the wealthy coastline of Santa Barbara, Malibu, and Santa Monica; and across Los Angeles. Even the once firmly conservative bastion of Orange County, while still more Republican than Democratic, and formerly Republican-majority San Diego, are much more moderate than their peers elsewhere in the country, as can be seen by voter support for stem cell research even as it was stymied in D.C. However, the Central Valley counties, all the way from the Tehachapi Mountains to the Oregon border, voted against the initiative, whether out of fiscal conservatism or religious objections to experimenting with embryos or, most likely, both.

This reality, then, is that California is not a united state but one starkly divided along several fault lines other than its infamous geologic ones. Economically, it is seeing yet another new boom for the "winners"—those with the right skills, education, real estate, or connections to earn some of the highest salaries in the country—even as millions of workers in the unskilled labor and manufacturing sectors are seeing their wages plunging in real dollars. Politically, the partisan fragmentation seen nationally has receded somewhat, as Democrats have come to dominate Sacramento. Yet there are many, especially in that "red state" central corridor, who see the urbanites as aliens, and vice versa—politically, morally, and culturally.

The state's cosmopolitan diversity blurs hard ideological lines that have come to immobilize Congress to a great extent. The best explanation given me as to why California does not have the same level of political polarization that plagues Washington, and why the Tea Party lost its mojo in California, came from one of the state's most influential politicians ever to walk the halls of the state capital, the powerful former speaker of the assembly and former mayor of San Francisco, Willie Brown:

> California politically has never become subservient to the movement in the nation that is now called the Tea Party.... The Republicans who were of that opinion and of that view were never able to even dominate the Republican Party in California, in part because there were so many independent Republicans.
>
> One example, the Republicans lost any possibility of any change in . . . Pat Brown's legacy when the Reagan revolution in California never took hold. There are examples of how it allegedly took hold with Prop 13, et cetera, but it never really took hold.
>
> His successor was George Deukmejian, who had no interest in the Republican Party at all. He was a registered Republican, but he did not allow for any development. And then when Pete Wilson came along, Pete Wilson had too many years of having been in the mainstream of the Republican Party rather than the fringe of the Republican Party, so the Republican Party never had a [Tea Party congressman] Tom McClintock toehold on California. Period.
>
> And that made it literally possible for us, sometimes haltingly, but in many cases enthusiastically, to keep moving forward. Because the tax in-

creases for California on an as-needed basis were orchestrated in some cases
by Republican administrations. . . .

And then in the nineties, it was again Republican administrations—in
part Deukmejian with the standby tax, et cetera—that were stronger; it
wasn't all cut, cut, cut, cut, cut. It was things that happened to be done, that
needed to be done. They still have their hostile attitude toward welfare recipients . . . but it was not the insanity of Texas and the insanity of Oklahoma
and the insanity of Arizona.

Yeah, they came along with the nonsense about trying to figure out how
to dismember Latinos and keep them from being able to vote. But they were
never able to cause viral pneumonia politically to set in, in California, because
the inoculation had so happened over the years that the patient didn't get
sick.[24]

The pendulum has swung far back since Proposition 13 toward more optimistic, liberal, technocratic, forward-thinking governance in all areas: reversal of decades-long resistance to public welfare taxation, a new pragmatism
toward unauthorized immigrants and the criminal justice system, stricter climate change mandates, equal pay for similar work regardless of gender, and
so on. The scale and scope of California would suggest that the repercussions
of this shift resonate far beyond the state's borders, though the sheer diversity
and complexity of its population and economy also caution us to be realistic
about a tsunami of challenges.

Epilogue

The diversity of the state's resources is matched by
the constant diversity of its population. Preoccupied
with its peculiar problems, isolated from the rest of
the nation during two crucial decades in its early
history, California develops a remarkable energy and
resourcefulness in the solution of its problems without
consultation or assistance—from the other Western
states or the federal government.

—CAREY MCWILLIAMS, *CALIFORNIA:*
THE GREAT EXCEPTION, 1949[1]

When this book was conceived several years ago in the wake of the Great Recession, it was intended to directly answer a question the nation's pundits were posing with some ferocity: Whatever happened to California? Implicit in the question was the belief that the Golden State, floundering through a terrible economic crisis and, to its great embarrassment, issuing IOUs to pay its bills, was a terminal case, a near "failed state" in hopeless decline.

Conveniently for this oft-recycled narrative, rival "red" Texas was then enjoying a boom under the reign of an enthusiastic presidential candidate who crisscrossed the country touting his state's "miracle" to all who would listen—and the media was all ears—boasting that California businesses were fleeing to the Lone Star State. To the north, in heartland Kansas, another Republican governor, abetted by the Republican-majority legislature, was garnering national press by dramatically wiping out his state's income tax in a pointed rebuke to the progressive government model pioneered by California and the industrial states of the Northeast.

To witness firsthand what California might learn from this "miracle," governor in waiting Gavin Newsom made a pilgrimage to Texas to see how the magic was made. "I say, 'Learn from, don't follow, others,'" the lieutenant governor said, as if he were a football coach facing a losing streak. "We've got to get back in the game."

Now, in 2016, that all seems a bit silly.

Since reaching its fiscal bottom, California has surged back into the black from a $26.6 billion deficit when Jerry Brown took office in 2010, its underlying economy displaying its traditional resilience as a massive, diversified, creative, and global force. The drumbeat of criticism about California's alleged hostility toward business and high taxation muted, and moderate and right-wing voices grew faint during the slow yet steady recovery.

"California is [still] a high-cost, high-benefit state," reminded the nonpartisan Public Policy Institute of California's 2015 annual report. "California workers, on average, earn 12 percent more than the national average—even after adjusting for differences in workers, occupations, and industries. But output per worker in California is 13 percent above the national average, and this higher productivity fully offsets the higher average wages. All of California's immediate neighbors—Nevada, Oregon, and Arizona—have lower wages and lower output per worker."[2]

Since 2011, the state's growth rate has been a healthy 4.1 percent, and in 2014 alone, the state added half a million new jobs, by far the most in the nation. The surge in the state's GDP saw it pass that of Russia, Italy, and Brazil; its economy once again would be ranked seventh in the world if it were a separate country.[3]

Meanwhile, Texas's boom began to flag as oil prices fell drastically. J. P. Morgan's chief U.S. economist, Michael Feroli, said in late September that the state might be headed for recession if they remained so low,[4] and it was expected to add fewer jobs than the national average for the first time this century. This, even as Kansas's governor, humiliated, has been forced to sign on to the biggest tax *increase* in his state's history in a desperate attempt to balance the books he shredded.

"Governor Sam Brownback, tearing up and warning that the nation is watching Kansas, pleaded with Republican lawmakers . . . to pass a tax hike to keep the state financially solvent,"[5] reported the *Kansas City Star* on June 11, 2015, as the state's legislature debated massive cuts to education and regressive tax increases. The Republican senate president, Susan Wagle, who suggested the joint meeting, also stressed urgency. "It's a crisis. We have not served Kansans well. And the time is short."[6]

In contrast, California, after suffering cumulative deficits of more than $100 billion from 2000 to 2010, was stacking a series of budget surpluses that had Wall Street cheering.

"With slowing growth in the oil states, we believe California may quickly become the most important state driver of national growth in 2015. This is due in part to the incredible trends seen in Silicon Valley and the high tech industry," Dr. Christopher Thornberg, a founding partner at Beacon Economics, said prophetically in a report for City National Bank. "The state outperformed the nation in terms of growth [in the second quarter of 2015], a pattern we have consistently seen over the last few years."[7]

The state's new rainy-day fund was expected to grow to $3.5 billion by mid-2016, according to state administration sources cited by the *Los Angeles Times*.[8] One clear upshot of this movement toward budget stability has been a steep ascent in the state's credit rating to its highest point in fourteen years, making it the second-best performer in the tax-exempt bond market as it offloaded nearly $2 billion in general obligations.

"Governor Brown has put the fiscal house in order," Ben Woo, senior municipal analyst at Columbia Threadneedle Investments, which manages about $30 billion in local debt, told *Bloomberg News*.[9] "Compared to the chaotic political environment we're seeing in New Jersey and Illinois, California is a much better credit environment than some other states."

In fact, while the postrecession recovery has been slow and weak nationwide, California has been outperforming the country as a whole. "Since reaching bottom in February 2010, California has been the single largest source of new jobs in the United States," reported the Public Policy Institute of California.[10] "With 1.86 million jobs created, California accounts for 16.2% of all new jobs created in the nation since 2010—that's over 350,000 more jobs than the next closest competitor, Texas." This placed the state fourth in per capita job generation, nationally; meanwhile, the natural-resource-extraction-based economies of the top three players in the fracking boom (North Dakota, Utah, and Texas) were all headed for a shock with the plummet in energy prices.

In reality, this interstate grudge match, largely a political and media creation, was never much of a contest. As it has been since roughly World War II, California is the ascending giant of American states, economically, demographically, and culturally. Those who want to belittle its strength and importance for ideological reasons are simply ignoring the facts.

Consider, for example, that 111 billionaires live in California—only the United States and China had more in 2015, according to *Forbes,* and they are both countries. They, and nearly thirty-nine million other humans, call the state home because it is pretty and there is a lot of money to be made here. Rents are soaring along its 840 miles of coastline for the same reason, while the once smaller towns of the Central Valley continue to rapidly sprawl. Even the beleaguered agriculture sector somehow made huge profits in the fourth year of a now historic drought.

However, for California boosters, gloating over fending off the "haters" would be a terrible mistake. As Newsom, an early 2016 gubernatorial candidate, pointed out after Brown's 2015 State of the State speech, "We've got 6.1 million people living in poverty in two Californias: a very wealthy coastal economy in contrast to a struggling inland economy."[11] The state is not immune to the condition of much of the country, one starkly divided between haves and have-nots.

Yet for so many—from the young unauthorized immigrant going to college under the state Dream Act to the entrepreneur who received a GO-Biz grant to expand his business in the state, the California dream does exist. And this dream, amorphous as it may be, is precisely why California can't measure its success against Texas or Kansas. As a nation-size state famous for its progressive models, it has to shoot higher because it is bigger, richer, better educated, more diverse, more advanced, and more closely watched than almost anywhere else on this surprisingly small planet. What happens in California really does matter more, not only because of the scale of our consumption and production, but because the rest of the nation and world actually do look to it for new ways of doing things.

In fact, it is not hyperbolic to argue that California is the key test case not only for the United States but also for the entire world. With their eyes turned to California, observers will learn if a multicultural, democratic, and postindustrial society can remain united, functional, and progressive in the face of globalized, high-tech capitalism. Is there another political unit on the planet that combines an economy this advanced with a population this large and diverse?

This is all the more reason, then, why California's leaders must act like adults. And unlike Texas or Kansas or Wisconsin, where elected Republican leaders have used the cover of the recession to push a radical laissez-faire, "trickle-down" economic agenda, in California the state's voters and leaders have been shocked into maturity and moderation—raising taxes to pay for schools, investing in infrastructure, saving for the next economic bust, and attempting wholesale changes to slow climate change. It may not be sexy or fit the "kooky California" narrative, but it is a real model for seeking sustainability in a world that often seems to be moving in the opposite direction.

In keeping with the state's embrace of moderation and compromise, perhaps we should pause here to make clear what the current California is not. It is neither a liberal fantasy nor a progressive's proto-utopia. Just as, in the 1960s, it was never as conservative as its governor, Ronald Reagan (who was himself never as far to the right as his latter-day fanboys would pretend), or as "wild" as the hippies, the anti–Vietnam War movement, and the Black Panthers seemed to the world (as they were making Reagan's life miserable), so today the mammoth state holds its complex multitudes in simultaneity.

There are hipsters and yuppies, anarchists and fascists, down-homers and cosmopolitans, all speaking more than a hundred different languages with different value systems—and all of it is held together by a state government historically hamstrung by conflicting populist initiatives, severe restrictions on taxation and budgeting, term limits, and an often polarized legislature. The state's diversity and democracy ensure that nobody can ever be completely happy with the direction it is going at any time; sometimes it is enough to find that the ship is at least moving generally toward a safe harbor in heavy seas and not listing so far to port or starboard it will capsize.

As the current captain of this vessel, Jerry Brown is an apt symbol of the state's political trend lines. He is not a radical, after all, nor is he any longer "Governor Moonbeam," if he ever really was. Or perhaps it is better to say that he is a radical moderate, attempting aggressively to advance a middle-path liberal and pragmatic agenda. While progressive activists in California certainly find fault with his fiscal conservatism, profracking sympathies, and quiescence to the prison industrial complex, corporate lobbyists and Republican stalwarts alike disdain his emphasis on regulation, deeming it antibusiness and antijobs.

A less stubborn politician facing such vituperative critics on all sides might be inclined to abandon the field. Certainly that appeared to be Arnold Schwarzenegger's approach after he had his ears boxed by the voters during the special election. He just sort of faded out, only to rise to some definition of prominence again by taking Donald Trump's place on *Celebrity Apprentice* and starring in a video game commercial during the Super Bowl. Brown, in his last years of his fourth term, certainly could coast to the finish line of his career, with most of an apathetic public none the wiser. Instead, whether out of ambition or a true sense of responsibility, he has doubled down on seeking game-changing legacy legislation.

The blow he suffered at the end of his last term, when oil-company lobbyists got enough legislators to gut the key element of his 2015 climate change program and he was unable to negotiate a last-minute compromise, was an outlier in recent years. More typically, cautious but forward-thinking pragmatism, defying the general drift of national political discourse toward gridlock and extremism, could be seen throughout the $167.6 billion 2015 budget approved by Brown after he beat back appeals from his Democratic Party brethren to spend more lavishly. Even as the budget paid into the new rainy-day fund, however, it showed an old-school liberal bias by expanding school funding after the severe cuts of the recession; setting aside $380 million for an earned income tax credit for an estimated 825,000 poor families; and, for the first time, opening Medi-Cal, the state-funded public health-care program, to the children of undocumented immigrants, at an expected cost of $132 million annually.

"For a relatively small investment, every child in every California classroom and playground will now have access to care and coverage," Anthony Wright, executive director of the advocacy organization Health Access California, said in a statement reported by the *Los Angeles Times*. "We all benefit from that."[12]

Still to be determined were how to use hundreds of millions of dollars raked in from polluters through the state's pioneering cap-and-trade program, as well as how to manage a budgetary time bomb posed by baby-boomer state workers who are expecting pensions and retirement health care (the latter alone is expected to cost $78.1 billion more than currently set aside). Yet that officials, corporations, and unions were discussing these matters with serious purpose far ahead of any deadlines was itself a sign that adults are minding the store, so to speak.

Of course, that we are even noting this trend as newsworthy, which we certainly are, is itself a sign of low expectations. Yet here we are; as of this writing, three of the original Republican primary candidates—Donald Trump, Dr. Ben Carson, and Carly Fiorina—had never held office, and the party they were seeking to represent, which controls both houses of Congress, actually considered shutting down the entire federal government to block funding of Planned Parenthood and wishes to abrogate its Constitutional responsibility by refusing to consider a Supreme Court nominee of President Obama. For a large part of the country, the once uncontroversial concept of "good government" was seen as an oxymoron.

As always, though, California is zigging while much of the country zags. And so it goes, California as the model—not of utopia but of serious attempts to find solutions rather than wasting time and energy looking for scapegoats. And it is not just the politicians, of course. They are responding to a well-educated electorate that is civically engaged. In California, even the corporate titans of Silicon Valley and Hollywood must at least pretend to care about the future of the world, whether it is Google or Tesla seeking ways to decrease auto pollution, Twitter claiming credit for helping the Arab Spring, or creatives at Pixar pushing messages of empowerment and equality in their films.

Sure, it can be gross when these executives exaggerate the good they do as they become billionaires simply by selling stuff, but how often do you hear of an oil baron or Wall Street bond trader even suggesting that morality has a place in business? In fact, it is just this stance of responsibility to the future and the greater good—sometimes made with more sincerity than others, of course—that so often has enraged those elsewhere, who have so mocked our hippies and punks, dreamers and leaders, unconventional governors and outspoken celebrities.

Yet there is something different happening now. Certainly, it is less colorful than the rollicking gold rush, the race to lay the golden spike, the World War II boom, and the wild ride of the 1960s and '70s. This is more serious business: the trials of a state reaching maturity. A place that for so long seemed to each new wave of arrivals like an empty, blank slate upon which they could write their destiny now is full, expensive, difficult, and yet still pretty amazing. Nobody can pretend anymore that we are all going to be wealthy, that water will always flow from the mountains, that the soil will keep disgorging its riches at the slightest touch. If we are not to become a dystopia, we will have to figure some things out; encouragingly, we seem to have begun to do so.

According to the Public Policy Institute of California's 2016 annual survey, 60 percent of Californians support government regulation of business as a way to protect the public interest, 57 percent support a bigger government providing more services over a smaller government providing fewer services, and 61 percent would favor an extension of Prop 30's tax increase on those making more than $250,000 a year. A majority favors continuing to build the nation's first high-speed bullet train, which is projected to run from San Francisco to Los Angeles in less than three hours by 2029.[13]

This then is the California model after the Great Recession: tackling seemingly intractable, even possibly hopeless problems with solutions developed by a government neither abdicating its responsibility to the civic good nor acting without limits or good sense. It is correcting the course when the ship runs aground, as the state did in its costly experiment with energy deregulation and imposition of a costly corrections policy dictated by fear and social whim.

The California model has the adults agreeing to mind the store, to put aside despair or fatalism, to face problems squarely—adults who are not hoping for a religious deus ex machina to rescue us all. It builds policies to lessen the problem and then revises and reconfigures those policies as new evidence becomes available while seeking a symbiosis between the economic and environmental.

This has meant, despite not being an independent nation, that California has faced environmental catastrophe like no other state, instead of putting its head in the sand or waiting for the rest of the world to act first. It has meant that, when the nation overhauled its health-care systems through the Affordable Care Act, California led the way as the state with the best and most comprehensive implementation of the reforms, enrolling 1.4 million Californians in the program by February 2016, 12 percent of the nation's total. And it has meant that, accustomed to receiving waves of migrants every decade, California has responded to the complex economic, legal, and humanitarian consequences of unauthorized immigration with a harm-reduction approach instead of caving to demagogues who seek to vilify or create crusades; most Californians understand that the state became the giant it is because it has remained so attractive to hardworking people since gold was found at Sutter's Mill.

It has meant not only renewing a commitment to the state's public universities and colleges, long the envy of the rest of the country and the world, with the opening of the first new University of California campus in Merced but also struggling to regain—with the help of taxpayers who voted themselves a tax increase—as much as possible the affordability and accessibility that made the system so uniquely transformative in a more equitable era. So too is there a commitment to the K–12 children, giving a larger share of funds to K–12 schools with low-income parents than those in districts with high-income parents.

Realizing that its taxation system and dynamic economy make it vulnerable to wild budget swings, California has finally put in place more reliable revenue streams and a rainy-day fund approved by voters and pushed by a governor who put more money into this campaign than his own reelection race.[14] Is it enough? Clearly, the stunning economic inequality, huge prison population, significant air pollution, and continued water shortages, terrible traffic, and lack of affordable housing all say no. Brown, in particular, is famous for emphasizing limits, that there are no magic bullets, no golden geese laying golden eggs. Yet in a world where extremism and glibness often dominate the news cycle day after day, California is undergoing a quiet revolution of sorts.

The biggest industry in California is real estate, the biggest cash crop is marijuana, and the biggest employer is the state government. Hollywood is still a global cultural force, and the state's farms are the nation's produce section. Yet it is the techies of Silicon Valley and Silicon Beach who currently rule the zeitgeist, and their word of the moment is "disruption," as in the ability of a new technology to disrupt a society, an economic sector, or the way we work or play.

Disruption has always been a California specialty, from the gold rush to the beatniks, the antiwar movement to gangster rap, car culture to celebrity culture, *Birth of a Nation* to the iPhone, always spawning an unplanned cascade of negative and positive consequences with each new cultural, economic, or technological innovation. It is not an exaggeration to claim that explosive innovation is part of the place's essential DNA, nor that this is both a blessing and a curse.

As exemplified by the avowedly pragmatic leadership of Governor Brown 2.0, the current California is attempting to respond to those disruptions, to ameliorate the worst consequences and multiply the positive ones. Of course, governments are clumsy, ponderous things, and California's is no different; the attempt to shape history through bureaucratic and legal means is no clean science.

No matter how powerful the Democratic Party grows in California, the state will never look like high-tax, high-wage northern Europe—it is too diverse, too globalized; its underclass too entrenched, its radical political left too small and neutered. Yet the alternative does not have to be a complete abandonment of the commons by an increasingly resented and resentful ruling class, as we see in much of the world throughout history. A line—muddled and meandering, to be sure—is being drawn in the sand: we can provide good schools, clean water, working democracy, and meaningful work at a decent wage.

For decades, scholars and journalists have called California "ungovernable," conservative alarmists have howled that the state was being "overrun" by successive immigrant waves making it "the capital of the Third World," and liberals have often sunk into passive fatalism about its future in the aftermath of their bête noire, Proposition 13. Yet here we are in 2016, in a place that is damn interesting, for all its real flaws an astonishingly vibrant place to be, work, and live. If the present is not what we want it to be, we at least are viscerally aware that the resources, brainpower, diversity, and historical momentum are all here to make it much better and dare one say it, once again a beacon of progress for the rest of the world.

ACKNOWLEDGMENTS

This book project began with a call from a book agent, referred by a friend, who wondered if I would be interested in writing a book about California. This was during the worst of the financial meltdown. California was being crushed by a multibillion-dollar deficit that forced services and funding to be slashed and unemployment to soar. Critics and commentators calling it a "failed state" humiliated California, and the publisher wanted a book to explain the working title, "Whatever Happened to California?"

I had been a *Los Angeles Times* reporter, government and politics editor, and bureau chief in Sacramento before becoming editor of the Orange County edition and associate editor of the newspaper, and I was interested. I began writing that book, but thankfully, my prescient journalist-and-author husband Robert Scheer cautioned me: Don't write that book. California is still golden, it will bounce back from this adversity as it always has, and your book will be quickly outdated.

I hesitated, and then along came Jerry Brown. I had been state capital bureau chief toward the end of his previous term as governor (1974–1982), and I asked for a reprieve on the deadline; Jerry Brown could be the game-changer, I argued. My very patient and kind publisher Tom Dunne agreed to an extension, as he did again when Brown's tax-increase measure, Proposition 30, was on the ballot and I said its passage would alter the state's downward trajectory. It did, and thus was born *California Comeback*.

My husband Bob has been my rock, supporting me in all matters professional and personal, as well as being my best friend. The work of my sons—Josh, a professional researcher, and Christopher, a gifted writer—was of enormous help in completing this book. So, too, was the editing of good friend Heidi Swillinger, who volunteered days of her time to this book, and Kay Gallin, who helped me through endnote chaos.

My son Peter and brother Pete brought me joy and calmness in stressful times, and my grandsons Tamayo and Ben delight me and are the reason I am grateful for California's vigorous leadership in the fight against climate change.

A special shout-out goes to Josh's exceptional wife Isabel, a force unto herself, wrapped in a bundle of warmth, humor, compassion, and competence in everything she does, who takes care of problems before we even know they exist. Isa's family has seamlessly merged with our family and enriched our lives. Her mother Lucrecia Aguilar provides me with sustenance—both moral and gastronomic.

I thank family members and attorneys Anne Weills and Dan Siegel for their wise counsel, literally. Their tireless efforts and dedication to making life better for the 99 percent is unparalleled. Anne was also a valuable source on criminal justice issues for this book, having been one of the attorneys who settled her solitary confinement case with the state, which became a model for the nation. My love and gratitude go to friends Sara Beladi and Luke Bowerman, from whom I have learned so much, and Dr. Mary Powers (who buys our books to give out as Christmas presents!). I thank friends Larry Gross and Scott Tucker, and the crew from the Annenberg Center for Communication Leadership and Policy—particularly Geoff Cowan, Geoff Baum, and Susan Goeltz—for providing support, moral and otherwise.

My agent, the writer and attorney Ron Goldfarb, had me with his contract, a simple one-page agreement to represent me, as he has done so well. Of course I am grateful for my publisher, Thomas Dunne and his colleagues, Emily Angell, Jennifer Letwack, and especially Will Anderson, with whom I worked most closely.

I thank my friend Jean Stein, who empathized with my lament about missing deadlines, though she beat me to publication with her *West of Eden: An American Place,* which became a *New York Times* bestseller. Not bad, Jean!

NOTES

1: The California Dream

1 Tristram Korten, "Governor Rick Scott's Ban on Climate Change Term Extended to Other State Agencies," *Miami Herald,* March 11, 2015, http://miamiherald.com/news /state/florida/article13576691.html.

2 James Fallows, "Jerry Brown's Political Reboot," *The Atlantic,* June 2013, http://www .theatlantic.com/magazine/archive/2013/06/the-fixer/309324/.

3 Henry William Brands, *The Age of Gold: The California Gold Rush and the New American Dream* (New York: Anchor Books, 2003), 458.

4 "Modern Economy." Department of Finance, California, http://www.dof.ca.gov /HTML/FS_DATA/HistoryCAEconomy/modern_economy.htm.

5 Claudia K. Jurmain, David Lavender, and James J. Rawls, eds., *California: A Place, a People, a Dream* (San Francisco: Chronicle Books, 1986), 141.

6 James J. Berg and Chris Freeman, eds., *Conversations with Christopher Isherwood* (Jackson: *University Press of Mississippi,* 2001), 91.

7 Paul Harris, "Will California Become America's First Failed State?" *Guardian,* October 3, 2009, http://www.theguardian.com/world/2009/oct/04/california-failing-state-debt.

8 Julie Pace and Philip Elliott, "Romney Compares California's Economy to Greece," *Yahoo!,* August 8, 2012, http://news.yahoo.com/romney-compares-californias-economy -greece-185358845.html.

9 Bill Watkins, "First Step for California: Admit There's a Problem," *New Geography,* September 27, 2011, http://www.newgeography.com/content/002460-first-step -california-admit-theres-a-problem.

10 Torey Van Oot, "California Officials Announce Closure of 70 State Parks," *Sacramento Bee*, May 13, 2011, http://blogs.sacbee.com/capitolalertlatest/2011/05/california-officials -70-state-parks.html.

11 Harris, "Will California Become America's First Failed State?"

12 Robert Greenstein, "Tax Cuts and Consequences: The States That Cut Taxes the Most During the 1990s Have Suffered Lately," Center on Budget Priorities, January 12, 2005, http://www.cbpp.org/research/tax-cuts-and-consequences-the-states-that-cut -taxes-the-most-during-the-1990s-have-suffered.

13 Newt Gingrich, "Texas Leads as California Dreams On," *Financial Times*, September 1, 2009, http://www.ft.com/cms/s/0/7e5945b4-9725-11de-83c5-00144feabdc0.html.

14   Texas Legislative Study Group, *Texas on the Brink,* March 2013, http://texaslsg.org
     /texas-on-the-brink/.

15   Max Pringle, "California Regains Economic Ranking," Capital Public Radio, July 11,
     2013, http://www.capradio.org/articles/2013/07/11/california-regains-economic-ranking/.

16   State of California Employment Development Department, "Unemployment Rate and
     Labor Force," Historical Unemployment and Labor Force Data Tables, http://www
     .labormarketinfo.edd.ca.gov/data/unemployment-and-labor-force.html.

17   Phillip Longman, "Oops: The Texas Miracle That Isn't," *Washington Monthly,*
     March-April-May 2014, http://www.washingtonmonthly.com/magazine/march_april
     _may_2014/features/oops_the_texas_miracle_that_is049289.php?page=all.

18   Ibid.

19   Ibid.

20   Jeffery Kahn, "Ronald Reagan Launched Political Career Using the Berkeley Campus
     as a Target," *UC Berkeley News,* June 8, 2004.

21   Jerry Brown, State of the State Address, January 7, 1976, Sacramento, http://governors
     .library.ca.gov/addresses/s_34-JBrown1.html.

2: The Pendulum Swings Right

1   "California Real Estate Median Prices of Existing Homes since 1968," 2005, http://
    www.realestateabc.com/graphs/calmedian.htm.

2   Peter Schrag, *Paradise Lost: California's Experience, America's Future* (Berkeley:
    University of California Press, 1999), 133.

3   Howard Jarvis and Robert Pack, *I'm Mad as Hell: The Exclusive Story of the Tax Revolt
    and Its Leader* (New York: Times Books, 1979), 30.

4   Ibid., 41.

5   Rose Institute of State and Local Government, California Initiatives in Perspective
    1966-2002, "Prop. 14: Property Tax Limitations," p. 17, October 2003, Claremont
    McKenna College, file:///Users/rscheer/Downloads/8116%20(1).pdf.

6   "Report on the 1973 Campaign of California Gov. Reagan for Prop 1 (Spending
    Limit)," YouTube, May 15, 2011, https://www.youtube.com/watch?v=_QroATIRO4k.

7   Lou Cannon, *Governor Reagan: His Rise to Power* (New York: Public Affairs,
    2003), 385.

8   "Report on the 1973 Campaign."

9   Jarvis and Pack, *I'm Mad as Hell,* 52.

10 Schrag, *Paradise Lost,* 142.

11 Jarvis and Pack, *I'm Mad as Hell,* 112.

12 Ibid., 113.

13 Schrag, *Paradise Lost,* 146.

14 Ibid., 147.

15 Jane Gross and Katherine Bishop, "The 1992 Campaign: Candidate's Record; Brown
    Opened Doors but Failed to Build Coalitions," *New York Times,* April 5, 1992,
    http://www.nytimes.com/1992/04/05/us/1992-campaign-candidate-s-record-brown
    -opened-doors-but-failed-build-coalitions.html.

16 Interview with the author, Los Angeles, October 28, 2011.
17 Ibid.
18 Dorothy Townsend, "Arts Backers Hold Protest," *Los Angeles Times,* May 24, 1978, OC14.
19 Schrag, *Paradise Lost,* 146.
20 Sid Bernstein and Barbara Baird, "County Assessments to Be Mailed Before Election," *Los Angeles Times,* May 17, 1978.
21 Ibid.
22 Alexander Pope, "The Assessor's Perspective," *University of Southern California Law Review,* Volume 53, 1979–80, 156, https://www.evernote.com/shard/s4/sh/99912af6 -ef92-4a9a-ac37-afdc53b16723/cdef794544ef570e1da28da1215d2c17/res/3748ba41-d811 -47cd-92d6-fb4ebcb1f6dc/Pope%20Assessors%20Perspective.pdf.
23 Ibid., 155.
24 Schrag, *Paradise Lost,* 150.
25 Interview with the author, August 10, 2011.
26 Joe Garofoli, "What 'Third Rail'? CA Democrats Support Changes to Prop 13," *SF Gate,* April 14, 2013, http://blog.sfgate.com/politics/2013/04/14/what-third-rail-ca -democrats-support-changes-to-prop-13/.
27 Christopher Palmeri, "California Diminished by 1978 Tax Revolt Shows U.S. in Decline," *Bloomberg,* October 16, 2011, http://www.bloomberg.com/news/2011-10-17 /california-diminished-by-1978-tax-revolt-shows-u-s-in-decline.html.
28 Chris Isidore, "Buffett Says He's Still Paying Lower Tax Rate Than His Secretary," *CNN Money,* http://money.cnn.com/2013/03/04/news/economy/buffett-secretary-taxes/.
29 Jodi Wilgoren and Ann Conway, "60 Emerald Bay Houses Lost in Fire: Community Homeowners Whose Properties Were Threatened Include Ex-Astronaut Buzz Aldrin and the Nation's Richest Man, Warren E. Buffett," *Los Angeles Times,* October 28, 1993, http://articles.latimes.com/1993-10-28/news/mn-50578_1_emerald-bay.
30 Elizabeth Lesly Stevens, "On Gold Coast, a Legacy of Low Taxes," *Bay Citizen,* May 26, 2010, https://www.baycitizen.org/columns/elizabeth-lesly-stevens/death-and -taxes-sfs-gold-coast/.
31 Garofoli, "What 'Third Rail'?"
32 Palmeri, "California Diminished by 1978 Tax Revolt Shows U.S. in Decline."
33 Ibid.
34 Jarvis and Pack, *I'm Mad as Hell,* 147.
35 Ibid., 148.
36 Interview with the author, December 10, 2011.
37 Jarvis and Pack, *I'm Mad as Hell,* 147.
38 Interview with the author, Los Angeles, February 11, 2013.
39 Interview with the author, October 28, 2011.
40 Jarvis and Pack, *I'm Mad as Hell,* 151.
41 Ibid., 152.
42 Ibid., 156.
43 Ibid., 157.
44 Interview with the author, San Francisco.

3: Moonbeam to Laser Beam

1   Dick Shoemaker, "Jerry Brown's First Term as California Governor—Part I,"
    YouTube, August 23, 1975, uploaded by ABC News, https://www.youtube.com/watch
    ?v=9XVXcTqeMkI.

2   Dan Walters, "Dan Walters Daily: Jerry Brown's 'Canoe Theory' of Politics," YouTube,
    September 29, 2014, uploaded by the *Sacramento Bee,* https://www.youtube.com/watch
    ?v=yxzlHFu2VzY.

3   Wyatt Buchanan and Marisa Lagos, "Jerry Brown Vetoes Budget—Democrats
    'Dismayed,' " *SF Gate,* June 17, 2011, http://www.sfgate.com/news/article/Jerry-Brown
    -vetoes-budget-Democrats-dismayed-2367281.php.

4   Jessica Calefati and Theresa Harrington, "California, Suffering with a $26 Billion
    Deficit Not Long Ago, Now Has an $8 Billion Surplus," Tribune News Service,
    Governing the States and Localities, May 7, 2013, http://www.governing.com/topics
    /finance/tns-california-surplus.html.

5   "Governor Brown Proposes 2015-16 State Budget," Office of Governor Edmund G.
    Brown Jr. January 9, 2015, https://www.gov.ca.gov/news.php?id=18834.

6   "Governor Brown Signs Immigration Legislation," Office of Governor Edmund G.
    Brown Jr. Newsroom, October 5, 2013, http://gov.ca.gov/news.php?id=18253.

7   Phillip Reese and Stephen Magagnini, "Census: Hispanics Overtake Whites to Become
    California's Largest Ethnic Group," *Sacramento Bee,* June 30, 2015, http://www.sacbee
    .com/news/local/article25940218.html.

8   *New York Times* Editorial Board, "Fixing Immigration from the Ground Up," *New
    York Times,* October 6, 2013, http://www.nytimes.com/2013/10/07/opinion/fixing
    -immigration-from-the-ground-up.html.

9   Alexei Koseff, "Jerry Brown Approves Loan Program for Undocumented Students,"
    Sacramento Bee, September 29, 2014, http://www.sacbee.com/news/politics-government
    /capitol-alert/article2615437.html.

10 Roger Rapoport, *California Dreaming: The Political Odyssey of Pat & Jerry Brown,*
    (Berkeley: Nolo Press, 1982), 56.

11 Seth Rosenfeld, "The Governor's Race," *SF Gate,* June 9, 2002, http://www.sfgate.com
    /news/article/The-governor-s-race-3311801.php.

12 Martin Schiesl, "Residential Opportunity for All Californians: Governor Edmund G.
    'Pat' Brown and the Struggle for Fair Housing Legislation, 1959–1963," Pat Brown
    Institute, August 2013, http://www.patbrowninstitute.org/up/documents/publications/
    HistoricalEssayFairHousingOpportunities.pdf.

13 Mervyn D. Field, "Public Opposed to Rumford Act, Want Repeal or Modification,"
    California Poll, Field Research Corporation, September 15, 1966, http://ucdata.berkeley
    .edu/pubs/CalPolls/540.pdf.

14 Lisa McGirr, *Suburban Warriors: The Origins of the New American Right* (Princeton:
    Princeton University Press, 2001), 205.

15 Edmund G. Brown, *Reagan and Reality: The Two Californias* (New York: Praeger,
    1970), 17–18.

16   Orville Schell, *Brown* (New York: Random House, 1978), 125.

17   Morrie Ryskind, "Academic Chutzpah," *Sarasota Herald-Tribune,* August 19, 1969, https://news.google.com/newspapers?nid=1774&dat=19690819&id=Pr0qAAAAIBAJ&s jid=-WUEAAAAIBAJ&pg=5095,5125562&hl=en.

18   Ibid.

19   Susan Stocking, "College Trustees Clash Over Office Furniture," *Los Angeles Times,* August 13, 1969, http://search.proquest.com.libproxy2.usc.edu/docview/156226791 ?accountid=14749.

20   Rapoport, *California Dreaming,* 123.

21   "MLK's Name Proposed for Southwest Junior College," *Los Angeles Sentinel,* January 29, 1970, A4.

22   Carl Greenberg, "Edmund Brown Jr. Enters Race for Secretary of State," *Los Angeles Times,* March 3, 1970, A3.

23   William Endicott, "134 Candidates Get Ultimatum on Filing Financial Reports," *Los Angeles Times,* September 17, 1971. A3, http://search.proquest.com.libproxy2.usc.edu /docview/156879464?accountid=14749.

24   William Endicott, "The New Brown in State Politics Moves Boldly," *Los Angeles Times,* September 27, 1971, A3, http://search.proquest.com.libproxy1.usc.edu/news /docview/156796444/68676315F99846E6PQ/2?accountid=14749.

25   UPI, "Brown Hits Reagan's Use of Leased Jet," *Los Angeles Times,* December 30, 1973, 20.

26   William Endicott, "Reagan Accuses Brown of Lies and Distortions," *Los Angeles Times,* November 1, 1974, A3.

27   Chuck McFadden, *Trailblazer: A Biography of Jerry Brown* (Berkeley: University of California Press, 2013), 55.

28   Paul Glastris, "How the Trial Lawyers (and the Doctors!) Sold Out to the Tobacco Companies," *Washington Monthly,* December 1987, https://industrydocuments.library .ucsf.edu/documentstore/l/r/y/f//lryf0037/lryf0037.pdf.

29   Richard Reeves, "How Does the Governor Differ from a Shoemaker? And Why Is He So Popular?" *New York Times Magazine,* August 24, 1975, 20.

30   George Skelton, "A More Mature Gov. Brown Has Less to Say in Speeches, Plenty to Do," *Los Angeles Times,* December 10, 2014, http://www.latimes.com/local/politics/la -me-cap-jerry-brown-20141211-column.html.

31   "Text of Gov. Jerry Brown's First Inaugural Address," *Los Angeles Times,* January 6, 1975, California State Library, http://governors.library.ca.gov/addresses/34-Jbrown01.html.

32   Ibid.

33   Ibid.

34   Interview with the author, October 28, 2013.

35   Murray Fromson, May 19, 1976, "Jerry Brown's First Term as California Governor—Part I," uploaded by CBS News, https://www.youtube.com/watch?v =9XVXcTqeMkI.

36   Dick Shoemaker, "Jerry Brown's First Term as California Governor—Part I," uploaded by CBS News, https://www.youtube.com/watch?v=9XVXcTqeMkI.

37   Fromson, "Jerry Brown's First Term."

38 Manuel Klausner, "Inside Ronald Reagan," *Reason,* July 1, 1975, http://reason.com/archives/1975/07/01/inside-ronald-reagan/5.

39 Jesse Walker, "Five Faces of Jerry Brown," *American Conservative,* November 1, 2009, http://www.theamericanconservative.com.

40 Jesse McKinley, "How Jerry Brown Became 'Governor Moonbeam,'" *New York Times,* March 6, 2010, http://www.nytimes.com/2010/03/07/weekinreview/07mckinley.html?_r=0.

41 Maureen Dowd, "Governor Brown Redux: The Iceman Melteth," *New York Times,* March 5, 2011, http://www.nytimes.com/2011/03/06/opinion/06dowd.html.

42 Fred Branfman, "The Salon Interview: Jerry Brown: Moving Toward the Abyss," *Salon,* June 3, 1996, http://www.salon.com/1996/06/03/interview960603/.

43 Ibid.

44 Ibid.

45 Ibid.

46 Ibid.

4: The Enron Assault

1 Snohomish County Public Utility District, "Our Fight Against Enron," Newsroom, Special Reports, audio files, http://www.snopud.com/Site/Content/Documents/sno-525%20powerpoint.wav.

2 Taped Conversation, "Enron Traders Phone Call—Secret Scandals," YouTube, uploaded November 20, 2010, https://www.youtube.com/watch?v=nWCtKqYnLXA.

3 Interview with the author, October 28, 2011.

4 Ibid.

5 Rebecca Smith, "California Legislators Approve Deregulation of Utilities," *San Jose Mercury News,* September 2, 1996, http://www.highbeam.com/doc/1G1-18643558.html.

6 Nancy Vogel, "How State's Consumers Lost with Electricity Deregulation," *Los Angeles Times,* December 9, 2000, http://articles.latimes.com/print/2000/dec/09/news/mn-63325.

7 Christopher Keating, "Electric Rates Vex Governors," *Hartford Courant,* December 4, 1996, http://articles.courant.com/1996-12-14/news/9612140335_1_deregulation-new-hampshire-electric-utilities.

8 John Dunbar and Robert Moore, "California Power Politics," Center for Public Integrity, May 2001, https://www.publicintegrity.org/files/manual/pdf/corporate/2001_CPI_Highlights.pdf.

9 Ibid.

10 "The California Crisis: California Timeline," *Frontline,* PBS, http://www.pbs.org/wgbh/pages/frontline/shows/blackout/california/timeline.html.

11 Ibid.

12 Vogel, "How State's Consumers Lost."

13 Dan Morain, "Deregulation Bill Signed by Wilson," *Los Angeles Times,* September 24, 1996, http://articles.latimes.com/1996-09-24/news/mn-47043_1_wilson-signed-legislation.

14 Vogel, "How State's Consumers Lost."

15 Eric Lipton, "Gramm and the 'Enron Loophole,'" *New York Times,* November 14, 2008, http://www.nytimes.com/2008/11/17/business/17grammside.html.

16 Tyson Slocum, *Blind Faith: How Deregulation and Enron's Influence Over Government Looted Billions from Americans,* Public Citizen Report, December 2001, https://www .citizen.org/documents/Blind_Faith.pdf.

17 Ibid.

18 John W. Dean, "Some Questions About Enron's Campaign Contributions: Did Enron Successfully Buy Influence with the Money It Spent?" *FindLaw,* January 18, 2002, http://writ.news.findlaw.com/dean/20020118.html.

19 Vogel, "How State's Consumers Lost."

20 "California Crisis."

21 Thomas Leavitt, "Enron Tapes—Enron Audio Tapes Now Public," *Seeing the Forest,* June 4, 2004, http://elibrary.ferc.gov/idmws/common/opennat.asp?fileID =10161550.

22 Jonathan Peterson, "Tapes Reveal Enron's Power Plant Rigging," *Los Angeles Times,* February 4, 2005, http://articles.latimes.com/2005/feb/04/business/fi-enron4/2.

23 Mark Baldassare, "PPIC Statewide Survey: Californians and Their Government," Public Policy Institute of California, October 2000, vi, http://www.ppic.org/content /pubs/survey/S_1000MBS.pdf.

24 *Democratic Underground,* "The Enron Tapes: Unbleeped," June 3, 2004, http://www .democraticunderground.com/discuss/duboard.php?az=view_ all&address=104x1711340.

25 Vogel, "How State's Consumers Lost."

26 Interview with the author.

27 Kevin O'Connor, "Celebrating Ten Years of Derivatives Deregulation," *Huffington Post,* December 21, 2012, http://www.huffingtonpost.com/kevin-connor/celebrating-ten -years-of_b_799981.html.

28 Kurt Eichenwald, *Conspiracy of Fools: A True Story* (New York: Broadway Books, 2005), 402.

29 Ibid.

30 Ibid., 403.

31 Ibid., 204.

32 O'Connor, "Celebrating Ten Years of Derivatives Deregulation."

33 Slocum, *Blind Faith.*

34 Interview with the author, October 28, 2011.

35 Ibid.

36 Thomas DeLay, "Bringing Consumer Choice to Electricity," *Heritage Foundation,* April 18, 1997, http://www.heritage.org/research/lecture/hl582nbsp-bringing-consumer -choice.

37 Marego Athans, "Energy's Future in a New Market," *Baltimore Sun,* January 11, 2001, http://articles.baltimoresun.com/2001-01-11/news/0101110029_1_natural-gas-price-of -natural-electricity/2.

38 R. A. ("Jake") Dyer, "Deregulated Electricity in Texas," *Texas Coalition for Affordable*

Power, March 2014, p. 16, http://tcaptx.com/wp-content/uploads/2014/02/TCP-793
-Deregulation2014-A-1.7.pdf.

39 Ibid., 2.

40 Ibid., 28.

5: A Tale of Two States

1   Mark Leibovich, "Rick Perry's 'Groundhog Day,'" *New York Times Magazine,* June 17,
    2014, http://www.nytimes.com/2014/06/22/magazine/rick-perrys-groundhog-day
    .html.

2   Will Weissert, "Could Texas Gov. Rick Perry Be Mulling Move to . . . California?"
    Dallas Morning News, June 17, 2014, http://www.dallasnews.com/news/politics/state
    -politics/20140617-could-texas-gov.-rick-perry-be-mulling-move-to- . . . -california.ece.

3   Ibid.

4   Julie Wiener, "Rick Perry, the Jew," *Jewish Telegraphic Agency,* June 17, 2014, http://
    www.jta.org/2014/06/17/default/rick-perry-the-jew.

5   Hunter Schwarz, "California's Economy Is Large Enough It Could Be Admitted into
    G8," *Washington Post,* July 8, 2014, http://www.washingtonpost.com/blogs/govbeat/wp
    /2014/07/08/californias-economy-is-large-enough-it-could-be-admitted-into-g-8/.

6   Alex Rogers, "Rick Perry Goes Job Rustling, Again," *Time,* February 5, 2013,
    swampland.time.com/2013/02/05/rick-perry-goes-job-rustling-again/.

7   *ABC News,* "California, Texas Governors Spar Over Jobs," http://abcnews.go.com
    /Politics/video/california-texas-governors-spar-jobs-18414237.

8   Kish Rajan, "GO-Biz Quoted Response to Rick Perry Trying to Poach Jobs from
    California," *California Association for Local Economic Development,* December 8, 2014,
    http://www.caled.org/go-biz-quoted-response-poach-jobs-california/.

9   Jed Kolko, "Business Relocation and Homegrown Jobs, 1992–2006," Public Policy
    Institute of California, September 2010, http://www.ppic.org/content/pubs/report/R
    _910JKR.pdf.

10 Rajan, "GO-Biz Quoted Response."

11 Greg LeRoy, Kasia Tarczynska, Leigh McIlvaine, Thomas Cafcas, and Philip Mattera,
    "The Job-Creation Shell Game," *Good Jobs First Report,* January 2013, 4–5, http://www
    .goodjobsfirst.org/sites/default/files/docs/pdf/shellgame.pdf.

12 Boris Epshteyn, "Republicans, All We Need Is Six Little Words to Get Our Message
    Out," *Fox News Opinion,* September 27, 2010, http://www.foxnews.com/opinion/2010
    /09/27/boris-epshteyn-pledge-america-republicans-small-government-low-taxes
    -national.html.

13 G. Scott Thomas, "California Loses Most Amount of Jobs Since Recession," *Sacra-
    mento Business Journal,* March 26, 2012, http://www.bizjournals.com/sacramento/news
    /2012/03/26/california-job-loss-recession-analysis.html.

14 FactCheck.org, "Texas-Size Recovery: Here's a Look at the Facts Behind Job Growth
    in the Lone Star State," August 31, 2011, http://www.factcheck.org/2011/08/texas-size
    -recovery/.

15 Claudia Grisales, "Experts: Lower Oil Prices a Threat to Texas Oil Economy,"

Statesman, December 18, 2014, http://www.statesman.com/news/business/experts-lower
-oil-prices-a-threat-to-texas-economy/njWwN/.

16   Ibid.

17   Josh Zumbrun, "Oil States See Slumping Employment as Texas Loses 25,000 Jobs in
      March," *Wall Street Journal,* April 21, 2015, http://blogs.wsj.com/economics/2015/04/21
      /oil-states-see-slumping-employment-as-texas-loses-25000-jobs-in-march/.

18   *Union Pacific,* "Current West Texas Intermediate Crude Oil (WTI) Prices," http://
      www.up.com/customers/surcharge/wti/prices/.

19   Lori Robertson, "A Tale of Two Jobs Numbers," FactCheck.org, January 20, 2015,
      http://www.factcheck.org/2015/01/a-tale-of-two-jobs-numbers/.

20   Ibid.

21   Office of the Governor, "Texas Enterprise Fund Graphic as of June 30, 2015," http://gov
      .texas.gov/files/ecodev/TEF_Listing.pdf.

22   Dave Mann, "Slush Fun," *Texas Observer,* March 11, 2010, http://www.texasobserver
      .org/slush-fun/.

23   Texans for Public Justice, "Phantom Jobs: The Texas Enterprise Fund's Broken
      Promises," September 8, 2010, http://info.tpj.org/watchyourassets/enterprise3/index
      .html.

24   Ibid.

25   Texans for Public Justice, "Perry's Piggybank: Texas Enterprise Fund Recipients Gave
      $7 Million to Rick Perry and His Republican Governors Association," October 2011,
      http://info.tpj.org/reports/pdf/PerryPiggybankTEF.pdf.

26   Mark Maremont, "Behind Perry's Jobs Success, Numbers Draw New Scrutiny," *Wall
      Street Journal,* October 11, 2011, http://www.wsj.com/articles/SB1000142405297020379190457660685282305894 0.

27   Ibid.

28   John Keel, "An Audit Report on the Texas Enterprise Fund at the Office of the
      Governor," State Auditor's Office, September 2014, http://www.sao.state.tx.us/reports
      /main/15-003.pdf.

29   Christy Hoppe, "Firms Got Millions from Texas Enterprise Fund Without Applications,
      Specific Job Goals," *Dallas Morning News,* September 25, 2014, http://www.dallasnews
      .com/news/state/headlines/20140925-firms-got-millions-from-texas-enterprise-fund
      -without-applications-specific-job-goals.ece.

30   Ibid.

31   Office of the Governor, "Texas Enterprise Fund, the Deal Closer. TEF Award Listing—
      All Projects to Date Graphic," http://gov.texas.gov/files/ecodev/TEF_Listing.pdf.

32   Charles Dameron, "Rick Perry's Crony Capitalism Problem," *Wall Street Journal,*
      August 13, 2011, http://www.wsj.com/articles/SB1000142405270230476060457642862897285614.

33   Texas Wide Open for Business, "Gov. Perry Announces Toyota Moving North
      American Headquarters to Plano, Generating 4,000 Jobs," April 28, 2014, https://
      texaswideopenforbusiness.com/news/gov-perry-announces-toyota-moving-north
      -american-headquarters-plano-generating-4000-jobs.

34   Texas Legislative Study Group, *Texas on the Brink.*

35   Jerry Hirsch and Tim Logan, "Was Toyota Driven Out of California? Not So Fast," *Los Angeles Times,* May 1, 2014, http://www.latimes.com/business/autos/la-fi-toyota -economy-20140502-story.html.

36   Ibid.

37   Ibid.

38   Ibid.

39   Governor's Office of Business and Economic Development, "California Competes Tax Credit Program," http://www.business.ca.gov/Portals/0/CA%20Competes/Docs /Meeting%20Agendas/CCTC%20June%2019%202014%20Committee%20Meeting.pdf.

40   Ibid.

41   John Woolfolk, "San Jose Approves $7 Million Samsung Incentives," *Contra Costa Times,* March 27, 2013, http://www.contracostatimes.com/ci_22877593/san-jose -approves-7-million-samsung-incentives.

42   Bryce Druzin, "Gov. Jerry Brown Gets Thumbs Up from Silicon Valley CEOs, Survey Says," *Silicon Valley Business Journal,* April 13, 2016, http://www.bizjournals.com /sanjose/news/2016/04/13/gov-jerry-brown-gets-thumbs-up-from-silicon-valley.html.

43   *CB Insights,* "For Venture Capital, It's Still California or Bust: 2014 Sees Funding Up 81% YoY," February 2, 2015, https://www.cbinsights.com/blog/california-venture-capital-2014/.

44   SSTI, "Useful Stats: Venture Capital Dollars and Deals by State, 2010–2015," February 4, 2016, ssti.org/blog/useful-stats-venture-capital-dollars-and-deals-state-2010–2015.

45   Interview with Los Angeles Port commissioner Robin Kramer, Los Angeles.

46   Texas Legislative Study Group, *Texas on the Brink.*

47   "Cross-State Air Pollution Rule (CSAPR)," United States Environmental Protection Agency, http://www.epa.gov/airtransport/CSAPR/.

48   Paul Burka, "True to Form, Perry Blasts EPA," *Texas Monthly,* July 1, 2010, http://www .texasmonthly.com/burka-blog/true-to-form-perry-blasts-epa/.

49   Letter from Rick Perry, Texas governor, to Barack Obama, U.S. president, Office of the Governor, May 28, 2010, http://gov.texas.gov/files/press-office/O -ObamaBarack201005280133.pdf.

50   Lawrence Hurley, "Update 4: In Win for Obama, Top Court Revives Cross-State Air Pollution Rule," *Reuters,* April 29, 2014, http://www.reuters.com/article/2014/04/29 /usa-court-environment-idUSL2N0NL0V320140429.

51   Brad Johnson, "Rick Perry Wants to Frack Iowa," *Climate Progress,* August 16, 2011, http://thinkprogress.org/climate/2011/08/16/296821/rick-perry-loves-fracking/.

52   Alexandra Petri, "Rick Perry, Global Warming and Those Durn Scientists," *Washington Post,* August 17, 2011, http://www.washingtonpost.com/pb/blogs/compost/post/rick -perry-global-warming-and-those-durn-scientists/2011/08/17/gIQAccZoLJ_blog.html.

53   Joe Romm, "Rick Perry's Inane Miscue on Galileo and Climate Change," *Think Progress,* September 8, 2012, http://thinkprogress.org/climate/2011/09/08/315220/rick -perry-galileo-climate-change/.

54   Brad Johnson, "Perry Reveals Plan for Total U.S. Anarchy: 'Put A Moratorium On All Regulations.'" *Think Progress,* August 15, 2011, http://thinkprogress.org/climate/2011 /08/15/296314/perry-reveals-plan-for-total-u-s-anarchy-put-a-moratorium-on-all -regulations/.

55   Ibid.

56   Tea Party News Network, "Rick Perry Rocks CPAC: 'A Little Rebellion Now and Then Is a Good Thing,'" March 7, 2014, http://www.tpnn.com/2014/03/07/rick-perry -rocks-cpac-a-little-rebellion-now-and-then-is-a-good-thing/.

57   Covered California, "Covered California Open Enrollment 2013–2014," October 2014, https://www.coveredca.com/pdfs/10-14-2014-Lessons-Learned-final.pdf.

58   Dan Mangan, "Don't Mess with Medicaid Expansion? A Lesson from Texas," CNBC, May 29, 2015, http://www.cnbc.com/2015/05/29/texas-pays-a-big-price-for-saying-no-to -medicaid-expansion.html.

59   Texas Legislative Study Group, *Texas on the Brink*.

60   Ibid.

61   Mangan, "Don't Mess with Medicaid Expansion?"

62   Ibid.

63   Nick Swartsell, "Minimum Wage Boost Could Help Texans—or Hurt," *Dallas Morning News,* March 6, 2014, http://www.dallasnews.com/news/metro/20140306 -minimum-wage-boost-could-help-texans—or-hurt.ece.

64   James Nash, "California Lawmakers Pass Toughest U.S. Law Requiring Equal Pay," *Bloomberg Politics,* August 27, 2015, http://www.bloomberg.com/politics/articles/2015 -08-27/california-lawmakers-pass-toughest-u-s-law-requiring-equal-pay.

65   Interview with author, February 9, 2013.

66   Gene Stone, "I'm Okay, You're a Gay," *Huffington Post,* June 9, 2005, http://www .huffingtonpost.com/gene-stone/im-okay-youre-a-gay_b_2355.html.

67   "Rick Perry Transcript: June 11, 2014," Commonwealth Club of California, June 11, 2014, http://www.commonwealthclub.org/about/press-room/rick-perry-transcript-and -multimedia-61114.

68   Wade Goodwyn, "New Texas Governor Adds to Tension Between State, City Governments," National Public Radio, January 15, 2015, http://www.npr.org/2015/01 /15/377526831/new-texas-governor-adds-to-tension-between-state-city-governments.

69   Patrick McGreevy, "Gov. Brown Approves Legal Help for Minors in the Country Illegally," *Los Angeles Times,* September 27, 2014, http://www.latimes.com/local /political/la-me-pc-gov-brown-approves-legal-help-for-minors-in-the-country-illegally -20140927-story.html.

70   Molly Hennessy-Fiske, "Texas Gov. Rick Perry Orders 1,000 National Guard Troops to Border," *Los Angeles Times,* July 21, 2014, http://www.latimes.com/nation/la-na-texas -perry-national-guard-border-20140721-story.html.

71   Interview with the author, February 9, 2013.

6: Diversity Trumps

1   "Republican Presidential Debate with Ronald Reagan and George H. W. Bush," YouTube, 45:30–48:10, April 24, 1980, https://www.youtube.com/watch ?v=YfHN5QKq9hQ.

2   Ibid.

3   Sharon Bernstein, "Californians Say Undocumented Immigrants Should Get to Stay," *Reuters,* October 1, 2015, http://www.reuters.com/article/2015/10/01/us-usa-poll -california-immigration-idUSKCN0RV3DB20151001.

4   Ibid.

5   Emiko Omori, "The Rabbit in the Moon," Television Race Initiative, January 1999, 8, http://www-tc.pbs.org/pov/tvraceinitiative/gr/rabbit_guide.pdf.

6   Audrey McAvoy, "Internments Can Happen Again, Scalia Warns," *Star-Advertiser,* February 4, 2014, http://www.staradvertiser.com/news/hawaiinews/20140204 _Internments_can_happen_again_Scalia_warns.html?id=243454461.

7   *This American Life,* WBEZ Radio Archive, Number 41: Politics, November 8, 1996, 26:19, http:thisamericanlife.org/radio-archives/episode/41/politics?/act=2#play.

8   Leslie Berestein Rojas, "The Original 'Self-Deportationist' Finally Gets His Due," 89.3 KPCC, February 1, 2012, http://www.scpr.org/blogs/multiamerican/2012/02/01/8362 /the-original-self-deportationist-finally-gets-his-/.

9   William Safire, "Essay: Self-Deportation?" *New York Times,* November 21, 1994, http://www.nytimes.com/1994/11/21/opinion/essay-self-deportation.html.

10 Lucy Madison, "Romney on Immigration: 'I'm for Self-Deportation,'" *CBS News,* January 24, 2012, http://www.cbsnews.com/news/romney-on-immigration-im-for-self -deportation/.

11 Aaron Blake, "Priebus: Romney's Self-Deportation Comment Was 'Horrific,'" *Washington Post,* August 16, 2013, http://www.washingtonpost.com/news/post-politics /wp/2013/08/16/priebus-romneys-self-deportation-comment-was-horrific/.

12 Alan Greenblatt, "Kris Kobach Tackles Illegal Immigration." *Governing the States and Localities,* March 2012, http://www.governing.com/topics/politics/gov-kris-kobach -tackles-illegal-immigration.html.

13 *ImmigrationProf Blog,* "Proposition 187, Twenty Years Later," November 10, 2014, http://lawprofessors.typepad.com/immigration/2014/11/proposition-187-twenty-years -later.html.

14 "Illegal Aliens: Ineligibility for Public Services. Verification and Reporting," *UC Hastings College of the Law,* 1994, http://repository.uchastings.edu/cgi/viewcontent.cgi ?article=2103&context=ca_ballot_props.

15 Ibid.

16 Ibid.

17 William Safire, "Essay: Self-Deportation?"

18 Ibid.

19 "Illegal Aliens: Ineligibility."

20 *Time,* "Texas Gov-Elect Just Says No to Prop 187," December 2, 1994, http://content .time.com/time/nation/article/0,8599,2482,00.html.

21 Jesse Katz, "Prop 187 Gives Texas a Selling Point in Mexico," *Los Angeles Times,* February 6, 1995, P1, http://articles.latimes.com/1995-02-06/news/mn-28768_1_mexico -city.

22 Ibid.

23 Ibid.

24 "Pete Wilson 1994 Campaign Ad on Illegal Immigration," YouTube, 1994, https://
    www.youtube.com/watch?v=lLIzzs2HHgY.

25 Ibid.

26 Roxana Kopetman, "Politics, Activism, Families: How Prop. 187 Is Still Being Felt
    20 Years Later," *Orange County Register,* October 30, 2014, http://www.ocregister.com
    /articles/california-640388-prop-state.htm.

27 Ron Unz, "Value Added: Why *National Review* Is Wrong," *National Review,* Novem-
    ber 7, 1994.

28 Gebe Martinez, "California Elections/Proposition 187: Kemp Defends Criticism Before
    Hostile Audience," *Los Angeles Times*, October 20, 1994, http://articles.latimes.com
    /1994-10-20/news/mn-52440_1_jack-kemp.

29 Patrick J. McDonnell and Dave Lesher, "Clinton, Feinstein Declare Opposition to Prop
    187: Immigration: President Calls Measure Unconstitutional. Senator Admits Her
    Stance Could Cost Her the Election," *Los Angeles Times,* October 22, 1994, http://
    articles.latimes.com/1994-10-22/news/mn-53251_1_illegal-immigrants.

30 Ibid.

31 Michael R. Alvarez and Tara L. Butterfield. "The Resurgence of Nativism in
    California? The Case for Proposition 187 and Illegal Immigration," California Institute
    of Technology, September 25, 1997, http://polmeth.wustl.edu/media/Paper/alvar97d
    .pdf.

32 Ibid.

33 Daniel Politi, "Donald Trump in Phoenix: Mexicans Are 'Taking Our Jobs' and
    'Killing Us,'" *Slate,* July 12, 2015, http://www.slate.com/blogs/the_slatest/2015/07/12
    /donald_trump_in_phoenix_mexicans_are_taking_our_jobs_and_killing_us.html.

34 Patrick J. McDonnell and Dave Lesher, "Clinton, Feinstein Declare Opposition to Prop
    187."

35 Ibid.

36 Daniel HoSang, *Racial Propositions: Ballot Initiatives and the Making of Postwar
    California* (Berkeley: University of California Press, 2010), 187.

37 Ibid., 179.

38 "Illegal Aliens: Ineligibility."

39 Patrick J. McDonnell and Robert J. Lopez, "L.A. March Against Prop. 187 Draws
    70,000: Immigration: Protesters Condemn Wilson for Backing Initiative That They
    Say Promotes 'Racism, Scapegoating,'" *Los Angeles Times,* October 17, 1994, http://
    articles.latimes.com/1994-10-17/news/mn-51339_1_illegal-immigrants.

40 Michael Haas, "Captive Thai Workers," *Immigration to the United States,* http://
    immigrationinamerica.org/405-captive-thai-workers.html.

41 "California Department of Industrial Relations, Targeted Industries Partnership
    Program, Fifth Annual Report," 1997, https://www.dir.ca.gov.dise.tipp1997.htm.

42 Kopetman, "Politics, Activism, Families."

43 Frank James, "Meg Whitman Blames Jerry Brown for Housekeeper 'Smear,'" NPR,
    September 30, 2010, http://www.npr.org/sections/itsallpolitics/2010/09/30/130243424
    /meg-whitman-discusses-nanny-gate.

44   Associated Press, "Meg Whitman Settles for $5,500 with Former Housekeeper," *Christian Science Monitor,* November 18, 2010, http://www.csmonitor.com/USA/Latest-News-Wires/2010/1118/Meg-Whitman-settles-for-5-500-with-former-housekeeper.

45   Matt Barreto, "The Prop 187 Effect: How the California GOP Lost Their Way and Implications for 2014 and Beyond," *Latino Decisions,* October 17, 2013, http://www.latinodecisions.com/blog/2013/10/17/prop187effect/.

46   Interview with the author, January 13, 2015.

47   Ibid.

48   Luis F. B. Plascencia, *Disenchanting Citizenship: Mexican Migrants and the Boundaries of Belonging* (New Brunswick: Rutgers University Press, 2012), 152.

49   Interview with the author.

50   Barreto, "The Prop 187 Effect."

51   Jennifer Medina, "House Republicans in California Find a Struggle on Immigration," *New York Times,* September 7, 2013, http://www.nytimes.com/2013/09/08/us/politics/house-republicans-in-california-find-a-struggle-on-immigration.html.

52   Ibid.

53   Ryan Lizza, "The Party Next Time: As Immigration Turns Red States Blue, How Can Republicans Transform Their Platform?" *The New Yorker,* November 19, 2012, http://www.newyorker.com/magazine/2012/11/19/the-party-next-time.

54   Ibid.

55   Medina, "House Republicans."

56   Kopetman, "Politics, Activism, Families."

57   Patrick McGreevy, "Gov. Brown Signs Bill Repealing Unenforceable Parts of Prop. 187," *Los Angeles Times,* September 15, 2014, http://www.latimes.com/local/politics/la-me-pol-brown-bills-20140916-story.html.

58   Josh Richman and David E. Early, "Twenty Years After Prop. 187, Attitudes Toward Illegal Immigration Have Changed Dramatically in California," *San Jose Mercury News,* November 22, 2014, http://www.mercurynews.com/census/ci_26994670/twenty-years-after-prop-187-attitudes-toward-illegal.

59   John F. Kennedy, "Executive Order 10925: Establishing the President's Committee on Equal Employment Opportunity," White House, March 6, 1961, http://www.eeoc.gov/eeoc/history/35th/thelaw/eo-10925.html.

60   Michael R. Alvarez and Tara L. Butterfield, "The Revolution Against Affirmative Action in California: Politics, Economics, and Proposition 209," California Institute for Technology, April 7, 1998, http://www.polmeth.wustl.edu/media/Paper/alvar98a.pdf.

61   "*Los Angeles Times* Poll: Study #389, Exit Poll the General Election," *Los Angeles Times,* November 5, 1996, http://media.trb.com/media/acrobat/2008-10/43120439.pdf.

62   "University of California, Application, Admission and Enrollment of California Resident Freshmen for Fall 1995 through 2014," www.ucop.edu/news/factsheets/2-14/flow-frosh-ca-14.pdf.

63   Frank Shyong, "Affirmative Action Amendment Divides State's Asian-Americans," *Los Angeles Times,* May 18, 2014, http://www.latimes.com/local/la-me-asian-divisions-20140519-story.html.

64 Andrea Lampros, "Foes say Prop. 227 is Racist," *Contra Costa Times,* April 26, 1998, http://www.languagepolicy.net/archives/CCT6.htm.

65 Ibid.

66 Ibid.

67 Marisol Cuellar Mejia and Hans Johnson, "Immigrants in California," *Public Policy Institute of California Report,* May 2013, http://www.ppic.org/main/publication_show .asp?i=258.

68 Kopetman, "Politics, Activism, Families."

69 Ibid.

70 Jeremy White, "California Legislature Sends Undocumented Immigrant Driver's License Bill to Gov. Jerry Brown," *Sacramento Bee,* September 12, 2013, http://blogs .sacbee.com/capitolalertlatest/2013/09/california-sends-undocumented-immigrant -license-bill-to-gov-jerry-brown.html#storylink=cpy.

71 Matt O'Brien, "Undocumented Immigrants Crowd California DMV Offices for New Licenses," *San Jose Mercury News,* January 2, 2015, http://www.mercurynews.com /immigration/ci_27247711/undocumented-immigrants-crowd-dmv-offices-new-licenses.

72 Mark Hugo, "The Latino Vote in the 2010 Elections," Pew Research Center, November 3, 2010, http://www.pewhispanic.org/2010/11/03/the-latino-vote-in-the-2010-elections/.

73 Seema Mehta and Melanie Mason, "State GOP Formally Welcomes Gays to the Party," *Los Angeles Times,* March 1, 2015, http://www.latimes.com/local/politics/la-me -california-republicans-20150302-story.html.

74 Christopher Cadelago and David Siders, "California Republicans Softening Platform on Immigration," *Sacramento Bee,* September 19, 2015, http://www.sacbee.com/news /politics-government/capitol-alert/article35855355.html.

75 John Ellis, "State Republican Party Votes to Alter Its Immigration Plank," *Fresno Bee,* September 21, 2015, http://www.fresnobee.com/news/politics-government/politics -columns-blogs/political-notebook/article36070563.html.

76 Ibid.

77 Cadelago and Siders, "California Republicans."

78 Chris Megerian, "California Republicans Set to Soften Stance on Immigrants in the Country Illegally, *Los Angeles Times,* September 19, 2015, http://www.latimes.com /local/political/la-me-ln-california-republicans-soften-stance-on-immigrants-in-the -country-illegally-20150919-story.html.

79 Cathleen Decker, "California GOP Softens Its Message on Immigration in a Bid for Survival," *Los Angeles Times,* September 21, 2015, http://www.latimes.com/local /politics/la-pol-ca-california-politics-convention-20150921-story.html.

80 Megerian, "California Republicans."

81 Cadelago and Siders, "California Republicans."

7: Gold Rush, Fracking, and Electric Cars

1 Powell Greenland, *Hydraulic Mining in California: A Tarnished Legacy* (Washington, D.C.: Arthur H. Clark Company, 2001).

2   Don Baumgart, "Pressure Builds to End Hydraulic Gold Mining," *Sierra County Gold,* http://www.sierracountygold.com/History/BecomingCA_Archive26.html.

3   1849.org, "Gold, Greed & Genocide: Legacy of Poison," http://www.1849.org/ggg /legacy.html.

4   "Opinions of Lorenzo Sawyer, Circuit Judge, and Matthew P. Deady, District Judge, in the Matter of Case 2900, *Edwards Woodruff v. North Bloomfield Mining Company,*" *National Archives Catalog,* https://research.archives.gov/id/295945.

5   1849.org, "Gold, Greed & Genocide: Legacy of Poison."

6   Jon Hamilton, "Tips for Surviving a Mega Disaster," Morning Edition, National Public Radio, June 28, 2013.

7   *Los Angeles Times,* "Smog," September 29, 2007, http://latimesblogs.latimes.com /thedailymirror/2007/09/smog.html.

8   South Coast Air Quality Management District, "The Southland's War on Smog: Fifty Years of Progress Toward Clean Air (through May 1997)," http://www.aqmd.gov/home /library/public-information/publications/50-years-of-progress.

9   California Air Resources Board, "Key Events in the History of Air Quality in California," http://www.arb.ca.gov/html/brochure/history.htm.

10 Ibid.

11 Maudie, "October 2008 Dashboard: Hybrid Sales Up, Despite Economy," *Hybrid Cars,* November 12, 2008, http://www.hybridcars.com/october-2008-dashboard-55132/.

12 Carolyn Whetzel, "California Adopts Strict New Car Standards, Updates Zero-Emissions Vehicle Mandate," *Bloomberg BNA,* January 30, 2012, http://www.bna.com /california-adopts-strict-n12884907528/.

13 David R. Baker, "California Electric Car Sales Pass Major Milestone," *SF Gate,* September 9, 2014, http://blog.sfgate.com/energy/2014/09/09/california-electric-car-sales -pass-major-milestone/.

14 Dan Walters, "Opinion: Fixing California's Roads Will Be Tough Chore," *Sacramento Bee,* January 18, 2015, http://www.sacbee.com/news/politics-government/dan-walters /article7280315.html.

15 CA Department of Motor Vehicles, "State of California Department of Motor Vehicles Statistics for Publication January Through December 2014," March 2015, https://www .dmv.ca.gov/portal/wcm/connect/5aa16cd3-39a5-402f-9453-0d353706cc9a/official.pdf ?MOD=AJPERES.

16 Eric Schaal, "10 Best-Selling Electric Vehicles and Hybrids in 2014," *CheatSheet,* June 9, 2014, http://www.cheatsheet.com/automobiles/10-best-selling-electric-vehicles-and -hybrids-in-2014.html.

17 California Air Resources Board, "Hydrogen Fuel Cell," *Drive Clean,* http://www .driveclean.ca.gov/Search_and_Explore/Technologies_and_Fuel_Types/Hydrogen _Fuel_Cell.php.

18 Ibid.

19 California Natural Resource Agency, "Frequently Asked Questions About CEQA," http://resources.ca.gov/ceqa/more/faq.html.

20 Lee Smith, "Coke and Pepsi to Change Formula to Avoid Prop 65 Labeling," *Food Liability Law,* March 16, 2012, http://www.foodliabilitylaw.com/2012/03/articles

/legislation-and-regulation/coke-and-pepsi-to-change-formula-to-avoid-prop-65
-labeling/.

21 Juan Carlos Rodriguez, "Suits Say Pepsi, Goya Masked Caramel Color Content," *Law
360,* January 24, 2014, http://www.law360.com/articles/503857/suits-say-pepsi-goya
-masked-caramel-color-content.

22 San Diego County Water Authority, "Seawater Desalination," February 2016,
http://www.sdcwa.org/sites/default/files/desal-carlsbad-fs-single.pdf.

23 Colin Sullivan, "Jerry Brown's Environmental Record Runs Deep," *New York Times,*
October 8, 2010, http://www.nytimes.com/gwire/2010/10/08greenwire-jerry-browns
-environmental-record-runs-deep-44334.html?pagewanted=all.

24 Ibid.

25 Ibid.

26 "The California Legislative 2013 Report Card," Sierra Club California, October 2013,
http://www.sierraclub.org/sites/www.sierraclub.org/files/sce/sierra-club-california
/PDFs/FINAL%202013%20Report%20Card%20for%20Website.pdf.

27 Robert Gammon, "Fracking Jerry Brown," *East Bay Express,* October 2, 2013,
http://www.eastbayexpress.com/oakland/fracking-jerry-brown/Content?oid
=3726533.

28 Alex Epstein, "If California Gets Its 'Fracking' Act Together, a Boom Awaits," *Forbes,*
September 6, 2013, http://www.forbes.com/sites/alexepstein/2013/09/06/if-california
-gets-its-fracking-act-together-a-boom-awaits/.

29 Mike Mills, "It's Said and Done—Governor Brown Signs SB 4 into Law," *California
Environmental Law,* September 23, 2013, http://www.californiaenvironmentallawblog
.com/oil-and-gas/its-said-and-done-governor-brown-signs-sb-4-into-law/.

30 Timothy Cama, "GOP Moves to Block Obama's Fracking Regs," *The Hill,* March 20,
2015, http://thehill.com/policy/energy-environment/236444-gop-gears-up-to-fight
-obamas-fracking-rules.

31 David Siders, "Jerry Brown Followed to Events, Heckled by California Environmentalists over Fracking," *Sacramento Bee,* December 2, 2013, http://www.sacbee.com/news
/politics-government/article2584546.html.

32 "Jerry Brown Talks About Fracking," Soundcloud, uploaded by *Mercury News,*
October 29, 2013, https://soundcloud.com/mercurynews/gov-jerry-brown-talks-about.

33 Ibid.

34 Siders, "Jerry Brown Followed to Events."

35 David R. Baker, "Poll: Two-Thirds of CA Voters Want Fracking Moratorium," *SF
Gate,* May 22, 2014, http://blog.sfgate.com/energy/2014/05/22/poll-two-thirds-of-ca
-voters-want-fracking-moratorium/.

36 Dan Bacher, "CA Fracking Moratorium Bill Defeated by Oil Industry Lobby," *San
Diego Free Press,* May 30, 2014. http://sandiegofreepress.org/2014/05/ca-fracking
-moratorium-bill-defeated-by-oil-industry-lobby/.

37 Center for Biological Diversity, "Documents Reveal Billions of Gallons of Oil
Industry Wastewater Illegally Injected into Central California Aquifers," October 6,
2014, http://www.biologicaldiversity.org/news/press_releases/2014/fracking-10-06-2014
.html.

38   Julie Cart, "High Levels of Benzene Found in Fracking Waste Water," *Los Angeles Times,* February 11, 2015, http://www.latimes.com/local/california/la-me-fracking -20150211-story.html.

39   Ibid.

40   Ibid.

41   Julie Cart, "Water and Wildlife May Be at Risk from Fracking's Toxic Chemicals, Panel Finds," *Los Angeles Times,* August 6, 2015, http://www.latimes.com/local/lanow /la-me-california-science-panel-warns-that-fracking-poses-unknown-risk-20150709 -story.html.

42   Ibid.

43   David Baker, "In-State Oil Fields Don't All Meet Standard," *SF Gate,* February 10, 2013, http://www.sfgate.com/business/article/In-state-oil-fields-don-t-all-meet-standard -4267131.php.

44   Zain Shauk, "Oklahoma Temblors Outpace California as Fracking Booms," *Bloomberg Business,* July 7, 2014, http://www.bloomberg.com/news/articles/2014-07-07/oklahoma -temblors-outpace-california-as-fracking-booms.

45   Amberlee P. Darold, Austin A. Holland, Jennifer K. Morris, and Amie R. Gibson, "Oklahoma Earthquake Summary Report 2014," Oklahoma Geological Survey, Sarkeys Energy Center, February 19, 2015.

46   Louis Sahagun, "U.S. Officials Cut Estimate of Recoverable Monterey Shale Oil by 96%," *Los Angeles Times,* May 20, 2014, http://www.latimes.com/business/la-fi-oil -20140521-story.html.

47   Office of Governor Edmund G. Brown Jr., "Governor Brown Addresses Global Leaders at United Nations Climate Summit," September 23, 2014, https://www.gov.ca .gov/news.php?id=18724.

48   Michael B. Marois and Alison Vekshin, "California Leading on Emissions as Brown Signs New Laws," *Bloomberg Business,* September 23, 2014, http://www.bloomberg .com/news/articles/2014-09-23/california-leading-on-emissions-as-brown-signs-new -laws.

49   Ibid.

50   Office of Governor Edmund G. Brown Jr., "Governor Brown to World's Mayors: It's Up to Us to Make It Happen," June 21, 2015, https://www.gov.ca.gov/news.php ?id=19047.

51   Ibid.

52   Tom Kington, "Jerry Brown, at the Vatican, Tells Mayors to 'Light a Fire' on Climate Change," *Los Angeles Times,* July 21, 2015, http://www.latimes.com/world/europe/la-fg -brown-vatican-mayors-climate-20150721-story.html.

53   Office of Governor Edmund G. Brown Jr., "Governor Brown Sworn in, Delivers Inaugural Address," January 5, 2015, https://www.gov.ca.gov/news.php?id=18828.

54   Mike De Souza, "Trailblazing California-Quebec Climate Plan Faces Fossil Fuel Industry Pushback," *InsideClimate News,* June 12, 2014, http://insideclimatenews.org /news/20140612/trailblazing-california-quebec-climate-plan-faces-fossil-industry -pushback.

55   Chris Lang, "Pope Francis Rejects Carbon Credits as a Solution to Climate Change," *Redd-Monitor,* June 17, 2015, http://www.redd-monitor.org/2015/06/17/pope-francis -rejects-carbon-credits-as-a-solution-to-climate-change/.

56   Ibid.

57   Sierra Club, "2014: Environmental Power Unifies and Wins," *Sierra Club 2014 Report Card,* October 2014, http://www.sierraclub.org/sites/www.sierraclub.org/files/sce/sierra -club-california/PDFs/FINAL%20Scorecard%202014%20WEB.pdf.

58   Philip Elliott, "Ted Cruz Says Climate-Change Fears Falsified by Scientists and Politicians," *Time,* August 2, 2015, http://time.com/3981623/ted-cruz-climate-change/.

59   David Cohen, "Jerry Brown: Ted Cruz 'Absolutely Unfit to be Running for Office,'" *Politico,* March 22, 2015, http://www.politico.com/story/2015/03/jerry-brown-ted-cruz -2016-elections-116292.html.

60   Elliott, "Ted Cruz."

61   Cohen, "Jerry Brown."

62   Tony Barboza, "California Is Ahead of the Game as Obama Releases Clean Power Plan," *Los Angeles Times,* August 4, 2015, http://www.latimes.com/science/la-me -climate-change-20150804-story.html.

63   Ibid.

64   Lauren Raab, "How Bad Was L.A.'s Smog When Barack Obama Went to College Here?" *Los Angeles Times,* August 3, 2015, http://www.latimes.com/local/lanow/la-me -ln-obama-smog-20150803-htmlstory.html.

65   Louis Jacobson, "Barack Obama Says When He Went to College in Los Angeles, the Pollution Was Often So Bad That 'Folks Couldn't Go Outside,'" PolitiFact.com, *Tampa Bay Times,* June 26, 2013, http://www.politifact.com/truth-o-meter/statements /2013/jun/26/barack-obama/barack-obama-says-when-he-went-college-los-angeles/.

66   Raab, "How Bad Was L.A.'s Smog?"

67   American Lung Association, "State of the Air 2014: Most Polluted Cities," 2014 http://www.stateoftheair.org/2014/city-rankings/most-polluted-cities.html.

68   Chris Megerian, "Oil Industry, Environmentalists in Ad War Over Bill to Cut Gasoline Use," *Los Angeles Times,* September 3, 2015, http://www.latimes.com/local /politics/la-me-pol-ad-war-20150904-story.html.

69   Judy Lin, "Governor, Legislative Democrats Scale Back Ambitious Proposal to Cut Energy Use in California," *U.S. News,* September 5, 2015, http://www.usnews.com /news/science/news/articles/2015/09/09/gov-brown-legislative-democrats-scale-back -climate-package.

70   Jessica Calefati and Tracy Seipel, "California Climate Change Bill: Jerry Brown, Democrats Drop Oil-Reduction Target; Talks on Taxes Stall," *San Jose Mercury News,* September 9, 2015, http://www.mercurynews.com/health/ci_28784374/california-bills -climate-change-taxes.

71   Jessica Calefati, Tracy Seipel, and Paul Rogers, "Gov. Jerry Brown Loses 'Invincible' Image in Climate Change, Tax Battles," *San Jose Mercury News,* September 10, 2015, http://www.mercurynews.com/california/ci_28793268/california-climate-change-taxes -jerry-brown-invincible.

8: Crime and Punishment

1   Ruth Wilson Gilmore, *Golden Gulag: Prisons, Surplus, Crisis, and Opposition in Globalizing California* (Berkeley: University of California Press, 2007), 26.

2   Jack Leonard, " 'Pizza Thief' Walks the Line," *Los Angeles Times,* February 10, 2010, http://articles.latimes.com/2010/feb/10/local/la-me-pizzathief10-2010feb10.

3   Ballotpedia, "California Proposition 36, Changes in the 'Three Strikes' Law (2012)," http://ballotpedia.org/California_Proposition_36,_Changes_in_the_%22Three _Strikes%22_Law_(2012).

4   Interview with the author, February 9, 2013.

5   Office of Governor Edmund G. Brown Jr., "Governor Brown Sworn In, Delivers Inaugural Address," January 1, 2015, https://www.gov.ca.gov/news.php?id=18828.

6   David Siders, "Jerry Brown Signs Racial Profiling Bill, Vetoes Date Rape Measure," *Sacramento Bee,* October 3, 2015.

7   Ibid.

8   Marissa Gerber, Abby Sewell, and Cindy Chang, "Prop. 47 Brings a Shift to Longer Time Spent Behind Bars," *Los Angeles Times,* January 28, 2015, http://www.latimes .com/local/crime/la-me-early-release-20150128-story.html.

9   Sam Stanton, "Prop. 47 Victory Shows California Embracing 'Smart on Crime' Approach, Supporters Say," *Sacramento Bee,* November 5, 2014, http://www.sacbee.com /news/politics-government/election/article3591130.html.

10 Gilmore, *Golden Gulag,* 7.

11 Ibid., 4.

12 Vauhini Vara, "Will California Again Lead the Way on Prison Reform?" *The New Yorker,* November 7, 2014, http://www.newyorker.com/business/currency/will-california -lead-way-prison-reform.

13 Jenifer Warren, "Jerry Brown Calls Sentence Law a Failure," *Los Angeles Times,* February 28, 2003, http://articles.latimes.com/2003/feb/28/local/me-prisoners28.

14 Mark Niquette, Michael B. Marois, and Rodney Yap, "$822,000 Worker Shows California Leads U.S. Pay Giveaway," *Bloomberg,* December 10, 2012, http://www.bloomberg.com /news/articles/2012-12-11/-822-000-worker-shows-california-leads-u-s-pay-giveaway.

15 Interview with the author, January 9, 2013.

16 Tessa Murphy, "Solitary Confinement Is Cruel and All Too Usual. Why Is It Only Getting Worse?" Amnesty International, October 14, 2014, http://www.amnesty.ca /blog/solitary-confinement-is-cruel-and-all-too-usual-why-is-it-only-getting-worse.

17 Ian Lovett, "Inmates End Hunger Strike in California," *New York Times,* September 5, 2013, http://www.nytimes.com/2013/09/06/us/inmates-end-hunger-strike-in-california .html.

18 Peter Baker and Erica Goode, "Critics of Solitary Confinement Are Buoyed as Obama Embraces Their Cause," *New York Times,* July 21, 2015, http://www.nytimes.com/2015 /07/22/us/politics/critics-of-solitary-confinement-buoyed-as-obama-embraces-cause .html.

19 Ibid.

20 Paige St. John, "Gov. Jerry Brown's Prison Reforms Haven't Lived Up to His Billing," *Los Angeles Times,* June 21, 2014, http://www.latimes.com/local/politics/la-me-ff-pol -brown-prisons-20140622-story.html.

21 Timm Herdt, "Brown Says Prison Emergency Is Over, Asks Court to Lift Inmate Cap," *Ventura County Star,* January 8, 2003, http://www.vcstar.com/news/brown-says -prison-emergency-is-over-asks-court-to-lift-inmate-cap-ep-293227749-351845681.html.

22 St. John, "Gov. Jerry Brown's Prison Reforms."

23 Ibid.

24 Public Policy Institute of California, "Corrections Realignment Largely Successful but Challenge's Remain," press release, September 28, 2015, http://www.ppic.org/main /pressrelease.asp?i=1863.

25 St. John, "Gov. Jerry Brown's Prison Reforms."

26 Ibid.

27 Haya El Nasser, " 'Walking Out of Jail': Prop 47 Frees Felons with Downgraded Charges," Al Jazeera America, November 14, 2014, http://america.aljazeera.com /articles/2014/11/14/california-feloniestomisdemeanors.html.

28 Newt Gingrich and Wayne B. Hughes, "What California Can Learn from the Red States on Crime and Punishment," *Los Angeles Times,* September 27, 2014.

29 Christopher Cadelago, "Jerry Brown: 'I Can Clean Up' Sentencing Problems He Created," *Sacramento Bee,* April 11, 2016, http://www.sacbee.com/news/politics -government/capitol-alert/article71193792.html.

30 "Proposition 47: Criminal Sentences. Misdemeanor Penalties. Initiative Statute,"Legislative Analyst's Office, November 4, 2014, http://www.lao.ca.gov/ballot /2014/prop-47-110414.aspx.

31 Adam Serwer, "California's Attorney General Thinks Legal Weed Is Inevitable," *BuzzFeed News,* November 17, 2014, http://www.buzzfeed.com/adamserwer/californias -attorney-general-thinks-legal-weed-is-inevitable.

32 Public Policy Institute of California, "Nearly All Say They Have Cut Water Use— Half of Likely Voters Support Water Bond," March 26, 2014, http://www.ppic.org /main/pressrelease.asp?i=1483.

33 Richard Halstead, "Gavin Newsom Voices Support for Legal Pot in Marin Appear- ance," *Marin Independent Journal,* August 5, 2014, http://www.marinij.com/general -news/20140805/gavin-newsom-voices-support-for-legal-pot-in-marin-appearance.

34 Dan Schneider, "Pot Economics," *Dollars and Sense,* March/April 2014, http:// dollarsandsense.org/archives/2014/0314schneider.html.

Chapter 9: To Teach His Own

1 University of California, Berkeley, Office of Planning and Analysis, "UC Berkeley in the *U.S. News & World Report*'s 2015 Guide to America's Best Colleges," September 2014, http://opa.berkeley.edu/sites/default/files/2015_us_news_release_v3.pdf.

2 "Top Colleges Doing the Most for Low-Income Students," *New York Times,* Septem- ber 16, 2015, http://www.nytimes.com/interactive/2015/09/17/upshot/top-colleges-doing -the-most-for-low-income-students.html.

3   Clark Kerr, *The Great Transformation in Higher Education, 1960–1980* (Albany: State University of New York Press, 1991), 210.

4   "Education: Master Planner," *Time Magazine,* October 17, 1960, http://www.time.com/time/magazine/article/0,9171,895026,00.html.

5   Andy Kroll, "Tomgram: Andy Kroll, the Death of the Golden Dream of Higher Education," *Tom Dispatch,* October 2, 2012, http://www.tomdispatch.com/blog/175600/tomgram%3A_andy_kroll,_the_death_of_the_golden_dream_of_higher_education/.

6   Carla Rivera, "Californians' Enrollment in UC, CSU Declines, Study Finds," *Los Angeles Times,* May 10, 2012, http://articles.latimes.com/2012/may/10/local/la-me-0510-college-report-20120510.

7   Saul Geiser and Richard C. Atkinson, "Beyond the Master Plan: The Case for Restructuring Baccalaureate Education in California," University of California, Berkeley, November 2010, http://files.eric.ed.gov/fulltext/ED517762.pdf.

8   Public Policy Institute of California, "State Faces Shortfall of 1.1 Million College Graduates in 2030," October 12, 2015, http://www.ppic.org/main/pressrelease.asp?i=1873.

9   Mark DiCamillo and Mervin Field, "Majorities Rate Jobs/The Economy, The State Budget Deficit, Education and Health Care as Top Issues in This Year's Governor's Race," The Field Poll, March 23, 2010, http://www.field.com/fieldpollonline/subscribers/Rls2334.pdf.

10 Lisa Delpit, *Other People's Children: Cultural Conflict in the Classroom* (New York: New Press, 2006).

11 Center for Educational Policy, "Oakland Unified School District," 1, https://cse.google.com/cse?cx=001382591411870128679%3Ail0cupb_8ya&ie=UTF-8&q=www.cep-dc.org%2Fcfcontent_file.cfm%3F . . . NCLB4_Case06-OaklandCA.pdf&sa=Search&siteurl=www.cep-dc.org%2Findex.cfm%3FDocumentTopicID%3D12&ref=www.cep-dc.org%2F&ss=0j0j1#gsc.tab=0&gsc.q=www.cep-dc.org%2Fcfcontent_file.cfm%3F . . . NCLB4_Case06-OaklandCA.pdf&gsc.page=1.

12 John Rogers, Sophie Fanelli, Rhoda Freelon, David Medina, Melanie Bertrand, and Maritza Del Razo, "California Educational Opportunity Report," UCLA IDEA, UC/ACCORD, January 2010, http://idea.gseis.ucla.edu/educational-opportunity-report/files-and-documents/Ed%20Op%20in%20Hard%20Times.pdf.

13 The Leadership Conference, "California a Pioneer," April 2013, http://www.civilrights.org/publications/reports/education-equity-report/california-a-pioneer.html.

14 David Black, "The State of Our Schools," Eyes on Phillips 66 Rodeo, December 8, 2009, http://crgna.org/blog/2009/12/the-state-of-our-schools/.

15 Brent Staples, "Editorial Observer: The 'Mississippification' of California Schools," *New York Times,* June 23, 2000, http://www.nytimes.com/2000/06/23/opinion/editorial-observer-the-mississippification-of-california-schools.html.

16 U.S. Department of Commerce, "Public Education Finances: 2013," table 8, June 2015, http://www2.census.gov/govs/school/13f33pub.pdf.

17 Interview with the author, February 9, 2013.

18 Sherry Posnick-Goodwin, "Ravitch: 'Poverty Clearly Affects Children's Readiness,'" *California Educator* 16, no. 3 (1999), http://www.cta.org/RavitchQA.

19 Ibid.

20   Eleanor Yang Su, "Fewer Schools Keep Librarians on Staff," Center for Investigative Reporting, *San Diego Union Tribune,* December 2, 2011, http://www .sandiegouniontribune.com/news/2011/dec/02/fewer-schools-keep-librarians-on-staff/.

21   John Rosales, "Checking Out," National Education Association, *NEA Today,* May 2011, http://www.nea.org/home/43952.htm.

22   California Department of Education, "The *Williams* Case—an Explanation," http://www.cde.ca.gov/eo/ce/wc/wmslawsuit.asp.

23   Louis Harris, "Report on the Status of Public School Education in California 2004," UCLA IDEA, May 2004, http://idea.gseis.ucla.edu/publications/report-on-the-status-of -public-school-education-in/Harris.pdf.

24   Interview with the author.

25   Stephen J. Carroll, Cathy Krop, Jeremy Arkes, Peter A. Morrison, and Ann Flanagan, *California's K-12 Public Schools: How Are They Doing?* (Santa Monica: RAND Corporation, 2005), http://www.rand.org/pubs/monographs/MG186.

26   "Quality Counts Introduces New State Report Card: U.S. Earns C, and Massachusetts Ranks First in Nation," *Education Week,* January 8, 2015, http://www.edweek.org /media/qualitycounts2015_release.pdf.

27   Anthony Cody, "Jerry Brown to Arne Duncan: Think Again!" *Education Week Teacher,* September 1, 2009, http://blogs.edweek.org/teachers/living-in-dialogue/2009 /09/jerry_brown_to_arne_duncan_thi.html.

28   Ibid.

29   Interview with the author, February 9, 2013.

30   Ibid.

31   Sandy Banks, "Prop 30 Isn't Perfect, but if It Fails, the Results Will Be Tragic," *Los Angeles Times,* September 28, 2012, http://articles.latimes.com/2012/sep/28/local/la-me -banks-school—tax-20120929.

32   Andrew Gumbel, "California Schools on the Brink," *Salon,* October 4, 2012, http:// www.salon.com/2012/10/04/california_schools_on_the_brink/.

33   Vauhini Vara, "California Voters Approves Higher Taxes," *Wall Street Journal,* November 8, 2012, http://www.wsj.com/articles/SB10001424127887324439804578104854 095658918.

34   Juliet Williams, "Gov. Jerry Brown Signs Bill for Education Funding," *San Jose Mercury News,* July 2, 2013, http://www.mercurynews.com/breaking-news/ci_23580334 /gov-jerry-brown-signs-bill-education-funding.

35   "Fairly Funding California's Schools," *Los Angeles Times,* editorial, May 28, 2013, http://articles.latimes.com/2013/may/28/opinion/la-ed-school-funding-jerry-brown -20130528.

36   Alan Greenblatt, "California Upends School Funding to Give Poor Kids a Boost," National Public Radio, August 19, 2013, http://www.npr.org/2013/08/19/212294111 /california-upends-school-funding-to-give-poor-kids-a-boost.

37   Interview with the author, February 2013.

10: Jerry Brown 2.0

1 Brooks Barnes, "Pornography and Politics," *New York Times,* October 19, 2012, http://www.nytimes.com/2012/10/21/fashion/larry-flynt-pornography-and-politics .html.

2 Ibid.

3 Interview with the author, August 10, 2013.

4 California Secretary of State Contributions Database, Flynt contributions to Edmund G (Jerry) Brown Jr., http://powersearch.sos.ca.gov/advanced.php.

5 Kevin Yamamura, "Gov. Jerry Brown's Budget Plans Threatened by a Determined Molly Munger," *Sacramento Bee,* October 10, 2012, http://www.freerepublic.com/focus /news/2943890/posts.

6 Judy Lin, "California Employees Forced to Take Day Off Without Pay," Associated Press, *Huffington Post,* March 9, 2009, http://www.huffingtonpost.com/2009/02/06 /california-employees-forc_n_164798.html.

7 Center for Public Education, "Cutting to the Bone: How the Economic Crisis Affects Schools," October 7, 2010, http://www.centerforpubliceducation.org/Main-Menu /Public-education/Cutting-to-the-bone-At-a-glance/Cutting-to-the-bone-How-the -economic-crisis-affects-schools.html.

8 Anna McCarthy, "The Battle for California's State Parks," *Outside Live Bravely,* June 19, 2012, http://www.outsideonline.com/1900806/battle-californias-state-parks.

9 *Calbuzz,* "Jerry Brown vs Four Horsemen of the Tax Apocalypse," September 26, 2011, http://www.calbuzz.com/2011/09/brown-gop-bows-to-four-horsemen-of-tax-apocalypse/.

10 Interview with the author, December 10, 2011.

11 Ibid.

12 "Text of California Proposition 30 (November 2012)," Ballotpedia, https://ballotpedia .org/Text_of_California_Proposition_30_(November_2012).

13 Fair Political Practices Commission, "Americans for Responsible Leadership Admits Campaign Money Laundering, Discloses $11 Million Donor," November 5, 2012, http://www.fppc.ca.gov/index.php?id=346.

14 Scott Wilson, "Obama Rekindles Talk About Boys Club After Comment About California Attorney General," *Washington Post,* April 4, 2013, http://www .washingtonpost.com/politics/obama-rekindles-talk-about-boys-club-after-comment -about-california-attorney-general/2013/04/04/edfb4c64-9d6b-11e2-9a79-eb5280c81c63 _story.html.

15 Chris Megerian, "Arizona Group Plans to Appeal to the U.S. Supreme Court in Funding Case," *Los Angeles Times,* November 4, 2012, http://latimesblogs.latimes.com /california-politics/2012/11/arizona-nonprofit-supreme-court.html.

16 Fair Political Practices Commission, "Americans for Responsible Leadership."

17 "Californians Say Yes to Taxes," *New York Times,* editorial, November 8, 2012, http://www.nytimes.com/2012/11/09/opinion/californians-say-yes-to-raising-their-taxes .html.

18 Wyatt Buchanan, "Prop 30 Wins, Prop 38 Flames Out," *SF Gate,* November 7, 2012, http://www.sfgate.com/politics/article/Prop-30-wins-Prop-38-flames-out-4014648.php.

19 Ibid.

20 William Bradley, "How Jerry Brown Pulled Off the Big Prop 30 Win," *Huffington Post,* November 8, 2012, http://www.huffingtonpost.com/william-bradley/jerry-brown-prop-30_b_2094749.html.

21 Juliet Williams, "Young Voters Turned the Tide for Brown's Prop 30," Associated Press, *San Jose Mercury News,* November 11, 2012, http://www.mercurynews.com/ci_21976176/young-voters-turned-tide-browns-prop-30.

22 Center for Responsive Politics, "Political Nonprofits (Dark Money)," 2014, https://www.opensecrets.org/outsidespending/nonprof_summ.php.

23 Fair Political Practices Commission, "FPPC Announces Record Settlement In $11 Million Arizona Contribution Case," press release, October 24, 2013, http://www.fppc.ca.gov/press_release.php?pr_id=783.

24 Anthony York, "List Unmasks Secret Donors to California Initiative Campaigns," *Los Angeles Times,* October 24, 2013, http://articles.latimes.com/2013/oct/24/local/la-me-pc-secret-donors-california-initiatives-20131024.

25 David Zahniser, "Philanthropist Eli Broad Endorses Brown's Call to Raise Taxes," *Los Angeles Times,* January 18, 2012, http://latimesblogs.latimes.com/lanow/2012/01/philanthropist-broad-endorses-browns-call-for-raising-taxes.html.

26 Fair Political Practices Commission, "Americans for Responsible Leadership."

27 Nicholas Confessore and Megan Thee-Brenan, "Poll Shows Americans Favor Overhaul of Campaign Financing," *New York Times,* June 2, 2015, http://www.nytimes.com/2015/06/03/us/politics/poll-shows-americans-favor-overhaul-of-campaign-financing.html?_r=2#story-continues-4.

28 Laurel Rosenhall, "Jerry Brown Signs Law Requiring Nonprofits Identify Donors," *Sacramento Bee,* May 14, 2014, http://blogs.sacbee.com/capitolalertlatest/2014/05/jerry-brown-signs-law-requiring-political-nonprofits-identify-donors.html.

29 Ibid.

30 Californians for the Right to Know, "What Is the Voters' Right to Know Act?" http://www.votersrighttoknow.org/faqs.

31 Californians for the Right to Know, "Why Is It Necessary?" http://www.votersrighttoknow.org/faqs.

32 Matea Gold, "Will California Guarantee the Right to Know the Names of Political Donors?" *Washington Post,* September 16, 2015, http://www.washingtonpost.com/politics/will-california-guarantee-the-right-to-know-the-names-of-political-donors/2015/09/16/2b232f62-5c78-11e5-b38e-06883aacba64_story.html.

33 Kim Barker and Theodoric Meyer, "The Dark Money Man: How Sean Noble Moved the Kochs' Cash into Politics and Made Millions," *ProPublica,* February 14, 2014, updated May 4, 2014, http://www.propublica.org/article/the-dark-money-man-how-sean-noble-moved-the-kochs-cash-into-politics-and-ma.

34 "Californians Say Yes to Taxes."

35 Interview with the author, January 10, 2013.

11: The Pendulum Swings Left

1   Howard Gleckman, "What's the Matter with Kansas and Its Tax Cuts? It Can't Do Math," *Forbes,* July 15, 2014, http://www.forbes.com/sites/beltway/2014/07/15/whats-the-matter-with-kansas-and-its-tax-cuts-it-cant-do-math/.

2   Ibid.

3   Mark Peters and Damian Paletta, "Sam Brownback's Tax-Cut Push Puts Kansas Out on Its Own," *Wall Street Journal,* June 10, 2014, http://www.wsj.com/articles/sam-brownbacks-tax-cut-push-puts-kansas-out-on-its-own-1402448126.

4   Thomas Frank, "In Brownbackistan, Everything Is Awesome! And Don't Let Any Liberal Tell You Different," *Salon,* September 21, 2014, http://www.salon.com/2014/09/21/in_brownbackistan_everything_is_awesome_and_don%E2%80%99t_let_any_liberal_tell_you_different/.

5   Nick Bilton, "The Housing Market with Nowhere to Go (but Up)," *New York Times,* March 2, 2014, http://bits.blogs.nytimes.com/2014/03/02/the-housing-market-with-nowhere-to-go-but-up/.

6   Kathryn Vasel, "America's Most Expensive Rental Markets," *CNN Money,* August 19, 2015, http://money.cnn.com/gallery/real_estate/2015/08/19/most-expensive-rental-markets/.

7   Sarah Bohn, Caroline Danielson, and Monica Bandy, "Poverty in California," Public Policy Institute of California Report, June 2015, http://www.ppic.org/main/publication_show.asp?i=261.

8   Kathleen Short, "The Supplemental Poverty Measure: 2013," U.S. Census Bureau, October 2014, https://www.census.gov/content/dam/Census/library/publications/2014/demo/p60-251.pdf.

9   Bohn, Danielson, and Bandy, "Poverty in California."

10 Susanna Kim, "10 Things You Didn't Know About Apple and Its Employees," ABC News, June 6, 2013, http://abcnews.go.com/Business/top-10-interesting-facts-apples-report-headquarters/story?id=19330088#1.

11 Tiffany Hsu, "El Centro's 21.1% Unemployment Rate Second Highest in U.S.," *Los Angeles Times,* July 1, 2014, http://www.latimes.com/business/la-fi-el-centro-unemployment-california-20140701-story.html.

12 Congressional Research Service, "CRS Report for Congress," December 12, 2005, http://fpc.state.gov/documents/organization/59030.pdf.

13 Alan Berube and Natalie Holmes, "Some Cities Are Still More Unequal Than Others—an Update," Brookings, March 17, 2015, http://www.brookings.edu/research/reports2/2015/03/city-inequality-berube-holmes.

14 Heather Long, "America's 10 Most Unequal Cities," CNN, December 14, 2014, http://money.cnn.com/2014/12/14/news/economy/america-inequality-10-worst-cities/.

15 Gale Holland, "13,000 Fall into Homelessness Every Month in L.A. County, Report Says," *Los Angeles Times,* August 25, 2015, http://www.latimes.com/local/california/la-me-homeless-pathways-20150825-story.html.

16 Kevin Rizzo, Chelsey Goff, and Anneliese Mahoney, "Crime in America 2015: Top 10

Most Dangerous Cities Over 200,000," Law Street, http://lawstreetmedia.com/crime
-america-2015-top-10-dangerous-cities-200000-2/.

17 Preston Grisham, "United States Tech Industry Employs 6.5 Million in 2014," Comp-
TIA, press release, February 10, 2015, https://www.comptia.org/about-us/newsroom
/press-releases/2015/02/10/united-states-tech-industry-employs-6.5-million-in-2014.

18 James Rainey and Jean Merl, "Garcetti Calls for $13.25 Minimum Wage by 2017," *Los
Angeles Times,* September 1, 2014, http://www.latimes.com/local/cityhall/la-me-garcetti
-wage-20140902-story.html.

19 California Stem Cell Agency, "Where CIRM Funding Goes," Accessed March 10,
2016, https://www.cirm.ca.gov/about/where-cirm-funding-goes.

20 Ibid.

21 Kevin McCormack and Cristy Lytal, "California Stem Cell Agency Celebrates
10 Years of Progress," University of Southern California, December 2, 2014, https://
news.usc.edu/71879/california-stem-cell-agency-celebrates-10-years-of-progress/.

22 Ibid.

23 "State Stem Cell Agency Hasn't Lived up to Its Hype," *SF Gate,* May 2, 2014, http://
www.sfgate.com/opinion/editorials/article/State-stem-cell-agency-hasn-t-lived-up-to-its
-hype-5449312.php.

24 Interview with the author, San Francisco, January 9, 2013.

Epilogue

1 Carey McWilliams, *California: The Great Exception* (Berkeley: University of California
Press, 1949), 364.

2 Public Policy Institute of California, "California's Future," January 15, 2014, http://
www.ppic.org/content/pubs/report/R_114BKR.pdf.

3 Juli Anne Patty, "Why California Leads the Nation in Private Sector Job Growth,"
Kern EDC, May 18, 2015, http://kedc.com/why-california-leads-the-nation-in-private
-sector-jobs-growth/.

4 Ananya Bhattacharya, "Is Texas America's Best State Economy?" CNN, June 10, 2015,
http://money.cnn.com/2015/06/10/news/economy/texas-big-economic-growth-2014/.

5 Brian Lowry, "Brownback and Other Republican Brass Plead for Tax Hike to Balance
Kansas Budget," *Kansas City Star,* June 11, 2015, http://www.kansascity.com/news
/government-politics/article23744494.html.

6 Ibid.

7 City National Bank, "City National Economy & Jobs Report Second Quarter 2015,"
News and Insights, June 24, 2015, http://newsroom.cnb.com/city-national-economy-jobs
-report-second-quarter-2015.

8 Chris Megerian and Phil Willon, "California Officials Eyeing Stock Market Plunge,
Hope It Won't Last," *Los Angeles Times,* August 24, 2015, http://www.latimes.com
/local/political/la-me-pol-california-officials-eyeing-stock-market-plunge-20150824
-story.html.

9 Romy Varghese, "California Rainy Day Fund Yields Results in Bond-Market

Recovery," *Bloomberg,* August 25, 2015, http://www.bloomberg.com/news/articles/2015 -08-25/california-rainy-day-fund-yields-results-in-bond-market-recovery.

10   Sarah Bohn et al., "California's Future," Public Policy Institute of California, February 2015, http://www.ppic.org/main/publication.asp?i=895.

11   David Siders and Christopher Cadelago, "Gov. Jerry Brown Takes Fourth Oath, Targets Climate Change," *Sacramento Bee,* January 5, 2015, http://www.sacbee.com /news/politics-government/capitol-alert/article5448294.html.

12   Chris Megerian, "Gov. Jerry Brown Signs New $167.6-Billion State Budget," *Los Angeles Times,* June 24, 2015, http://www.latimes.com/local/political/la-me-pc-jerry -brown-signs-california-budget-20150624-story.html.

13   Mark Baldassare, Dean Bonner, David Kordus, and Lunna Lopes, "Californians and Their Government," Public Policy Institute of California, March 2016, http://ppic.org /content/pubs/survey/S_316MBS.pdf.

14   Seema Mehta, "Gov. Jerry Brown Finally Spends Campaign Money, but Not on Himself," *Los Angeles Times,* October 23, 2014, http://www.latimes.com/local/political /la-me-pc-gov-brown-spends-campaign-money-propositions-20141023-story.html.

INDEX